The Politics and Economics of International Sanctions: International Justice or Playground Bullying?

The Politics and Economics of International Sanctions: International Justice or Playground Bullying?

Anne Wade

SOCIETY Publishing

www.societypublishing.com

The Politics and Economics of International Sanctions: International Justice or Playground Bullying?

Anne Wade

Society Publishing
224 Shoreacres Road
Burlington, ON L7L 2H2
Canada
www.societypublishing.com
Email: orders@arclereducation.com

ISBN: 978-1-77469-059-8 (Hardcover)

ABOUT THE AUTHOR

Dr. Anne Wade has been a researcher and an instruction in the Criminal Justice field for 27 years. She is currently an Associate Professor at a Community College in North Carolina. She holds an Ed.D. in Educational Leadership and a Ph.D. in Public Safety Leadership/Criminal Justice. Her research interests are in Criminology, Victimology, and the Human Services. She is married to Wesley Wade. She is an artist, writer, research, teacher, and trainer.

TABLE OF CONTENTS

LIST OF FIGURES

LIST OF ABBREVIATIONS

ANC	Constituent National Assembly
CPF	Cuba Policy Foundation
DISIP	Directorate of Intelligence and Prevention Services
EU	European Union
FARC	Revolutionary Armed Forces of Colombia
ICJ	International Court of Justice
IPO	International Progress Organization
IR	International relations
LCS	London controlling section
MIC	Military-industrial complex
MICC	Military-industrial-congressional complex
NGO	Non-Governmental Organization
NLF	National Liberation Front
OFAC	Office of Foreign Assets Control
PSYOPS	psychological operations
TSJ	Supreme Tribunal of Justice
UNICEF	United Nations Children's Fund

PREFACE

International sanctions are now closely associated with a world governance framework, whereas they are actually a relic of mercantilism. There was a time when nations behaved like territorial lions...one had to kill or risk being killed. Some of the effects of that approach were theendless and sometimes completely meaningless wars. Eventually, nations began to build fragile alliances when they realized that it was costlier to fight one another than to work together. Eventually, those alliances grew large and looser until we reached the age of the United Nations (a child of the toothless 'League of Nations'). The rationale behind international sanctions was that nations who did not play by the rules would be punished by the UN with the force of many nations acting in concert. Not only would a punishment meted out by the international community be heftier than an individual nation's response, but they would also be cloaked within the comforting language of international law.

Unfortunately, like everything else, international sanctions have come to represent the worst aspects of postcolonial hegemony and even outright international injustice. It seems that Western nations get away with what some refer to as atrocities while other countries that demonstrate any deviance from the status quo or prevailing approach are punished. Some examples of countries on the receiving end of international sanctions include Iran and North Korea. These two countries have been blighted by brutal regimes over the years which have systematically oppressed sections of their populace. Many of the crimes these nations are accused seem similar to the actions employed by colonial powers. Certainly, the atomic bombs launched by the USA to end World War II led to significant damage, but one which is ignored since they were launched during wartime. Iran and North Korea are repeatedly sanctioned for even suggesting nuclear ambitions, the former routinely highlighting the fact that it has never yet released an atomic bomb on another nation.

In effect, international sanctions have exposed contradictions inherent in modern implementations of international law. Some of the most vocal advocates for international sanctions are countries that are not actually signatories to many of the internationally accepted covenants. The USA argues that any attempt at UN oversight is tantamount to a usurpation of their own constitution. Yet, there r is insistence that other countries are monitored/ The victors do control the narrative of the future.

There is a festering resentment from some countries against the international because they deem it to be unfair. They feel many of the old colonial powers use international laws to oppress and bully their former colonies. Sometimes, it is those same powers as the United Kingdom which are directly responsible for creating the chaos that they now presume to be addressing through international sanctions. One just must look at the official borders that the British Empire set up to understand the disastrous impact that these "civilized democracies" have inflicted on the rest of the world. This book attempts to tell the story of international sanctions. Specifically, it highlights the political and economic interests that lay at the heart of this conflict among nations.

Chapter 1

Introduction to International Sanctions

CONTENTS

We begin this book by considering how international sanctions are defined. Reference will be made to the provisions of Chapter VII of the UN Charter. Other aspects that will be considered when conceptualizing international sanctions include their economic dimensions. We will review some of the historical landmarks in international sanctions, such as the 'continental system.' The chapter will close with an overview of the Rhodesia case study. By the end of this chapter, the reader will begin to understand the inherent contradictions in defining and conceptualizing international sanctions.

1.1. DEFINITION OF INTERNATIONAL SANCTIONS

International sanctions are political and economic decisions that are part of diplomatic efforts by countries, multilateral or regional organizations against states or organizations to protect national security interests (Afesorgbor, 2019; Alam, 2008; Al-Jawaheri, 2008). They can also be used to protect international law and to defend against threats to international peace and security (Askari et al., 2003; Attia, Grauvogel, and von Soest, 2020). These decisions principally include the temporary imposition on a target of economic, trade, diplomatic, cultural, or other restrictions (sanctions measures) that are lifted when the motivating security concerns no longer apply, or when no new threats have arisen (Bacchiega and Borzaga, 2003; Baldwin and Pape, 1998; Barber, 1979; Bederman and Keitner, 2016). Figure 1.1 highlights the current reach of USA sanctions. This is a country that uses sanctions more than most countries with having far more impact than virtually any other country on earth (Biersteker, Eckert, and Tourinho, 2016).

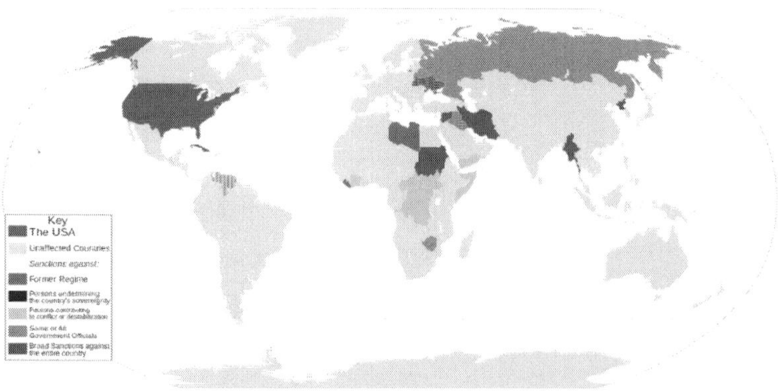

Figure 1.1. US sanctions across the globe.

Source: Wikipedia.

According to Chapter VII of the United Nations Charter, only the UN Security Council has a mandate by the international community to apply sanctions (Blyton, 2004; Bolander, 2011; Borszik, 2014, 2016; Bosco, 2012; Bradley and Galbraith, 2016; Brzoska, 2015). Hence, Article 41 must be complied with by all UN member states as stipulated in the provisions of Chapter I, Article 2.2 of the UN Charter (Buck, Gallant, and Nossal, 1998; Caron, 1989; Carter, 1987; Caruso, 2003; Chachavalpongpun, 2014). These sanctions serve as the international community's most powerful peaceful means to prevent threats to international peace and security or to settle them (Chan, 2000; Chan and Drury, 2000; Chen et al., 2019; Cheraghali, 2013; Chiquiar, 2008). Sanctions do not include the use of military force (Choi and Luo, 2013; Clegg and Palmer, 1996; Cleveland, 2001; Cortright et al., 2000; Cranmer, Heinrich, and Desmarais, 2014). However, if sanctions do not lead to the diplomatic settlement of a conflict, the use of force can be authorized by the Security Council separately under Article 42 (Crawford and Klotz, 1999; Crook, 2013; David and Holliday, 2012; Daviron and Ponte, 2007; De Visscher, 2015). UN sanctions should not be confused with unilateral sanctions that are imposed by individual countries in furtherance of their strategic interests (De Vos, 2010; Defourny, 2013; Denzin, 2008; Devarajan and Mottaghi, 2015; Dobler, 2008). Typically intended as strong economic coercion; measures applied under unilateral sanctions can range between coercive diplomatic efforts, economic warfare, or as preludes to war (Doxey, 1972, 1980, 1983, 1987; Drezner, 2000, 2011, 2015; Drezner and Drezner, 1999).

There are several types of sanctions. One category is that of economic sanctions which typically is a ban on trade and possibly limited to certain sectors such as armaments (Drury and Peksen, 2014; Dunn and Shaw, 2001; Dunoff, Ratner, and Wippman, 2015; Eliat and Einav, 2004; Eriksson, 2016). However, they may also be modified by certain exceptions such as food and medicine (Escribà-Folch, 2010, 2012; Escribà-Folch and Wright, 2010; Farzanegan, 2013; Farzanegan and Hayo, 2019). A second category is that of diplomatic sanctions in which there is reduction or removal of diplomatic ties, such as embassies (Franzway and Fonow, 2011; Frick, Humphreys, and Scheel, 2015; Fridell, 2014; Fu et al., 2020). The third category are military in nature and may involve an actual military intervention (Genzberger et al., 1994; Gharehgozli, 2017; Goodhart, 2016; Grauvogel and Von Soest, 2014). The 4th category is that of sport sanctions which prevent one country's people and teams from competing in international events (Grauvogel, Licht, and von Soest, 2017; Gui, 1991; Hafner-Burton and Montgomery, 2008).

Recently, there has been more attention being given to sanctions that are imposed on the environment (Hanushek and Woessmann, 2010; Haugh and Kitson, 2007; Hinds, 1997; Hiraide and Chakraborty, 2012; Ho-Chuan, Yi-Chen, and Chih-Chuan, 2012). For example, since the declaration of the United Nations Conference on the Human Environment, international environmental protection efforts have been increased gradually (Hovdenak, 2009; Huang, Xu, and Lu, 2011; Huebner, 2009; Hultman and Peksen, 2017; Hurd, 2017). Economic sanctions are distinguished from trade sanctions (Igami, 2015; Ivanov, Sypchenko, and Webster, 2017; James, 2013). The latter are applied for purely economic reasons, and typically take the form of tariffs or similar measures, rather than bans on trade (Jiang, Chen, and Liu, 2010; Jing, Kaempfer, and Lowenberg, 2003; Kaempfer and Lowenberg, 1999).

Sanction formulations are divided into three categories (Kaempfer and Lowenberg, 2000; Kaempfer, Lowenberg, and Mertens, 2004; Kendall, 2000). The categories are used to differentiate between the political contexts due to the global nature of the act (Kiriya, 2017; Kirshner, 1997; Klotz, 1995; Koskenniemi, 2014; Kunz, 1960; Laub, 2015; Lee, 2018). The first category involves such sanctions that are designed to force cooperation with international law (Levy, 1999; Leyton-Brown, 2017; Li and Saghaian, 2013; Lutz and Lux, 1995; Mahmud, 2001). This can be seen in the sanctions placed on Iraq in Resolution 661 on August 6, 1990, after the initial invasion of neighboring Kuwait (Matsushita et al., 2015; McCorkell and Gillard, 2010; Meyer and Thein, 2014; Mikhaylova, Babich, and Smirnova, 2017). The United Nations placed an embargo on the nation in an attempt to prevent armed conflict (Morgan and Schwebach, 1997; Mueller and Mueller, 1999). Resolution 665 and Resolution 670 were further added creating both a naval and an air blockade on Iraq (Nossal, 1989; Ogden, 2008; Ozawa and Castello, 2001). The purpose of the initial sanctions was to coerce Iraq into following international law, which included the recognized sovereignty of Kuwait (Pape, 1997, 1998; Ponte, 2004; Reilly, 2012; Reisman and Stevick, 1998).

The second category is those sanctions with the purpose to contain a threat to peace within a geographical boundary (Richard and Raimo, 1999; Ross, 1989; Rothwell and Stephens, 2016; Ryngaert, 2015). The 2010 Iran nuclear proliferation debate is a contemporary example (Saeidnia and Abdollahi, 2013; Seyfi and Hall, 2019). On June 9, the current United Nations Security Council passed Resolution 1929 providing restrictions on missile and weaponry materials that could be used for the creation of destructive weapons. This principle of restriction is to contain the possibility of Iranian aggression within the neighboring region (Solingen, 2012; Stephanides et al., 2002; Strack and Strack, 1978).

The third category involves the United Nations Security Councils condemnation of actions of a specific action or policy of a member or non-member nation (Takian, Raoofi, and Kazempour-Ardebili, 2020; Taylor, 2012; Thaver and Ekanayake, 2010). For example, the white minority declared Rhodesian Independence on November 11, 1965. The General assemble and United Nations, in a 107 to 2 vote, took to condemning Rhodesia on all military, economic, as well as oil and petroleum products (Tridimas and Guiterrex-Fons, 2008). The international display of disapproval forced sanctions onto the Rhodesian people, but without a clear goal as to a remedy for the economic sanctions (Von Glahn and Taulbee, 2015; Wallensteen and Staibano, 2005).

The three categories are a blanket explanation of the reason sanctions are applied to nations (Afesorgbor, 2019; Alam, 2008; Al-Jawaheri, 2008). However, it does not go as far as to say that voting members share the same political reasons for imposing them (Von Glahn and Taulbee, 2015; Wallensteen and Staibano, 2005). It is often the case for many nations to be driven by self-interests in one or more categories when voting on whether to implement sanctions (Tridimas and Guiterrex-Fons, 2008). Diplomatic sanctions are political measures taken to express disapproval or displeasure at a certain action through diplomatic and political means (Takian, Raoofi, and Kazempour-Ardebili, 2020; Taylor, 2012; Thaver and Ekanayake, 2010). This is seen as a better alternative than affecting economic or military relations (Solingen, 2012; Stephanides et al., 2002; Strack and Strack, 1978). Measures include limitations or cancellations of high-level government visits or expelling or withdrawing diplomatic missions or staff (Saeidnia and Abdollahi, 2013; Seyfi and Hall, 2019).

Economic sanctions can vary from imposing import duties on goods to blocking the export of certain goods from the target country, to a full naval blockade of the target's ports in an effort to verify, and curb or block specified imported goods (Richard and Raimo, 1999; Ross, 1989; Rothwell and Stephens, 2016; Ryngaert, 2015). Some examples of economic sanctions include Napoleon's Continental System of 1806–1814, which was directed against British trade (Pape, 1997, 1998; Ponte, 2004; Reilly, 2012; Reisman and Stevick, 1998). Another example are the UN sanctions against Zimbabwe, South Africa, Cuba, and Iraq (Nossal, 1989; Ogden, 2008; Ozawa and Castello, 2001). Sometimes there is almost universal condemnation of actions leading to wide-scale sanctions (Morgan and Schwebach, 1997; Mueller and Mueller, 1999). A case in point are the sanctions on Burma or Myanmar since 1993 for overthrowing a democratic government and replacing it with a military Junta (Matsushita et al., 2015; McCorkell and Gillard, 2010; Meyer and Thein, 2014; Mikhaylova, Babich, and Smirnova, 2017).

There are many examples of sanctions with mixed success and approval (Levy, 1999; Leyton-Brown, 2017; Li and Saghaian, 2013; Lutz and Lux, 1995; Mahmud, 2001). The case of South Africa gives rise to the typical example used for arguing for the effectiveness of sanctions, though that alleged effectiveness remains a matter of debate (Kiriya, 2017; Kirshner, 1997; Klotz, 1995; Koskenniemi, 2014; Kunz, 1960; Laub, 2015; Lee, 2018). In 2001 and 2002, the United States imposed economic sanctions against the state of Zimbabwe. This was codified through the Zimbabwe Democracy and Economic Recovery Act of 2001 or ZDERA, S. 494 (Kaempfer and Lowenberg, 2000; Kaempfer, Lowenberg, and Mertens, 2004; Kendall, 2000). This legislative instrument had the effect of vetoing or voting against access to financing, debt relief and rescheduling, and forcing the Zimbabwean government to operate on a cash-only basis (Jiang, Chen, and Liu, 2010; Jing, Kaempfer, and Lowenberg, 2003; Kaempfer and Lowenberg, 1999). On August 2, 2017, President Donald Trump signed into law the Countering America's Adversaries Through Sanctions Act that grouped together sanctions against Russia, Iran, and North Korea. There is a wide diversity of sanctions and their stipulations (Igami, 2015; Ivanov, Sypchenko, and Webster, 2017; James, 2013). Similarly, military sanctions can range from carefully targeted military strikes to degrade a nation's conventional or non-conventional capabilities, to the less aggressive form of an arms embargo to cut off supplies of arms or dual-use items (Hovdenak, 2009; Huang, Xu, and Lu, 2011; Huebner, 2009; Hultman and Peksen, 2017; Hurd, 2017).

Sport sanctions are used as a way of psychological warfare, intended to crush the morale of the general population of the target country (Hanushek and Woessmann, 2010; Haugh and Kitson, 2007; Hinds, 1997; Hiraide and Chakraborty, 2012; Ho-Chuan, Yi-Chen, and Chih-Chuan, 2012). Sports sanctions were imposed as part of the international sanctions against the Federal Republic of Yugoslavia between 1992 and 1995 (Grauvogel, Licht, and von Soest, 2017; Gui, 1991; Hafner-Burton and Montgomery, 2008). They were enacted by UN Security Council by resolution 757 (Genzberger et al., 1994; Gharehgozli, 2017; Goodhart, 2016; Grauvogel and Von

Soest, 2014). The Gleneagles Agreement approved by the Commonwealth of Nations in 1977, committed member nations to discourage contact and competition between their sportsmen and sporting organizations, teams, or individuals from South Africa (Franzway and Fonow, 2011; Frick, Humphreys, and Scheel, 2015; Fridell, 2014; Fu et al., 2020). However, it was not binding and unable to stop events such as the 1980 British Lions tour to South Africa or the 1981 South Africa rugby union tour of New Zealand (Escribà-Folch, 2010, 2012; Escribà-Folch and Wright, 2010; Farzanegan, 2013; Farzanegan and Hayo, 2019).

The United Nations Security Council can implement sanctions on political leaders or economic individuals (Drury and Peksen, 2014; Dunn and Shaw, 2001; Dunoff, Ratner, and Wippman, 2015; Eliat and Einav, 2004; Eriksson, 2016). These persons usually find ways of evading their sanction bccause of political connections within their nation (Doxey, 1972, 1980, 1983, 1987; Drezner, 2000, 2011, 2015; Drezner and Drezner, 1999). The sanctions on the environment include both economic and political issues such as trade since these are all interdependent (De Vos, 2010; Defourny, 2013; Denzin, 2008; Devarajan and Mottaghi, 2015; Dobler, 2008). The trade barriers and restrictions on trade are the key factors since they are engaged with the problems of endangered species, ozone-depleting chemicals, and environmental laws (Crawford and Klotz, 1999; Crook, 2013; David and Holliday, 2012; Daviron and Ponte, 2007; De Visscher, 2015). Although the sanctions and laws regarding the environment are relatively new; recent concerns over the environmental issues encouraged individuals and governments to actively cooperate in dealing the problems (Choi and Luo, 2013; Clegg and Palmer, 1996; Cleveland, 2001; Cortright et al., 2000; Cranmer, Heinrich, and Desmarais, 2014).

It is sometimes claimed that sanctions imposed by single countries or by an intergovernmental body like the United Nations are "illegal" or "criminal" (Chan, 2000; Chan and Drury, 2000; Chen et al., 2019; Cheraghali, 2013; Chiquiar, 2008). The opponents of this sanction refer to them as being illegal due to several conventions such as in the right to development and self-defense (Buck, Gallant, and Nossal, 1998; Caron, 1989; Carter, 1987; Caruso, 2003; Chachavalpongpun, 2014). A 1996 report by International Progress Organization (IPO) criticized sanctions as an illegitimate form of collective punishment of the weakest and poorest members of society, the infants, the children, the chronically ill, and the elderly (Blyton, 2004; Bolander, 2011; Borszik, 2014, 2016; Bosco, 2012; Bradley and Galbraith, 2016; Brzoska, 2015). Sanctions have long been the subject of controversy as scholars question their effects on citizens, the level of ethnocentrism involved when designing and implementing sanctions, and the possibility of ineffectiveness (Biersteker, Eckert, and Tourinho, 2016).

Supporters of sanctions argue that regardless of the sanctions effects on a group of people, those citizens were most likely already being oppressed by their government (Bacchiega and Borzaga, 2003; Baldwin and Pape, 1998; Barber, 1979; Bederman and Keitner, 2016). Supporters also argue that sanctions are the best alternative international tool, as opposed to taking no action (Askari et al., 2003; Attia, Grauvogel, and von Soest, 2020; Bacchiega and Borzaga, 2003; Baldwin and Pape, 1998). Furthermore, that in the absence of sanctions, oppressive regimes have no incentive to reform (Wallensteen and Staibano, 2005).

On the side of opposition, it is asserted that sanctions are a way to promote nationalistic values and diminish the culture of a state (Von Glahn and Taulbee, 2015; Wallensteen and Staibano, 2005). In a counterargument, support is argued on the basis that something must be done and democratic peace theory is cited as sound reasoning despite any possible cultural insensitivity (Von Glahn and Taulbee, 2015). In the case of the United States, it is important to note that the US has little to lose, in regard to public perception, as many around the world already have a distaste for American international policy and actions (Von Glahn and Taulbee, 2015). In regard to the effectiveness of the sanctions, supporters concede that multilateral sanctions have been found to work 33% of the time (Tridimas and Guiterrex-Fons, 2008).

There are several ways to remove and dissolve sanctions that have been imposed on a nation or nations (Tridimas and Guiterrex-Fons, 2008). In some cases, such as those imposed on Iraq in 1990, only a new resolution can be used to lift the sanctions (Tridimas and Guiterrex-Fons, 2008). This is done when no provision is put in the resolution for the lifting of sanctions (Thaver and Ekanayake, 2010; Tridimas and Guiterrex-Fons, 2008). Provisions for lifting sanctions only done if the sanctioned party has shown willingness to adopt certain conditions of the Security Council (Taylor, 2012; Thaver and Ekanayake, 2010; Tridimas and Guiterrex-Fons, 2008). Another way sanctions can be lifted is when time limits are implemented with the initial sanction (Takian, Raoofi, and Kazempour-Ardebili, 2020; Taylor, 2012; Thaver and Ekanayake, 2010). After an extended duration, the sanction will eventually be lifted off the nation, with or without cooperation (Strack and Strack, 1978; Takian, Raoofi, and Kazempour-Ardebili, 2020; Taylor, 2012;

Thaver and Ekanayake, 2010). The practice of time limitations has grown over the years and allows for a gradual removal of restrictions on nations conforming, at least in part, to conditions imposed by sanctioning bodies, such as the U.N. Security Council (Strack and Strack, 1978; Takian, Raoofi, and Kazempour-Ardebili, 2020; Taylor, 2012). In the next section, we will consider the enabling role of Chapter VII of the UN Charter.

1.2. CHAPTER VII OF THE UN CHARTER

Chapter VII of the United Nations Charter sets out the UN Security Council's powers to maintain peace (Stephanides et al., 2002; Strack and Strack, 1978; Takian, Raoofi, and Kazempour-Ardebili, 2020). It allows the Council to "determine the existence of any threat to the peace, breach of the peace, or act of aggression" and to take military and nonmilitary action to "restore international peace and security" (Solingen, 2012; Stephanides et al., 2002; Strack and Strack, 1978; Takian, Raoofi, and Kazempour-Ardebili, 2020). Chapter VII also gives the Military Staff Committee responsibility for strategic coordination of forces placed at the disposal of the UN Security Council (Solingen, 2012; Stephanides et al., 2002; Strack and Strack, 1978). It is made up of the chiefs of staff of the five permanent members of the Council (Solingen, 2012; Stephanides et al., 2002; Strack and Strack, 1978; Takian, Raoofi, and Kazempour-Ardebili, 2020). Figure 1.2 summarizes key aspects of the chapter.

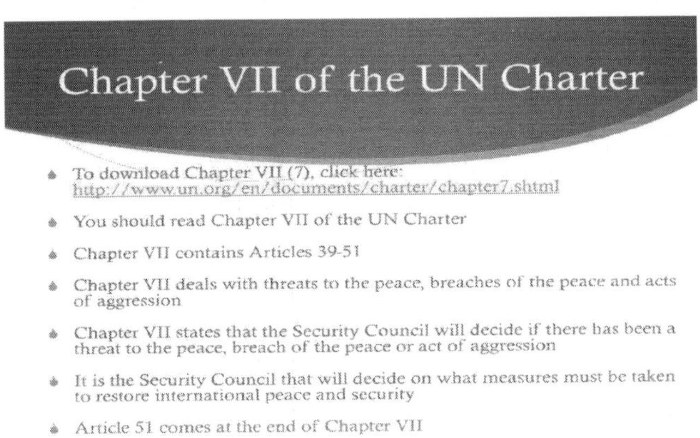

Figure 1.2. Key aspects of Chapter VII of the UN charter.

Source: Slide Serve.

The UN Charter's prohibition of member states of the UN attacking other UN member states is central to the purpose for which the UN was founded in the wake of the destruction of World War II which is to prevent war (Seyfi and Hall, 2019; Solingen, 2012; Stephanides et al., 2002). This overriding concern is also reflected in the Nuremberg Trials' concept of a crime against peace (Seyfi and Hall, 2019; Solingen, 2012; Stephanides et al., 2002). In that sense, the crime comprised starting or waging a war against the territorial integrity, political independence, or sovereignty of a state, or in violation of international treaties or agreements (Seyfi and Hall, 2019; Solingen, 2012; Stephanides et al., 2002). It was held to be the crime that makes all war crimes possible (Saeidnia and Abdollahi, 2013; Seyfi and Hall, 2019).

The United Nations was established after World War II (Saeidnia and Abdollahi, 2013; Seyfi and Hall, 2019). This followed the ultimate failure of diplomacy despite the existence of the League of Nations in the years between the First and Second World War (Ryngaert, 2015; Saeidnia and Abdollahi, 2013). The Security Council was thus granted broad powers through Chapter VII as a reaction to the failure of the League (Rothwell and Stephens, 2016; Ryngaert, 2015; Saeidnia and Abdollahi, 2013). These broad powers allow it to enjoy greater power than any other international organization in history (Ross, 1989; Rothwell and Stephens, 2016; Ryngaert, 2015; Saeidnia and Abdollahi, 2013). It can be argued that the strong executive powers granted to it give it the role of executive of the international community or even of an 'international government' (Richard and Raimo, 1999; Ross, 1989; Rothwell and Stephens, 2016; Ryngaert, 2015).

The covenant of the League of Nations provided, for the first time in history, enforcement of international responsibilities (i.e., adhering to the Covenant of the League of Nations) through economic and military sanctions (Reisman and Stevick, 1998; Richard and Raimo, 1999; Ross, 1989; Rothwell and Stephens, 2016; Ryngaert, 2015). Member states were also obliged, even without prior decision by the council to act against states that acted unlawfully in the eyes of the League's Covenant (Reilly, 2012; Reisman and Stevick, 1998; Richard and Raimo, 1999; Ross, 1989; Rothwell and Stephens, 2016). This meant that the peace process was largely dependent on the willingness of member states (Reilly, 2012; Reisman and Stevick, 1998; Richard and Raimo, 1999; Ross, 1989; Rothwell and Stephens, 2016). In fact, the Covenant of the League of Nations did not provide binding decisions (Ponte, 2004; Reilly, 2012; Reisman and Stevick, 1998; Richard and Raimo, 1999; Ross, 1989; Rothwell and Stephens, 2016).

The Council of the League was only responsible for recommending military force (Ponte, 2004; Reilly, 2012; Reisman and Stevick, 1998; Richard and Raimo, 1999; Ross, 1989). Moreover, Article 11 paragraph 1 of the covenant states that any war or threat of war, whether immediately affecting any of the Members of the League or not, is a matter of concern to the whole League, and the League shall take any action that may be deemed wise and effectual to safeguard the peace of nations (Ponte, 2004; Reilly, 2012; Reisman and Stevick, 1998; Richard and Raimo, 1999).

Such an assertion can be seen as an authorization of the use of force and other enforcement measures (Pape, 1998; Ponte, 2004; Reilly, 2012; Reisman and Stevick, 1998; Richard and Raimo, 1999). However, states repeatedly insisted that this did not make decisions by the League binding (Pape, 1997, 1998; Ponte, 2004; Reilly, 2012; Reisman and Stevick, 1998). This resulted in an unprecedented will by both the powers at the Dumbarton Oaks Conference and the states present at the San Francisco Conference to submit to a central organ like that of the Security Council (Ozawa and Castello, 2001; Pape, 1997, 1998; Ponte, 2004; Reilly, 2012). Despite long debate over whether the General Assembly should also have power over decisions made by the Security Council, it was eventually decided by a large majority vote that the Security Council should maintain its executive power (Ozawa and Castello, 2001; Pape, 1997, 1998; Ponte, 2004). This was because, as the major powers emphasized, a strong executive organ would be needed for the maintenance of world peace (Ozawa and Castello, 2001; Pape, 1997, 1998). This emphasis was advocated by the Chinese representative, recalling the powerlessness of the League during the Manchuria Crisis (Ozawa and Castello, 2001; Pape, 1997, 1998).

Article 42 states that should the Security Council consider that measures provided for in Article 41 would be inadequate or have proved to be inadequate, it may take such action by air, sea, or land forces as may be necessary to maintain or restore international peace and security (Ogden, 2008; Ozawa and Castello, 2001; Pape, 1997). Such action may include demonstrations, blockade, and other operations by air, sea, or land forces of Members of the United Nations (Nossal, 1989; Ogden, 2008; Ozawa and Castello, 2001). Article 51 provides for the right of countries to engage in self-defense, including collective self-defense, against an armed attack including cyber-attacks (Nossal, 1989; Ogden, 2008; Ozawa and Castello, 2001). Nothing in the Charter impaired the inherent right of individual or collective self-defense if an armed attack occurs against a Member of the

United Nations (Nossal, 1989; Ogden, 2008). Such defense could occur until the Security Council has taken measures necessary to maintain international peace and security (Mueller and Mueller, 1999; Nossal, 1989; Ogden, 2008). Measures taken by Members in the exercise of this right of self-defense shall be immediately reported to the Security Council (Morgan and Schwebach, 1997; Mueller and Mueller, 1999; Nossal, 1989; Ogden, 2008). In any case such actions shall not in any way affect the authority and responsibility of the Security Council under the Charter to take at any time such action as it deems necessary in order to maintain or restore international peace and security (Morgan and Schwebach, 1997; Mueller and Mueller, 1999; Nossal, 1989).

This chapter was the impetus for much international pact-making and has been cited by the United States as support for the Nicaragua case and the legality of the Vietnam War (Morgan and Schwebach, 1997; Mueller and Mueller, 1999). According to that argument, although South Vietnam is not an independent sovereign State or a member of the United Nations; it nevertheless enjoys the right of self-defense, and the United States is entitled to participate in its collective defense (Morgan and Schwebach, 1997; Mueller and Mueller, 1999). Article 51 has been described as difficult to adjudicate with any certainty in real-life (Mikhaylova, Babich, and Smirnova, 2017; Morgan and Schwebach, 1997).

Most Chapter VII resolutions first determine the existence of a threat to the peace, a breach of the peace, or an act of aggression in accordance with Article 39 (Meyer and Thein, 2014; Mikhaylova, Babich, and Smirnova, 2017). Secondly, they provide for deciding explicitly under Chapter VII (McCorkell and Gillard, 2010; Meyer and Thein, 2014; Mikhaylova, Babich, and Smirnova, 2017). However, not all resolutions are that explicit, there is disagreement about the Chapter VII status of a small number of resolutions (Matsushita et al., 2015; McCorkell and Gillard, 2010; Meyer and Thein, 2014; Mikhaylova, Babich, and Smirnova, 2017). As a reaction to this ambiguity, a formal definition of Chapter VII resolutions has recently been proposed (Matsushita et al., 2015; McCorkell and Gillard, 2010; Meyer and Thein, 2014; Mikhaylova, Babich, and Smirnova, 2017). A Security Council Resolution is considered to be 'a Chapter VII resolution' if it makes an explicit determination that the situation under consideration constitutes a threat to the peace, a breach of the peace, or an act of aggression and explicitly or implicitly states that the council is acting under Chapter VII in the adoption of some or all operative paragraphs (Mahmud, 2001; Matsushita et al., 2015; McCorkell and Gillard, 2010; Meyer and Thein, 2014).

Chapter VII resolutions are very rarely isolated measures (Lutz and Lux, 1995; Mahmud, 2001; Matsushita et al., 2015; McCorkell and Gillard, 2010; Meyer and Thein, 2014). Often the first response to a crisis is a resolution demanding the crisis be ended (Lutz and Lux, 1995; Mahmud, 2001; Matsushita et al., 2015; McCorkell and Gillard, 2010). This is only later followed by an actual Chapter VII resolution detailing the measures required to secure compliance with the first resolution (Lutz and Lux, 1995; Mahmud, 2001; Matsushita et al., 2015). Sometimes dozens of resolutions are passed in subsequent years to modify and extend the mandate of the first Chapter VII resolution as the situation evolves (Li and Saghaian, 2013; Lutz and Lux, 1995; Mahmud, 2001; Matsushita et al., 2015). The next section focuses on the economic aspects of international sanctions.

1.3. ECONOMIC INTERNATIONAL SANCTIONS

Economic sanctions are commercial and financial penalties applied by one or more countries against a targeted self-governing state, group, or individual (Leyton-Brown, 2017; Li and Saghaian, 2013; Lutz and Lux, 1995; Mahmud, 2001). Economic sanctions are not necessarily imposed because of economic circumstances (Levy, 1999; Leyton-Brown, 2017; Li and Saghaian, 2013; Lutz and Lux, 1995; Mahmud, 2001). Indeed, they may also be imposed for a variety of political, military, and social issues (Levy, 1999; Leyton-Brown, 2017; Li and Saghaian, 2013). Economic sanctions can be used for achieving domestic and international purposes in this respect (Lee, 2018; Levy, 1999; Leyton-Brown, 2017; Li and Saghaian, 2013). Economic sanctions generally aim to create good relationships between the country enforcing the sanctions and the receiver of said sanctions (Laub, 2015; Lee, 2018; Levy, 1999; Leyton-Brown, 2017; Li and Saghaian, 2013). However, the efficacy of sanctions is debatable, and sanctions can have unintended consequences (Kunz, 1960; Laub, 2015; Lee, 2018; Levy, 1999; Leyton-Brown, 2017; Li and Saghaian, 2013). Figure 1.3 highlights examples of targeted economic sanctions as used by the UN.

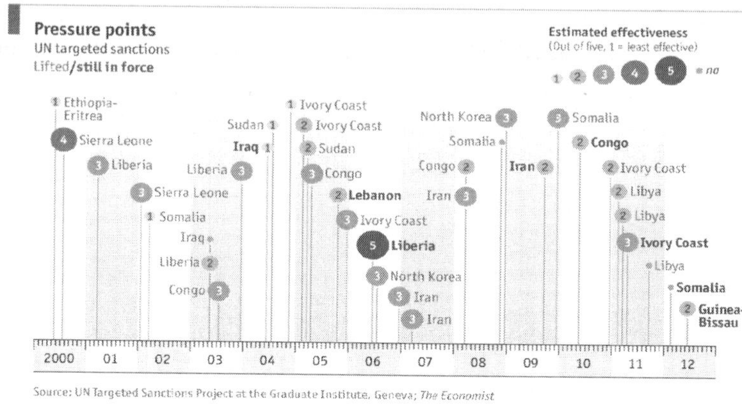

Figure 1.3. Pressure points and economic international sanctions.

Source: The Economist.

Economic sanctions may include various forms of trade barriers, tariffs, and restrictions on financial transactions (Koskenniemi, 2014; Kunz, 1960; Laub, 2015; Lee, 2018; Levy, 1999; Leyton-Brown, 2017). An embargo is similar, but usually implies a more severe sanction, often with a direct no-fly zone or naval blockade (Klotz, 1995; Koskenniemi, 2014; Kunz, 1960; Laub, 2015; Lee, 2018; Levy, 1999). An embargo is the partial or complete prohibition of commerce and trade with a particular country, state, or a group of countries (Kirshner, 1997; Klotz, 1995; Koskenniemi, 2014; Kunz, 1960; Laub, 2015; Lee, 2018). Embargoes are considered strong diplomatic measures imposed in an effort, by the imposing country, to elicit a given national-interest result from the country on which it is imposed (Kirshner, 1997; Klotz, 1995; Koskenniemi, 2014; Kunz, 1960; Laub, 2015; Lee, 2018). Embargoes are generally considered legal barriers to trade, not to be confused with blockades, which are often considered to be acts of war (Kiriya, 2017; Kirshner, 1997; Klotz, 1995; Koskenniemi, 2014; Kunz, 1960; Laub, 2015; Lee, 2018).

Embargoes can mean limiting or banning export or import, creating quotas for quantity, imposing special tolls, taxes, banning freight or transport vehicles, freezing, or seizing freights, assets, bank accounts, limiting the transport of particular technologies or products. A case in point is the COCOM conditions which were imposed during the cold war (Kendall, 2000; Kiriya, 2017; Kirshner, 1997; Klotz, 1995; Koskenniemi, 2014; Kunz, 1960; Laub, 2015; Lee, 2018). In response to embargoes, a closed economy or autarky often develops in an area subjected to heavy embargo (Kendall, 2000; Kiriya, 2017; Kirshner, 1997; Klotz, 1995; Koskenniemi, 2014; Kunz, 1960). Effectiveness of embargoes is thus in proportion to the extent and degree of international participation (Kaempfer, Lowenberg, and Mertens, 2004; Kendall, 2000; Kiriya, 2017; Kirshner, 1997). Embargoes can be an opportunity for some countries to develop faster a self-sufficiency (Kaempfer and Lowenberg, 2000; Kaempfer, Lowenberg, and Mertens, 2004; Kendall, 2000). However, an embargo may be necessary in various economic situations of the state forced to impose it, and not just in the case of a war (Kaempfer and Lowenberg, 1999; Kaempfer and Lowenberg, 2000; Kaempfer, Lowenberg, and Mertens, 2004).

Economic sanctions are used as a tool of foreign policy by many governments (Jing, Kaempfer, and Lowenberg, 2003; Kaempfer and Lowenberg, 1999, 2000). Economic sanctions are usually imposed by a larger country upon a smaller country for one of two reasons. First, the smaller country is a perceived threat to the security of the larger nation or the smaller country treats its citizens unfairly (Jiang, Chen, and Liu, 2010; Jing, Kaempfer, and Lowenberg, 2003; Kaempfer and Lowenberg, 1999). Second, they can be used as a coercive measure for achieving policy goals related to trade or for humanitarian violations (Jiang, Chen, and Liu, 2010; Jing, Kaempfer, and Lowenberg, 2003; Kaempfer and Lowenberg, 1999). Economic sanctions are used as an alternative weapon instead of going to war to achieve desired outcomes (Jiang, Chen, and Liu, 2010; Jing, Kaempfer, and Lowenberg, 2003). Some researchers argue that regime change is the most frequent foreign-policy objective of economic sanctions, accounting for just over 39% of cases of their imposition (James, 2013; Jiang, Chen, and Liu, 2010; Jing, Kaempfer, and Lowenberg, 2003).

Imposing sanctions on an opponent also affects the economy of the imposing country to some degree (Ivanov, Sypchenko, and Webster, 2017; James, 2013). If import restrictions are promulgated, consumers in the imposing country may have restricted choices of goods (Igami, 2015; Ivanov, Sypchenko, and Webster, 2017; James, 2013). If export restrictions are imposed or if sanctions prohibit companies in the imposing country from trading with the target country, the imposing country may lose markets and investment opportunities to competing countries (Igami, 2015; Ivanov, Sypchenko, and Webster, 2017; James, 2013). Critics of sanctions argue that in nondemocratic regimes, the extent to which this affects political outcomes is contested, because such regimes do not respond as strongly to the popular will (Hurd, 2017; Igami, 2015; Ivanov, Sypchenko, and Webster,

2017; James, 2013). Others suggest sanctions are popular not because they are known to be effective; but because there is nothing else between words and military action if you want to bring pressure upon a government (Hultman and Peksen, 2017; Hurd, 2017; Igami, 2015; Ivanov, Sypchenko, and Webster, 2017; James, 2013).

Sanctions have been criticized on humanitarian grounds, as they negatively impact a nation's economy and can also cause collateral damage on ordinary citizens (Huebner, 2009; Hultman and Peksen, 2017; Hurd, 2017; Igami, 2015; Ivanov, Sypchenko, and Webster, 2017). Some researchers imply that sanctions can degenerate human rights in the target country (Huang, Xu, and Lu, 2011; Huebner, 2009; Hultman and Peksen, 2017; Hurd, 2017; Igami, 2015). Certain policy analysts believe imposing trade restrictions only serves to hurt ordinary people as opposed to government elites (Hovdenak, 2009; Huang, Xu, and Lu, 2011; Huebner, 2009; Hultman and Peksen, 2017; Hurd, 2017). Moreover, others have likened the practice to siege warfare (Ho-Chuan, Yi-Chen, and Chih-Chuan, 2012; Hovdenak, 2009; Huang, Xu, and Lu, 2011; Huebner, 2009; Hultman and Peksen, 2017). Nevertheless, there is a substantial history of economic sanctions being used in one way or another (Hiraide and Chakraborty, 2012; Ho-Chuan, Yi-Chen, and Chih-Chuan, 2012; Hovdenak, 2009; Huang, Xu, and Lu, 2011).

The use of economic sanctions became much more common in the 20th century, particularly with the formation of The League of Nations in 1919 (Hinds, 1997; Hiraide and Chakraborty, 2012; Ho-Chuan, Yi-Chen, and Chih-Chuan, 2012; Hovdenak, 2009; Huang, Xu, and Lu, 2011). The Abyssinia Crisis resulted in League sanctions against Mussolini's Italy in 1935 under Article 16 of the Covenant (Haugh and Kitson, 2007; Hinds, 1997; Hiraide and Chakraborty, 2012; Ho-Chuan, Yi-Chen, and Chih-Chuan, 2012; Hovdenak, 2009). Petroleum supplies, however, were not stopped, nor the Suez Canal closed to Italy, and the conquest proceeded (Hanushek and Woessmann, 2010; Haugh and Kitson, 2007; Hinds, 1997; Hiraide and Chakraborty, 2012; Ho-Chuan, Yi-Chen, and Chih-Chuan, 2012). The sanctions were lifted in 1936 and Italy left the League in 1937 (Hafner-Burton and Montgomery, 2008; Hanushek and Woessmann, 2010; Haugh and Kitson, 2007; Hinds, 1997). After World War Two, the League was replaced by the more expansive United Nations in 1945 (Gui, 1991; Hafner-Burton and Montgomery, 2008; Hanushek and Woessmann, 2010; Haugh and Kitson, 2007). Sanctions have become a commonly used foreign policy tool in the 21st century in countless situations ranging from disputes to hostile confrontations (Gui, 1991; Hafner-Burton and Montgomery, 2008;

Hanushek and Woessmann, 2010). In the next section, we review an earlier form of sanctions in the form of the Continental System.

1.4. THE CONTINENTAL SYSTEM OF SANCTIONS

The Continental System or Continental Blockade was the foreign policy of Napoleon Bonaparte which he imposed on the United Kingdom during the Napoleonic Wars (De Visscher, 2015). This was a strategic response to the naval blockade of the French coasts (Aaslestad and Joor, 2014; Asprey, 2001; Corbett, 2017; Daly, 2007; Dwyer and Forrest, 2007). That blockade had been enacted by the British government on the 16th of May 1806 (Asprey, 2001; Corbett, 2017; Daly, 2007; Dwyer and Forrest, 2007; Ellis, 1981; Guillebaud, 1940; Hartley, 2003). Consequently, Napoleon issued the Berlin Decree on the 21st of November 1806 (Corbett, 2017; Daly, 2007; Dwyer and Forrest, 2007; Ellis, 1981; Guillebaud, 1940; Hartley, 2003; Heckscher, 1922). This decree created an embargo on British trade with the assistance of other European countries that were under the control or influence of Napoleon (Daly, 2007; Dwyer and Forrest, 2007; Ellis, 1981; Guillebaud, 1940; Hartley, 2003; Heckscher, 1922; Lefebvre and Case, 1969). The embargo was applied intermittently rather than as one process (Dwyer and Forrest, 2007; Ellis, 1981; Guillebaud, 1940; Hartley, 2003; Heckscher, 1922; Lefebvre and Case, 1969). It only ended on the 11th of April 1814 after Napoleon's first abdication (Ellis, 1981; Guillebaud, 1940; Hartley, 2003; Heckscher, 1922; Lefebvre and Case, 1969; Markham, 2003). Figure 1.4 is a geographical representation of the area that was affected by the Continental System.

In the event, this blockade caused little economic damage to the United Kingdom (Guillebaud, 1940; Hartley, 2003; Heckscher, 1922; Lefebvre and Case, 1969; Markham, 2003; Parry, 2001). However, British exports to the continent dropped from 55% to 25% between 1802 and 1806. This drop that was directly or indirectly attributable to the blockade (Hartley, 2003; Heckscher, 1922; Lefebvre and Case, 1969; Markham, 2003; Parry, 2001; Riley, 2013; Rose, 1893). When Napoleon recognized the fact that a lot of trade was ongoing via Spain and Russia, he launched a military assault on the two nations with a view to invading or otherwise subduing them(Heckscher, 1922; Lefebvre and Case, 1969; Markham, 2003; Parry, 2001; Riley, 2013; Rose, 1893; Ruppenthal, 1943). At this point, the Napoleonic army was bogged down by the effects of the Spanish war of independence which was simultaneously taking place (Lefebvre and Case, 1969; Markham, 2003;

Parry, 2001; Riley, 2013; Rose, 1893; Ruppenthal, 1943; Sloane, 1898a). The French forces were roundly beaten and had to withdraw from Russia by the end of 1812, a fact that severely hindered the ability of the French state to fully implement the dictates of the embargo on the United Kingdom (Markham, 2003; Parry, 2001; Riley, 2013; Rose, 1893; Ruppenthal, 1943; Sloane, 1898a, b; Ziller, 2007).

Figure 1.4. Geographical representation of the continental system.

Source: Wikipedia.

All these actions against the United Kingdom were enshrined in the Berlin Decree (Parry, 2001; Riley, 2013; Rose, 1893; Ruppenthal, 1943; Sloane, 1898a, b; Ziller, 2007). This was an order that forbade the import of British goods into any European countries allied with or dependent upon France (Riley, 2013; Rose, 1893; Ruppenthal, 1943; Sloane, 1898a, b; Ziller, 2007). This meant cutting off all contact with the United Kingdom, even if that contact was through nothing more than mail (Aaslestad and Joor,

2014; Asprey, 2001; Corbett, 2017; Daly, 2007; Dwyer and Forrest, 2007; Ellis, 1981). Despite all these restrictions, British merchants still managed to smuggle a substantial amount of goods (Guillebaud, 1940; Hartley, 2003; Heckscher, 1922; Lefebvre and Case, 1969; Markham, 2003; Parry, 2001). The result was that the Continental system was no longer as effective as it had been originally,(Riley, 2013; Rose, 1893; Ruppenthal, 1943; Sloane, 1898a, b; Ziller, 2007). In other words, France was unable to meet her strategic objectives of crippling the British economy (Aaslestad and Joor, 2014; Asprey, 2001; Corbett, 2017; Daly, 2007; Dwyer and Forrest, 2007). Just like contemporary sanctions are sometimes used to break the enemy (an example being the USA against Iran, North Korea, and Cuba); the Continental system was rendered ineffective by virtue of the loopholes that could be exploited by the European countries as well as the United Kingdom (Asprey, 2001; Corbett, 2017; Daly, 2007; Dwyer and Forrest, 2007; Ellis, 1981; Guillebaud, 1940; Hartley, 2003).

Despite the overall failure of the embargo, there was some damage to British trade during the critical period running from 1808 to 1812 (Corbett, 2017; Daly, 2007; Dwyer and Forrest, 2007; Ellis, 1981; Guillebaud, 1940; Hartley, 2003; Heckscher, 1922). Nevertheless, British supremacy on the seas helped the United Kingdom to turn to an alternative in the form of trade with North and South America (Daly, 2007; Dwyer and Forrest, 2007; Ellis, 1981; Guillebaud, 1940; Hartley, 2003; Heckscher, 1922; Lefebvre and Case, 1969). At the same time, the United Kingdom embarked on a program of large-scale smuggling in Europe. Ironically, France also suffered from the loss of its trading relationship with the United Kingdom (Dwyer and Forrest, 2007; Ellis, 1981; Guillebaud, 1940; Hartley, 2003; Heckscher, 1922; Lefebvre and Case, 1969). Those governments that had been harmed by the Continental System eventually started pulling away from Napoleon's coalition (Ellis, 1981; Guillebaud, 1940; Hartley, 2003; Heckscher, 1922; Lefebvre and Case, 1969; Markham, 2003).

This is true of modern sanctions as it was of the Napoleonic era (Guillebaud, 1940; Hartley, 2003; Heckscher, 1922; Lefebvre and Case, 1969; Markham, 2003; Parry, 2001). Often the price of an embargo takes in many people on both sides (Hartley, 2003; Heckscher, 1922; Lefebvre and Case, 1969; Markham, 2003; Parry, 2001; Riley, 2013; Rose, 1893). For an imperial power, there is the possibility of an even greater cost of engaging with very powerful enemies that can eventually diminish the colonial strength of the aggressor nation (Heckscher, 1922; Lefebvre and Case,

1969; Markham, 2003; Parry, 2001; Riley, 2013; Rose, 1893; Ruppenthal, 1943). In the case of sanctions against China, farmers in the USA have been significantly harmed by the lack of market for their soy as a case in point (Lefebvre and Case, 1969; Markham, 2003; Parry, 2001; Riley, 2013; Rose, 1893; Ruppenthal, 1943; Sloane, 1898a). It is for these reasons, that some prefer a diplomatic solution to outright embargos (Markham, 2003; Parry, 2001; Riley, 2013; Rose, 1893; Ruppenthal, 1943; Sloane, 1898a, b; Ziller, 2007).

Napoleon had planned to defeat the United Kingdom through the deliberate and sustained destruction of the island nation's ability to trade (Parry, 2001; Riley, 2013; Rose, 1893; Ruppenthal, 1943; Sloane, 1898a, b; Ziller, 2007). This is a tactic that is often used in international sanctions with a view that the nation that is being attacked will eventually moderate its behavior to avoid destroying its own economy (Riley, 2013; Rose, 1893; Ruppenthal, 1943; Sloane, 1898a, b; Ziller, 2007). As an island nation, trade was vital to the fortunes of the United Kingdom and its ability to avoid economic catastrophes (Aaslestad and Joor, 2014; Asprey, 2001; Corbett, 2017; Daly, 2007; Dwyer and Forrest, 2007; Ellis, 1981). Hence, Napoleon calculated that by isolating Britain economically, he would easily invade the nation following its economic collapse (Guillebaud, 1940; Hartley, 2003; Heckscher, 1922; Lefebvre and Case, 1969; Markham, 2003; Parry, 2001). However, like all sanctions regimes, the Continental System relied on two assumptions that were eventually confounded. First, it was assumed that the United Kingdom would not be able to access alternatives quickly enough to overcome the impact of the embargoes (Riley, 2013; Rose, 1893; Ruppenthal, 1943; Sloane, 1898a, b; Ziller, 2007). Secondly, that the impact of that embargo would not have such a significant effect on the aggressor (in this case, Napoleon's France) that the opportunity costs would render the entire arrangement unworkable (Aaslestad and Joor, 2014; Asprey, 2001; Corbett, 2017; Daly, 2007; Dwyer and Forrest, 2007). These are calculations that are routinely considered when engaging in international sanctions (Asprey, 2001; Corbett, 2017; Daly, 2007; Dwyer and Forrest, 2007; Ellis, 1981; Guillebaud, 1940; Hartley, 2003). The consistency with which this is done is up for debate (Corbett, 2017; Daly, 2007; Dwyer and Forrest, 2007; Ellis, 1981; Guillebaud, 1940; Hartley, 2003; Heckscher, 1922).

The actual mechanisms of the continental system are additionally interesting because they often mirror how sanctions regimes are conducted in the modern world (Daly, 2007; Dwyer and Forrest, 2007; Ellis, 1981; Guillebaud, 1940; Hartley, 2003; Heckscher, 1922; Lefebvre and Case,

1969). Napoleon decreed that all commerce ships wishing to do business in Europe must first stop at a French port to ensure that there was no trade with Britain (Dwyer and Forrest, 2007; Ellis, 1981; Guillebaud, 1940; Hartley, 2003; Heckscher, 1922; Lefebvre and Case, 1969). This meant that France now had oversight and the ability to determine what entered the United Kingdom, the quantities of those items, and the specific routes that it would take (Ellis, 1981; Guillebaud, 1940; Hartley, 2003; Heckscher, 1922; Lefebvre and Case, 1969; Markham, 2003). All European nations and French allies were ordered to stop trading with Britain (Guillebaud, 1940; Hartley, 2003; Heckscher, 1922; Lefebvre and Case, 1969; Markham, 2003; Parry, 2001). Moreover, France threatened Russia with an invasion if they did not comply with these dictates (Hartley, 2003; Heckscher, 1922; Lefebvre and Case, 1969; Markham, 2003; Parry, 2001; Riley, 2013; Rose, 1893). We have often seen this pattern take shape in international sanctions were the aggressor tries to find willing or unwilling allies to attain credibility for their actions (Heckscher, 1922; Lefebvre and Case, 1969; Markham, 2003; Parry, 2001; Riley, 2013; Rose, 1893; Ruppenthal, 1943). A sanctions regime that is sanctioned by the UN for example, is much more likely to succeed than one that is unilateral in nature (Lefebvre and Case, 1969; Markham, 2003; Parry, 2001; Riley, 2013; Rose, 1893; Ruppenthal, 1943; Sloane, 1898a).

Nevertheless, there are always problematic aspects of the implementation that often determine whether the entire endeavor will be a success (Markham, 2003; Parry, 2001; Riley, 2013; Rose, 1893; Ruppenthal, 1943; Sloane, 1898a, b; Ziller, 2007). In the case of Napoleon, his orders backfired in the Iberian Peninsula, especially in Portugal, which was an ally of Britain at the time (Parry, 2001; Riley, 2013; Rose, 1893; Ruppenthal, 1943; Sloane, 1898a, b; Ziller, 2007). This set off the Peninsular War which had far-reaching effects on the French economy and its ability to build alliances in Europe (Riley, 2013; Rose, 1893; Ruppenthal, 1943; Sloane, 1898a, b; Ziller, 2007). France had in effect pushed Russia too hard, both in terms of the Continental System (Aaslestad and Joor, 2014; Asprey, 2001; Corbett, 2017; Daly, 2007; Dwyer and Forrest, 2007; Ellis, 1981). There was consternation about France's demands for control over part of Poland, which many considered to be an invasion of sovereignty (Guillebaud, 1940; Hartley, 2003; Heckscher, 1922; Lefebvre and Case, 1969; Markham, 2003; Parry, 2001). Napoleon's attempted punishment of Russia through a massive invasion 1812 ended up being a military disaster which would eventually bring Napoleon's regime to an end (Riley, 2013; Rose, 1893; Ruppenthal, 1943; Sloane, 1898a, b; Ziller, 2007).

The system had mixed effects on British trade, a similar outcome for many sanctions regimes have also had unintended consequences. For example, the embargo encouraged British merchants to seek out new markets aggressively and to engage in smuggling with continental Europe (Aaslestad and Joor, 2014; Asprey, 2001; Corbett, 2017; Daly, 2007; Dwyer and Forrest, 2007). We already know that countries like Iran, North Korea, and Cuba have been able to survive despite the overwhelming US sanctions against them because they engage in smuggling and other clandestine activities (Alam, 2008; Bederman and Keitner, 2016; Dunoff et al., 2015). In the case of Napoleon's exclusively land-based customs enforcement regime, he was unable to stop British smugglers (Asprey, 2001; Corbett, 2017; Daly, 2007; Dwyer and Forrest, 2007; Ellis, 1981; Guillebaud, 1940; Hartley, 2003). This was mainly true because the smugglers operated with the connivance of Napoleon's chosen rulers of Spain, Westphalia, and other German states (Corbett, 2017; Daly, 2007; Dwyer and Forrest, 2007; Ellis, 1981; Guillebaud, 1940; Hartley, 2003; Heckscher, 1922). The vassal states that had driven Napoleon's imperial ambitions were turning out to be unreliable allies in much the same way as America has often been let down by the unwillingness of partners to go as far as the US government demands in implementing a sanctions regime (Daly, 2007; Dwyer and Forrest, 2007; Ellis, 1981; Guillebaud, 1940; Hartley, 2003; Heckscher, 1922; Lefebvre and Case, 1969).

That is not to say that there were no tangible impacts of the Continental System (Dwyer and Forrest, 2007; Ellis, 1981; Guillebaud, 1940; Hartley, 2003; Heckscher, 1922; Lefebvre and Case, 1969). For example, British exports to the continent fell between 25% and 55% compared to pre-1806 levels (Ellis, 1981; Guillebaud, 1940; Hartley, 2003; Heckscher, 1922; Lefebvre and Case, 1969; Markham, 2003). However, trade sharply increased with the rest of the world (Guillebaud, 1940; Hartley, 2003; Heckscher, 1922; Lefebvre and Case, 1969; Markham, 2003; Parry, 2001). This had the effect of covering much of the decline, and hence rendering the embargo counterproductive at best (Hartley, 2003; Heckscher, 1922; Lefebvre and Case, 1969; Markham, 2003; Parry, 2001; Riley, 2013; Rose, 1893). Britain issued several Orders in Council, which prohibited other countries from trading with France (Heckscher, 1922; Lefebvre and Case, 1969; Markham, 2003; Parry, 2001; Riley, 2013; Rose, 1893; Ruppenthal, 1943). Given the existence of other alliances, these orders provided to be a salvo for the effects of the Continental System (Lefebvre and Case, 1969; Markham, 2003; Parry, 2001; Riley, 2013; Rose, 1893; Ruppenthal, 1943;

Sloane, 1898a). The British also threatened to sink any ship that did not come to a British port or chose to comply with France (Markham, 2003; Parry, 2001; Riley, 2013; Rose, 1893; Ruppenthal, 1943; Sloane, 1898a, b; Ziller, 2007). This double threat created difficulties for neutral nations like the United States (Parry, 2001; Riley, 2013; Rose, 1893; Ruppenthal, 1943; Sloane, 1898a, b; Ziller, 2007). For example, the US government adopted the Embargo Act of 1807 and eventually Macon's Bill No. 2 which ensured that the American economy would not be harmed by the actions of either Britain or France (Riley, 2013; Rose, 1893; Ruppenthal, 1943; Sloane, 1898a, b; Ziller, 2007).

Although the Continental System was designed to hurt Britain, it proved even more damaging to American merchants (Aaslestad and Joor, 2014; Asprey, 2001; Corbett, 2017; Daly, 2007; Dwyer and Forrest, 2007; Ellis, 1981). Together with the issues of the impressment of foreign seamen, and British support for Indian raids in the American west, tensions led to a declaration of war by the US in the War of 1812 which reduced British trade with the United States (Guillebaud, 1940; Hartley, 2003; Heckscher, 1922; Lefebvre and Case, 1969; Markham, 2003; Parry, 2001). The British economy suffered high unemployment and inflation during the embargo. This led to widespread protest and violence (Riley, 2013; Rose, 1893; Ruppenthal, 1943; Sloane, 1898a, b; Ziller, 2007). However, the middle classes and upper classes strongly supported the government which used the army to suppress the working-class unrest, especially the Luddite Movement (Lefebvre and Case, 1969; Markham, 2003; Parry, 2001; Riley, 2013; Rose, 1893; Ruppenthal, 1943; Sloane, 1898a). In the next section, we consider a more recent example of sanctions against Rhodesia, which were somewhat more successful than the Continental System.

1.5. SANCTIONS AGAINST RHODESIA

Rhodesia was a rogue colony that unilaterally declared independence from the British Empire in 1965 and hence inspired significant sanctions from across the globe (Austin, 1966; Boczek, 1968; Cohen, 2011; Curtin, 1969; Fenwick, 1967; Galtung, 1967; Harris, 1968; Hintz, 1972). The minority government at the time instituted a quasi-apartheid system that oppressed the African majority in what is today's Zimbabwe (Boczek, 1968; Cohen, 2011; Curtin, 1969; Fenwick, 1967; Galtung, 1967; Harris, 1968; Hintz, 1972; Kreczko, 1980; Kuyper, 1975). Although the United Kingdom was ostensibly prepared to grant Rhodesia formal independence, this came with several conditions that were deemed unacceptable by the minority government (Cohen, 2011; Curtin, 1969; Fenwick, 1967; Galtung, 1967; Harris, 1968; Hintz, 1972; Kreczko, 1980; Kuyper, 1975). For example, the United Kingdom had adopted a policy of no independence before majority rule (Curtin, 1969; Fenwick, 1967; Galtung, 1967; Harris, 1968; Hintz, 1972; Kreczko, 1980; Kuyper, 1975; McDougal and Reisman, 1968). This meant dictating that in colonies with a population of both indigenous people and European settlers, independence would not be granted without majority rule (Fenwick, 1967; Galtung, 1967; Harris, 1968; Hintz, 1972; Kreczko, 1980; Kuyper, 1975; McDougal and Reisman, 1968).

White Rhodesians were outraged by the suggestion that they could lose their majority, which many of them saw as their God-given right and a form of colonial justice (Galtung, 1967; Harris, 1968; Hintz, 1972; Kreczko, 1980; Kuyper, 1975; McDougal and Reisman, 1968; McKinnell, 1968). There were members of a powerful white minority who felt entitled to absolute political control of the country (Harris, 1968; Hintz, 1972; Kreczko, 1980; Kuyper, 1975; McDougal and Reisman, 1968; McKinnell, 1968; Minter and Schmidt, 1988). Others did not see this as a permanent solution, but one which was the best option at least for the time being (Hintz, 1972; Kreczko, 1980; Kuyper, 1975; McDougal and Reisman, 1968; McKinnell, 1968; Minter and Schmidt, 1988). The white minority continued to exercise considerable influence over the state despite their relatively small numbers (Kreczko, 1980; Kuyper, 1975; McDougal and Reisman, 1968; McKinnell, 1968; Minter and Schmidt, 1988; Mlambo, 2005).

The Rhodesian authorities were also disturbed by the post-independence chaos that was plaguing other African nations at the time (Kuyper, 1975; McDougal and Reisman, 1968; McKinnell, 1968; Minter and Schmidt, 1988; Mlambo, 2005; Mobley, 2002). They therefore felt that if they did not curb the influence of the indigenous populations, they too would face the same chaos (McDougal and Reisman, 1968; McKinnell, 1968; Minter and Schmidt, 1988; Mlambo, 2005; Mobley, 2002; Porter, 1978). Matters came to a head once Rhodesia was introduced as a topic for discussion in international bodies (McKinnell, 1968; Minter and Schmidt, 1988; Mlambo, 2005; Mobley, 2002; Porter, 1978; Rowe, 1999, 2001). This discussion, by extension, touched on the status quo in the colonies at a time when many of them were successfully demanding for independence (Minter and Schmidt, 1988; Mlambo, 2005; Mobley, 2002; Porter, 1978; Rowe, 1999, 2001; Stephenson, 1975). The Rhodesian issue became a matter of concern to the world community (Mlambo, 2005; Mobley, 2002; Porter, 1978; Rowe,

1999, 2001; Stephenson, 1975; Strack and Strack, 1978). It turned into a serious embarrassment to the United Kingdom and its government (Mobley, 2002; Porter, 1978; Rowe, 1999, 2001; Stephenson, 1975; Strack and Strack, 1978). As Figure 1.5 shows, events in Rhodesia were leading to reactions from across the globe.

Figure 1.5. Image of boycotts against Rhodesia.

Source: Blasting News.

Following the federal break-up of Rhodesia which occurred in 1963; the then UK Prime Minister Alec Douglas-Home insisted that preconditions on independence talks hinge on a quintet of related principles (Porter, 1978; Rowe, 1999, 2001; Stephenson, 1975; Strack and Strack, 1978). The first condition was the achievement of unimpeded progress to majority rule (Rowe, 1999, 2001; Stephenson, 1975; Strack and Strack, 1978). The second touched on a firm assurance against any future legislation that could be decidedly detrimental to black interests (Austin, 1966; Boczek, 1968; Cohen, 2011; Curtin, 1969; Fenwick, 1967; Galtung, 1967; Harris, 1968; Hintz, 1972). The third condition was evidence of an improvement in the political status of local Africans (Kreczko, 1980; Kuyper, 1975; McDougal and Reisman, 1968; McKinnell, 1968; Minter and Schmidt, 1988). The fourth condition was evidence of concrete moves towards ending racial discrimination (Mlambo, 2005; Mobley, 2002; Porter, 1978; Rowe, 1999, 2001; Stephenson, 1975; Strack and Strack, 1978). The fifth and final condition was the agreement on a settlement that could be acceptable to the whole population (Austin, 1966; Boczek, 1968; Cohen, 2011; Curtin,

1969; Fenwick, 1967; Galtung, 1967; Harris, 1968; Hintz, 1972). These conditions meant that the white minority governments in colonies were bound to lose some or even most of their power (Boczek, 1968; Cohen, 2011; Curtin, 1969; Fenwick, 1967; Galtung, 1967; Harris, 1968; Hintz, 1972; Kreczko, 1980; Kuyper, 1975). In hindsight, it was inevitable that some of these minority communities would rise to rebel against the conditions that had been imposed on them (Cohen, 2011; Curtin, 1969; Fenwick, 1967; Galtung, 1967; Harris, 1968; Hintz, 1972; Kreczko, 1980; Kuyper, 1975).

The incoming Labor government of Harold Wilson took an even harder line on demanding that all these points be legitimately addressed before an independence agenda could be set (Curtin, 1969; Fenwick, 1967; Galtung, 1967; Harris, 1968; Hintz, 1972; Kreczko, 1980; Kuyper, 1975; McDougal and Reisman, 1968). By 1964, there was growing dissatisfaction with the ongoing negotiations (Fenwick, 1967; Galtung, 1967; Harris, 1968; Hintz, 1972; Kreczko, 1980; Kuyper, 1975; McDougal and Reisman, 1968). The Rhodesian government removed Salisbury's incumbent Winston Field, replacing him with Ian Smith (Harris, 1968; Hintz, 1972; Kreczko, 1980; Kuyper, 1975; McDougal and Reisman, 1968; McKinnell, 1968; Minter and Schmidt, 1988). Smith was the deputy chairman of the conservative Rhodesian Front party, a party that had decidedly pro-White minority inclinations (Galtung, 1967; Harris, 1968; Hintz, 1972; Kreczko, 1980; Kuyper, 1975; McDougal and Reisman, 1968; McKinnell, 1968). Smith became the colony's first Rhodesian-born leader. He soon came to personify resistance to liberals in the British government (Hintz, 1972; Kreczko, 1980; Kuyper, 1975; McDougal and Reisman, 1968; McKinnell, 1968; Minter and Schmidt, 1988). Smith was also perceived as a strong voice for those agitating for change in the negotiations process, with many perceiving delays and obstructions that were designed to thwart the needs and desires of the white minority in Rhodesia (Kreczko, 1980; Kuyper, 1975; McDougal and Reisman, 1968; McKinnell, 1968; Minter and Schmidt, 1988; Mlambo, 2005). There were some within the white community in Rhodesia which considered the conditions to be a symbol of UK interference in the affairs of the colony (Kuyper, 1975; McDougal and Reisman, 1968; McKinnell, 1968; Minter and Schmidt, 1988; Mlambo, 2005; Mobley, 2002). Others saw the crisis as an example of how Britain had meddled in colonies and left them in disarray on the dawn of independence (McDougal and Reisman, 1968; McKinnell, 1968; Minter and Schmidt, 1988; Mlambo, 2005; Mobley, 2002; Porter, 1978). In September of 1964, Smith visited Lisbon for a diplomatic mission designed to shore support for his government in its struggle against the British imperial power (McKinnell, 1968; Minter and Schmidt, 1988; Mlambo, 2005; Mobley, 2002; Porter, 1978; Rowe, 1999, 2001). The Portuguese prime minister António de Oliveira Salazar promised Smith "maximum support" if he should declare independence (Minter and Schmidt, 1988; Mlambo, 2005; Mobley, 2002; Porter, 1978; Rowe, 1999, 2001; Stephenson, 1975). Besides the common interest in maintaining security ties in southern Africa, Salazar expressed anger at Britain's refusal to support Portugal when India seized Goa in 1961 (Mlambo, 2005; Mobley, 2002; Porter, 1978; Rowe, 1999, 2001; Stephenson, 1975; Strack and Strack, 1978). Moreover, the Portuguese prime minister suggested that Britain was duplicitous and admonished Smith not to trust the British government (Mobley, 2002; Porter, 1978; Rowe, 1999, 2001; Stephenson, 1975; Strack and Strack, 1978). Following the visit, a Rhodesian Trade Office was opened in Lisbon (Porter, 1978; Rowe, 1999, 2001; Stephenson, 1975; Strack and Strack, 1978). This was put in place to co-ordinate breaking the anticipated sanctions in the event of a unilateral declaration of independence later that year (Rowe, 1999, 2001; Stephenson, 1975; Strack and Strack, 1978). Such actions by a European nation encouraged Smith not to compromise with the British (Austin, 1966; Boczek, 1968; Cohen, 2011; Curtin, 1969; Fenwick, 1967; Galtung, 1967; Harris, 1968; Hintz, 1972). Consequently, the Rhodesian Trade Office in Lisbon functioned as a de facto embassy (Kreczko, 1980; Kuyper, 1975; McDougal and Reisman, 1968; McKinnell, 1968; Minter and Schmidt, 1988). This turn of events caused tension with London, which objected to Rhodesia conducting its own foreign policy (Mlambo, 2005; Mobley, 2002; Porter, 1978; Rowe, 1999, 2001; Stephenson, 1975; Strack and Strack, 1978).

The support from Portugal was particularly important in making it even more difficult for Smith to compromise with the British (Austin, 1966; Boczek, 1968; Cohen, 2011; Curtin, 1969; Fenwick, 1967; Galtung, 1967; Harris, 1968; Hintz, 1972). As a land-locked country, Rhodesia shared a border with the Portuguese colony of Mozambique, and hence the support from Portugal was highly welcome (Boczek, 1968; Cohen, 2011; Curtin, 1969; Fenwick, 1967; Galtung, 1967; Harris, 1968; Hintz, 1972; Kreczko, 1980; Kuyper, 1975). Specifically, the promise of "maximum support" from gave Smith more grounds for self-confidence in his negotiations (Cohen, 2011; Curtin, 1969; Fenwick, 1967; Galtung, 1967; Harris, 1968; Hintz, 1972; Kreczko, 1980; Kuyper, 1975). For example, Smith ruled out acceptance for all five of the proposed principles (Curtin, 1969; Fenwick, 1967; Galtung, 1967; Harris, 1968; Hintz, 1972; Kreczko, 1980; Kuyper,

1975; McDougal and Reisman, 1968). He instead implied that Rhodesia was already legally entitled to independence (Fenwick, 1967; Galtung, 1967; Harris, 1968; Hintz, 1972; Kreczko, 1980; Kuyper, 1975; McDougal and Reisman, 1968). This was a claim that was overwhelmingly endorsed by registered white voters in a referendum (Galtung, 1967; Harris, 1968; Hintz, 1972; Kreczko, 1980; Kuyper, 1975; McDougal and Reisman, 1968; McKinnell, 1968).

Smith and his government were emboldened by the results of this referendum (Harris, 1968; Hintz, 1972; Kreczko, 1980; Kuyper, 1975; McDougal and Reisman, 1968; McKinnell, 1968; Minter and Schmidt, 1988). Those sentiments were then confirmed by the subsequent general election (Hintz, 1972; Kreczko, 1980; Kuyper, 1975; McDougal and Reisman, 1968; McKinnell, 1968; Minter and Schmidt, 1988). In effect, Rhodesia now threatened to assume her own sovereignty with or without British consent (Kreczko, 1980; Kuyper, 1975; McDougal and Reisman, 1968; McKinnell, 1968; Minter and Schmidt, 1988; Mlambo, 2005). For the British government, this represented a public relations disaster and a demonstration of the waning powers of the former global imperial power (Kuyper, 1975; McDougal and Reisman, 1968; McKinnell, 1968; Minter and Schmidt, 1988; Mlambo, 2005; Mobley, 2002). Harold Wilson and his government warned Smith that such an irregular procedure would be considered treasonous (McDougal and Reisman, 1968; McKinnell, 1968; Minter and Schmidt, 1988; Mlambo, 2005; Mobley, 2002; Porter, 1978). However, that implied threat was somewhat tempered by the fact that the British government also rejected the option of using armed force against people who could claim English heritage (McKinnell, 1968; Minter and Schmidt, 1988; Mlambo, 2005; Mobley, 2002; Porter, 1978; Rowe, 1999, 2001). Wilson's refusal to consider a military option encouraged Smith and Rhodesia to proceed with plans of independence (Minter and Schmidt, 1988; Mlambo, 2005; Mobley, 2002; Porter, 1978; Rowe, 1999, 2001; Stephenson, 1975). Consequently, talks quickly broke down and there was no settlement that was acceptable to either side (Mlambo, 2005; Mobley, 2002; Porter, 1978; Rowe, 1999, 2001; Stephenson, 1975; Strack and Strack, 1978).

The Rhodesian Front remained unwilling to accept what were regarded as unacceptably drastic terms and yet the British government was also not willing to compromise on its key preconditions for independence (Mobley, 2002; Porter, 1978; Rowe, 1999, 2001; Stephenson, 1975; Strack and Strack, 1978). On the 11th of November 1965, Smith issued a unilateral declaration of independence (Porter, 1978; Rowe, 1999, 2001; Stephenson,

1975; Strack and Strack, 1978). This was immediately denounced as an "act of rebellion against the Crown" in the United Kingdom (Rowe, 1999, 2001; Stephenson, 1975; Strack and Strack, 1978). Moreover, Harold Wilson promised that the illegal action would be short-lived (Austin, 1966; Boczek, 1968; Cohen, 2011; Curtin, 1969; Fenwick, 1967; Galtung, 1967; Harris, 1968; Hintz, 1972). However, the fact was that Rhodesia was no longer within the Commonwealth's direct sphere of influence (Kreczko, 1980; Kuyper, 1975; McDougal and Reisman, 1968; McKinnell, 1968; Minter and Schmidt, 1988). The United Kingdom risked looking ridiculous by claiming sovereignty over a territory that was well outside its reach (Mlambo, 2005; Mobley, 2002; Porter, 1978; Rowe, 1999, 2001; Stephenson, 1975; Strack and Strack, 1978).

On the 12th of October 1965, the United Nations General Assembly noted the repeated threats of the Rhodesian authorities "to declare unilaterally the independence of Southern Rhodesia, in order to perpetuate minority rule" (Austin, 1966; Boczek, 1968; Cohen, 2011; Curtin, 1969; Fenwick, 1967; Galtung, 1967; Harris, 1968; Hintz, 1972). The UN therefore called upon Wilson to use all means at his disposal (including military force) to prevent the Rhodesian Front from asserting independence (Boczek, 1968; Cohen, 2011; Curtin, 1969; Fenwick, 1967; Galtung, 1967; Harris, 1968; Hintz, 1972; Kreczko, 1980; Kuyper, 1975). After UDI was proclaimed, UN officials branded Ian Smith's government as an "illegal racist minority regime" (Cohen, 2011; Curtin, 1969; Fenwick, 1967; Galtung, 1967; Harris, 1968; Hintz, 1972; Kreczko, 1980; Kuyper, 1975). The UN also called on member states to sever economic ties with Rhodesia (Curtin, 1969; Fenwick, 1967; Galtung, 1967; Harris, 1968; Hintz, 1972; Kreczko, 1980; Kuyper, 1975; McDougal and Reisman, 1968). Furthermore, the UN recommended specific sanctions on petroleum products and military hardware to and from Rhodesia (Fenwick, 1967; Galtung, 1967; Harris, 1968; Hintz, 1972; Kreczko, 1980; Kuyper, 1975; McDougal and Reisman, 1968).

In December of 1966, these measures that had originally been recommended by the UN became mandatory (Galtung, 1967; Harris, 1968; Hintz, 1972; Kreczko, 1980; Kuyper, 1975; McDougal and Reisman, 1968; McKinnell, 1968). Furthermore, the restrictions were extended to the purchase of Rhodesian products including tobacco, chromium, copper, asbestos, sugar, meat, and hides (Harris, 1968; Hintz, 1972; Kreczko, 1980; Kuyper, 1975; McDougal and Reisman, 1968; McKinnell, 1968; Minter and Schmidt, 1988). The United Kingdom had already adopted extensive sanctions of its own against Rhodesia (Hintz, 1972; Kreczko, 1980; Kuyper,

1975; McDougal and Reisman, 1968; McKinnell, 1968; Minter and Schmidt, 1988). The British government additionally dispatched a Royal Navy squadron to monitor oil deliveries in the port of Beira in Mozambique. This was an important escalation of the crisis since this port was a strategic pipeline ran to Umtali in Rhodesia (Kreczko, 1980; Kuyper, 1975; McDougal and Reisman, 1968; McKinnell, 1968; Minter and Schmidt, 1988; Mlambo, 2005). The warships were given specific instructions to deter "by force, if necessary, vessels reasonably believed to be carrying oil destined for (Southern) Rhodesia." Not only was the United Kingdom using diplomatic pressure, but it was also prepared for military force if necessary (Kuyper, 1975; McDougal and Reisman, 1968; McKinnell, 1968; Minter and Schmidt, 1988; Mlambo, 2005; Mobley, 2002).

As was the case with the Continental System of Napoleon in the previous section, some countries did not join Britain in punishing Rhodesia (McDougal and Reisman, 1968; McKinnell, 1968; Minter and Schmidt, 1988; Mlambo, 2005; Mobley, 2002; Porter, 1978). For example, Switzerland and West Germany were not UN members and could therefore legally trade with Rhodesia (McKinnell, 1968; Minter and Schmidt, 1988; Mlambo, 2005; Mobley, 2002; Porter, 1978; Rowe, 1999, 2001). West Germany specifically remained the Smith government's largest trading partner in Western Europe until 1973 (Minter and Schmidt, 1988; Mlambo, 2005; Mobley, 2002; Porter, 1978; Rowe, 1999, 2001; Stephenson, 1975). This fissure coincided with the moment that Bonn joined the UN, reflecting subtle shifts in diplomatic priorities (Mlambo, 2005; Mobley, 2002; Porter, 1978; Rowe, 1999, 2001; Stephenson, 1975; Strack and Strack, 1978). For its part, Japan continued to accept more Rhodesian exports than any other nation (Mobley, 2002; Porter, 1978; Rowe, 1999, 2001; Stephenson, 1975; Strack and Strack, 1978). Moreover, Iran provided much needed oil to the beleaguered nation (Porter, 1978; Rowe, 1999, 2001; Stephenson, 1975; Strack and Strack, 1978). The Portuguese government further sabotaged the efforts by Britain when it marketed Rhodesian products as its own (Rowe, 1999, 2001; Stephenson, 1975; Strack and Strack, 1978). This was done via false certificates of origin and disguised trade channels (Austin, 1966; Boczek, 1968; Cohen, 2011; Curtin, 1969; Fenwick, 1967; Galtung, 1967; Harris, 1968; Hintz, 1972). South Africa openly refused to observe the UN sanctions, bearing in mind that it would soon similarly be labeled an international pariah for its more extreme form of apartheid (Kreczko, 1980; Kuyper, 1975; McDougal and Reisman, 1968; McKinnell, 1968; Minter and Schmidt, 1988). As the largest and most prosperous economy in the world, the USA's cooperation or lack of cooperation could prove decisive in terms of the success rate of the sanctions against Rhodesia (Mlambo, 2005; Mobley, 2002; Porter, 1978; Rowe, 1999, 2001; Stephenson, 1975; Strack and Strack, 1978). The message coming from Washington was mixed. For example, a 1971 law passed in the United States permitted American firms to go on importing Rhodesian chromium and nickel regardless of the sanctions (Austin, 1966; Boczek, 1968; Cohen, 2011; Curtin, 1969; Fenwick, 1967; Galtung, 1967; Harris, 1968; Hintz, 1972). However, there were other diplomatic effects of the sanctions which harmed Rhodesia which found it nearly impossible to obtain diplomatic recognition abroad (Boczek, 1968; Cohen, 2011; Curtin, 1969; Fenwick, 1967; Galtung, 1967; Harris, 1968; Hintz, 1972; Kreczko, 1980; Kuyper, 1975). In 1970, the US government indicated in no uncertain terms that the UDI would not be recognized (Cohen, 2011; Curtin, 1969; Fenwick, 1967; Galtung, 1967; Harris, 1968; Hintz, 1972; Kreczko, 1980; Kuyper, 1975). Even the National Party government in South Africa and the Estado Novo government of Portugal, did not recognize Rhodesia as an independent state (Curtin, 1969; Fenwick, 1967; Galtung, 1967; Harris, 1968; Hintz, 1972; Kreczko, 1980; Kuyper, 1975; McDougal and Reisman, 1968). This is despite their apparent sympathy for the stance that Rhodesia had taken (Fenwick, 1967; Galtung, 1967; Harris, 1968; Hintz, 1972; Kreczko, 1980; Kuyper, 1975; McDougal and Reisman, 1968). Instead, these countries insisted on only maintaining an Accredited Diplomatic Representative in Salisbury (Galtung, 1967; Harris, 1968; Hintz, 1972; Kreczko, 1980; Kuyper, 1975; McDougal and Reisman, 1968; McKinnell, 1968). This allowed Pretoria and Lisbon to continue to recognize British sovereignty while at the same time with the de facto authority of the Smith government (Harris, 1968; Hintz, 1972; Kreczko, 1980; Kuyper, 1975; McDougal and Reisman, 1968; McKinnell, 1968; Minter and Schmidt, 1988).

There had been signs that the white minorities in Rhodesia wanted to retain close ties with the British Crown if their demands were met (Hintz, 1972; Kreczko, 1980; Kuyper, 1975; McDougal and Reisman, 1968; McKinnell, 1968; Minter and Schmidt, 1988). The reluctance of the monarchy to support Smith and his government meant that these initial signs were soon quashed (Kreczko, 1980; Kuyper, 1975; McDougal and Reisman, 1968; McKinnell, 1968; Minter and Schmidt, 1988; Mlambo, 2005). Indeed, Rhodesia initially retained its pledged loyalty to Elizabeth II of the United Kingdom (Kuyper, 1975; McDougal and Reisman, 1968; McKinnell, 1968; Minter and Schmidt, 1988; Mlambo, 2005; Mobley, 2002). However, when Smith and Deputy Prime Minister Clifford Dupont called on colonial Governor Sir Humphrey Gibbs to formally notify him of the UDI, Gibbs condemned the UDI as an act of treachery (McDougal and Reisman, 1968; McKinnell, 1968; Minter and Schmidt, 1988; Mlambo, 2005; Mobley, 2002; Porter, 1978). Even when Smith formally announced the UDI on the radio, Gibbs used his reserve power to dismiss Smith and his entire cabinet (McKinnell, 1968; Minter and Schmidt, 1988; Mlambo, 2005; Mobley, 2002; Porter, 1978; Rowe, 1999, 2001). Gibbs was unable to enact any concrete actions to remove the Smith government (Minter and Schmidt, 1988; Mlambo, 2005; Mobley, 2002; Porter, 1978; Rowe, 1999, 2001; Stephenson, 1975).

Rhodesia simply ignored the Gibbs and Whitehall notices. Smith and his supporters contended that UDI made his office obsolete. Gibbs continued to occupy his residence in Salisbury until 1970, when he vacated the premises and left Rhodesia following the declaration of a republic (Mlambo, 2005; Mobley, 2002; Porter, 1978; Rowe, 1999, 2001; Stephenson, 1975; Strack and Strack, 1978). The Smith government stated that if the Queen did not appoint a Governor-General, it would name Dupont as "Officer Administering the Government." Queen Elizabeth II would not even consider this advice. Most of the international community backed Whitehall's assertion that Gibbs was the Queen's only legitimate representative (Mobley, 2002; Porter, 1978; Rowe, 1999, 2001; Stephenson, 1975; Strack and Strack, 1978). However, events on the ground were quickly overtaking any British assertions of rights over Rhodesia.

In September 1968, the Appellate Division of the High Court of Rhodesia ruled that Ian Smith's administration had become the de jure government of the country (Porter, 1978; Rowe, 1999, 2001; Stephenson, 1975; Strack and Strack, 1978). Chief Justice Sir Hugh Beadle referenced several statements made by Hugo Grotius when making his decision. Grotius had maintained that there was no way that a nation could claim to be governing a territory it was fighting against. Britain's economic war against Rhodesia could then be construed as war against the territory (Rowe, 1999, 2001; Stephenson, 1975; Strack and Strack, 1978). This was confirmed by subsequent judicial decisions that recognized the ability of the Smith government to act in much the same way as previous and other governments (Austin, 1966; Boczek, 1968; Cohen, 2011; Curtin, 1969; Fenwick, 1967; Galtung, 1967; Harris, 1968; Hintz, 1972). A Salisbury commission chaired by W.R. Waley was appointed to study constitutional implications and options in April 1968 noted that Europeans must give up any notion of domination (Kreczko, 1980; Kuyper, 1975; McDougal and Reisman, 1968; McKinnell, 1968; Minter and

Schmidt, 1988). However, that majority rule by the indigenous population was not yet appropriate (Mlambo, 2005; Mobley, 2002; Porter, 1978; Rowe, 1999, 2001; Stephenson, 1975; Strack and Strack, 1978).

Several attempts were made to reach a negotiated settlement (Austin, 1966; Boczek, 1968; Cohen, 2011; Curtin, 1969; Fenwick, 1967; Galtung, 1967; Harris, 1968; Hintz, 1972). For example, some of these talks took place on the Royal Navy vessels in December 1966 and October 1968 (Rowe, 1999, 2001; Stephenson, 1975; Strack and Strack, 1978). Whereas these diplomatic attempts at resolving the conflict did not achieve much concrete success, Harold Wilson added a 6th principle to the five he had previously stipulated (Porter, 1978; Rowe, 1999, 2001; Stephenson, 1975; Strack and Strack, 1978). This 6th condition would ensure that, race notwithstanding, there was no oppression of the majority by the minority or minority by the majority (Mobley, 2002; Porter, 1978; Rowe, 1999, 2001; Stephenson, 1975; Strack and Strack, 1978). The more radical elements of the Rhodesian Front response by calling for a republican government (Mlambo, 2005; Mobley, 2002; Porter, 1978; Rowe, 1999, 2001; Stephenson, 1975; Strack and Strack, 1978). During a two-proposition referendum held in 1969, the proposal for severing all remaining ties to the British Crown passed (Minter and Schmidt, 1988; Mlambo, 2005; Mobley, 2002; Porter, 1978; Rowe, 1999, 2001; Stephenson, 1975). Rhodesia declared itself a republic on 2nd of March 1970.

Under the new constitution, a president served as ceremonial head of state, with the prime minister nominally reporting to him (McKinnell, 1968; Minter and Schmidt, 1988; Mlambo, 2005; Mobley, 2002; Porter, 1978; Rowe, 1999, 2001). Independence did not bring about the international recognition that some in the government had hoped for (McDougal and Reisman, 1968; McKinnell, 1968; Minter and Schmidt, 1988; Mlambo, 2005; Mobley, 2002; Porter, 1978). Instead, the years following Rhodesia's UDI saw an unfolding series of economic, military, and political pressures placed on the country (Kuyper, 1975; McDougal and Reisman, 1968; McKinnell, 1968; Minter and Schmidt, 1988; Mlambo, 2005; Mobley, 2002). The combined weight of these pressures eventually brought about majority rule in Rhodesia and laid the foundation for its later evolution into modern day Zimbabwe (Kreczko, 1980; Kuyper, 1975; McDougal and Reisman, 1968; McKinnell, 1968; Minter and Schmidt, 1988; Mlambo, 2005). In 2005, a conference at the London School of Economics concluded that UDI was sparked by an existing racial conflict complicated by Cold War intrigues (Hintz, 1972; Kreczko, 1980; Kuyper, 1975; McDougal and Reisman, 1968; McKinnell,

1968; Minter and Schmidt, 1988). Critics of UDI sought to maintain that Ian Smith intended only to safeguard the privileges of an entrenched colonial elite (Harris, 1968; Hintz, 1972; Kreczko, 1980; Kuyper, 1975; McDougal and Reisman, 1968; McKinnell, 1968; Minter and Schmidt, 1988). This would inevitably be at the expense of the impoverished African community (Galtung, 1967; Harris, 1968; Hintz, 1972; Kreczko, 1980; Kuyper, 1975; McDougal and Reisman, 1968; McKinnell, 1968). In doing so, UDI created a vacuum of oppression that was eventually filled by Robert Mugabe's dictatorship. Smith and his supporters continued to defend their actions by claiming that the Rhodesian majority was too inexperienced at the time to manage the country (Fenwick, 1967; Galtung, 1967; Harris, 1968; Hintz, 1972; Kreczko, 1980; Kuyper, 1975; McDougal and Reisman, 1968).

Many white Rhodesians still considered themselves to be European elite that were entitled to rule over the black majority of the population, if only to save them from chaos (Curtin, 1969; Fenwick, 1967; Galtung, 1967; Harris, 1968; Hintz, 1972; Kreczko, 1980; Kuyper, 1975; McDougal and Reisman, 1968). After 1965, there were those who continued to claim that they were collectively upholders of justice and democracy against communism (as exemplified by militant black nationalists) on the one hand, and the decadence of British government on the other (Cohen, 2011; Curtin, 1969; Fenwick, 1967; Galtung, 1967; Harris, 1968; Hintz, 1972; Kreczko, 1980; Kuyper, 1975). These idealists often made repeated appeals to the Christian heritage of their pioneer ancestors in "defending the free world" (Boczek, 1968; Cohen, 2011; Curtin, 1969; Fenwick, 1967; Galtung, 1967; Harris, 1968; Hintz, 1972; Kreczko, 1980; Kuyper, 1975).

African parties were horrified by Smith's government and its attempt to hijack the rights of the indigenous population (Austin, 1966; Boczek, 1968; Cohen, 2011; Curtin, 1969; Fenwick, 1967; Galtung, 1967; Harris, 1968; Hintz, 1972). In the earlier phases of the Smith government, these nationalists relied on creating opportunities for external intervention (Harris, 1968; Hintz, 1972; Kreczko, 1980; Kuyper, 1975; McDougal and Reisman, 1968; McKinnell, 1968; Minter and Schmidt, 1988). It would, however, be several years before even the most radical nationalists chose to develop a coherent strategy revolving around armed resistance (McKinnell, 1968; Minter and Schmidt, 1988; Mlambo, 2005; Mobley, 2002; Porter, 1978; Rowe, 1999, 2001). A series of guerilla skirmishes and unworkable peace agreements ensued in the following years until Robert Mugabe was able to take over as the first elected black leader (Galtung, 1967; Harris, 1968; Hintz, 1972; Kreczko, 1980; Kuyper, 1975; McDougal and Reisman, 1968; McKinnell, 1968).

Later, Mugabe himself would endure the harsh reality of nearly universal international sanctions against his regime. It is debatable whether the end of UDI was mainly due to the sanctions imposed on the breakaway colony of Black nationalism (Kuyper, 1975; McDougal and Reisman, 1968; McKinnell, 1968; Minter and Schmidt, 1988; Mlambo, 2005; Mobley, 2002). Either way, this case demonstrated the possibilities and limits of a sanctions regime in bringing rogue governments to heel.

CHAPTER 1 SUMMARY

In conceptualizing international sanctions, it is always important to understand their instrumentality. Essentially, this chapter has shown that international sanctions are a means of achieving national, regional, and international objectives such as peace, security, and economic dominance. As we have seen with the Continental System and the sanctions against Rhodesia, sanctions can have unintended consequences which impact on their levels of success. The process of implementing such sanctions will be scrutinized further in the next chapter.

Chapter 2

Implementing an International Sanctions Regime

CONTENTS

As seen in the previous chapter, the actual implementation of international sanctions (in terms of scope, coverage, and adherence) is critical to their success. This chapter is an example of the implementation process with reference to the case studies of Iraq and Cuba in which the USA imposed sanctions against their opponents who were deemed to be weaker. The chapter will close with a comment on the role of sanctions in preventing, causing, sustaining, and ending international wars. By the end of this chapter, the reader should have a broad view of some of the challenges and considerations when implementing an international sanctions regime.

2.1. INTERNATIONAL SANCTIONS AGAINST IRAQ

A good starting point for this chapter in a reference to the multiple messes that have entangled the USA in the internal and foreign affairs of Iraq. The sanctions against Iraq were a comprehensive financial and trade embargo (Abunimah, 2002; Al-Ali, 2005; Bolton, 1997; Byman, Pollack, and Waxman, 1998; Clawson, 1993; Cordesman, 1999). These restrictions were imposed by the United Nations Security Council on the Ba'athist regime that dominated Iraq at the time (Al-Ali, 2005; Bolton, 1997; Byman, Pollack, and Waxman, 1998; Clawson, 1993; Cordesman, 1999, 2018; Delmonte, 2001). They began on the 6th of August 1990 (Bolton, 1997; Byman, Pollack, and Waxman, 1998; Clawson, 1993; Cordesman, 1999, 2018; Delmonte, 2001). This was exactly four days after Iraq's invasion of Kuwait. The sanctions regime stayed largely intact until the 22nd of May 2003 (Byman, Pollack, and Waxman, 1998; Clawson, 1993; Cordesman, 1999, 2018; Delmonte, 2001; Falk, 2002).

The end of the sanctions came immediately after Saddam Hussein had been forced from power (Clawson, 1993; Cordesman, 1999, 2018; Delmonte, 2001; Falk, 2002; Gause III, 1999). That is why some argue that these sanctions were in effect a form of regime change; at least in terms of intention, if not outcome (Cordesman, 1999, 2018; Delmonte, 2001; Falk, 2002; Gause III 1999; Ismael and Ismael, 2005). However, it should be noted that these sanctions have partially persisted to the present day, long after Saddam Hussein left the stage (Cordesman, 2018; Delmonte, 2001; Falk, 2002; Gause III, 1999; Ismael and Ismael, 2005; Joyner, 2003; Karsh and Rautsi, 1991). A case in point are the reparations to Kuwait which are ongoing (Karsh and Rautsi, 1991; Lopez, 1998; Lopez and Cortright, 2004; Mackey, 2003; Nagy, 2001). There has been some controversy surrounding the reasons for sanctioning Iraq and many of these reasons have never been fully explained or agreed upon (Bolton, 1997; Byman, Pollack, and Waxman, 1998; Clawson, 1993; Cordesman, 1999, 2018; Delmonte, 2001). For example, the original stated purposes of the sanctions were to compel Iraq to withdraw from Kuwait (Joyner, 2003; Karsh and Rautsi, 1991; Lopez, 1998; Lopez and Cortright, 2004; Mackey, 2003; Nagy, 2001). This action by Saddam Hussein to invade a sovereign nation without an internationally acceptable reason meant that the powers were worried about setting a dangerous precedent (Ismael and Ismael, 2005; Joyner, 2003; Karsh and Rautsi, 1991; Lopez, 1998; Lopez and Cortright, 2004; Mackey, 2003). If Iraq could do as it pleased against international norms, there was nothing stopping another rogue regime for doing the same (Gause III 1999; Ismael and Ismael, 2005; Joyner, 2003; Karsh and Rautsi, 1991; Lopez, 1998; Lopez and Cortright, 2004).

A second objective of the sanctions was to force Iraq to pay reparations to Kuwait for the invasion (Falk, 2002; Gause III 1999; Ismael and Ismael, 2005; Joyner, 2003; Karsh and Rautsi, 1991; Lopez, 1998; Lopez and Cortright, 2004). The invasion had harmed the economy and opened pathways for the oil-rich Kuwait to be exploited by Iraq (Delmonte, 2001; Falk, 2002; Gause III 1999; Ismael and Ismael, 2005; Joyner, 2003; Karsh and Rautsi, 1991; Lopez, 1998). The world powers saw this as an injustice that could only be partially redressed through significant penalties and reparations (Cordesman, 1999, 2018; Delmonte, 2001; Falk, 2002; Gause III, 1999; Ismael and Ismael, 2005). Nevertheless, it might be a curious anomaly that some of the countries that enthusiastically joined the USA in sanctioning Iraq (UK and France being examples) had significant and extensive colonial histories (Al-Ali, 2005; Bolton, 1997; Byman, Pollack, and Waxman, 1998; Clawson, 1993; Cordesman, 1999, 2018; Delmonte, 2001). However, these colonial powers had yet resisted any attempt to pay reparations for the countries that they had previously invaded, subjugated, and ruthlessly exploited.

The third stated purpose of the sanctions was to disclose and eliminate any weapons of mass destruction (Cordesman, 2018; Delmonte, 2001; Falk, 2002; Gause III, 1999; Ismael and Ismael, 2005; Joyner, 2003; Karsh and Rautsi, 1991). The rationale for this goal was that dangerous weapons in the hands of a dangerous and unpredictable dictator placed the world in unacceptable danger (Abunimah, 2002; Al-Ali, 2005; Bolton, 1997; Byman, Pollack, and Waxman, 1998; Clawson, 1993; Cordesman, 1999). As it later turned out, the search for these dangerous weapons ended up embarrassing the USA in later years when it was discovered that a lot of the evidence had been fabricated when the real intention was to remove Saddam Hussein (Clawson, 1993; Cordesman, 1999, 2018; Delmonte, 2001; Falk, 2002; Gause III, 1999). Others argue that Saddam Hussein was a dangerous tyrant who was not beyond using deadly weapons on his own people and neighbors, hence the justification for his removal from power (Byman, Pollack, and Waxman, 1998; Clawson, 1993; Cordesman, 1999, 2018; Delmonte, 2001; Falk, 2002). As Figure 2.1 shows with reference to the "oil for food" program, the Western powers engaged in self-deception and disingenuousness throughout the Iraq intervention.

Figure 2.1. Contradictions in the oil for food program.

Source: Slide Player.

The actual mechanisms for the sanctions were couched in international law and practice (Delmonte, 2001; Falk, 2002; Gause III 1999; Ismael and Ismael, 2005; Joyner, 2003; Karsh and Rautsi, 1991; Lopez, 1998). For example, initially the UN Security Council imposed stringent economic sanctions on Iraq by adopting and enforcing United Nations Security Council Resolution 661 (Falk, 2002; Gause III 1999; Ismael and Ismael, 2005; Joyner, 2003; Karsh and Rautsi, 1991; Lopez, 1998; Lopez and Cortright, 2004). At the close of the 1991 Persian Gulf War, existing sanctions were extended and elaborated (Gause III 1999; Ismael and Ismael, 2005; Joyner, 2003; Karsh and Rautsi, 1991; Lopez, 1998; Lopez and Cortright, 2004). For example, this involved linked these sanctions to removal of weapons of mass destruction as stated by Resolution 687 (Ismael and Ismael, 2005; Joyner, 2003; Karsh and Rautsi, 1991; Lopez, 1998; Lopez and Cortright, 2004; Mackey, 2003). The sanctions banned all trade and financial resources except for medicine (Joyner, 2003; Karsh and Rautsi, 1991; Lopez, 1998; Lopez and Cortright, 2004; Mackey, 2003; Nagy, 2001). There was an exception "in humanitarian circumstances" where foodstuffs could be exchanged (Karsh and Rautsi, 1991; Lopez, 1998; Lopez and Cortright,

2004; Mackey, 2003; Nagy, 2001). However, the import of food into Iraq was tightly regulated (Abunimah, 2002; Al-Ali, 2005; Bolton, 1997; Byman, Pollack, and Waxman, 1998; Clawson, 1993).

The effects of the sanctions on the civilian population of Iraq have been disputed in existing literature. For example, it was widely and initially believed that the sanctions caused a major rise in child mortality. However, there was subsequent research following the 2003 invasion of Iraq which suggested that the commonly cited data in the original papers had been doctored by the Saddam Hussein regime. Indeed, some suggested that there was no significant rise in child mortality in Iraq after 1990.

The sanctions also had the effect of weakening Iraq militarily, a direct response to its earlier aggression against Kuwait (Cordesman, 1999, 2018; Delmonte, 2001; Falk, 2002; Gause III, 1999). For example, Resolutions 660–662, 664–667, 669–670, 674, 677–678, and 687 expressed the goals of eliminating weapons of mass destruction and extended-range ballistic missiles (Ismael and Ismael, 2005; Joyner, 2003; Karsh and Rautsi, 1991; Lopez, 1998; Lopez and Cortright, 2004; Mackey, 2003; Nagy, 2001). The resolutions had the effect of prohibiting any support for terrorism, a practice that Iraq was widely suspected of among the major powers (Abunimah, 2002; Al-Ali, 2005; Bolton, 1997; Byman, Pollack, and Waxman, 1998; Clawson, 1993; Cordesman, 1999). Through the punitive sanctions, the global community aimed to achieve the goal of forcing Iraq to pay war reparations and all foreign debt (Al-Ali, 2005; Bolton, 1997; Byman, Pollack, and Waxman, 1998; Clawson, 1993; Cordesman, 1999, 2018; Delmonte, 2001). This would have adverse effects on the economic and political integrity of the nation; almost certainly threatening the hold that Saddam Hussein had over the government (Bolton, 1997; Byman, Pollack, and Waxman, 1998; Clawson, 1993; Cordesman, 1999, 2018; Delmonte, 2001).

International institutions were used in imposing and justifying the sanctions regime (Byman, Pollack, and Waxman, 1998; Clawson, 1993; Cordesman, 1999, 2018; Delmonte, 2001; Falk, 2002). For example, the United Nations Office of the Iraq Program was responsible for the management and monitoring of key aspects of the sanctions(Clawson, 1993; Cordesman, 1999, 2018; Delmonte, 2001; Falk, 2002; Gause III 1999). These sanctions included strict limits both on the items that could be imported into Iraq (Cordesman, 1999, 2018; Delmonte, 2001; Falk, 2002; Gause III 1999; Ismael and Ismael, 2005). The sanctions regime also specified the items that could be exported and the circumstances in which they could be exported (Cordesman, 2018; Delmonte, 2001; Falk, 2002; Gause III 1999; Ismael and Ismael, 2005; Joyner, 2003; Karsh and Rautsi, 1991). Initially, the UN Sanctions did not issue a complete list of items that could not be imported into Iraq (Karsh and Rautsi, 1991; Lopez, 1998; Lopez and Cortright, 2004; Mackey, 2003; Nagy, 2001). Instead, it evaluated applications for importing items to Iraq on a case-by-case basis (Joyner, 2003; Karsh and Rautsi, 1991; Lopez, 1998; Lopez and Cortright, 2004; Mackey, 2003; Nagy, 2001). Hence, in theory, the sanctions allowed for foodstuffs, medicines, and products for essential civilian needs (Ismael and Ismael, 2005; Joyner, 2003; Karsh and Rautsi, 1991; Lopez, 1998; Lopez and Cortright, 2004; Mackey, 2003). In reality, there were many more restrictions on Iraq, and often the rules were tightened throughout the course of the sanctions (Gause III 1999; Ismael and Ismael, 2005; Joyner, 2003; Karsh and Rautsi, 1991; Lopez, 1998; Lopez and Cortright, 2004).

The terms that were imposed by the sanctions could be quite onerous on individuals and institutions that wished to do business in Iraq or with Iraq communities (Falk, 2002; Gause III 1999; Ismael and Ismael, 2005; Joyner, 2003; Karsh and Rautsi, 1991; Lopez, 1998; Lopez and Cortright, 2004). For example, any person wishing to deliver items to Iraq was required to apply for export licenses to the designated authorities of one or more UN member state. Some have argued that this amounted to an affront to the territorial integrity of Iraq and made it something of a vassal state to the sanctioning powers. It also made trade difficult (Delmonte, 2001; Falk, 2002; Gause III 1999; Ismael and Ismael, 2005; Joyner, 2003; Karsh and Rautsi, 1991; Lopez, 1998). These conditions applied regardless of whether the transaction involved trade or charitable activities. This was a controversial clause because it meant that even those sending much needed aid to Iraq citizens were being systematically frustrated by the sanction's regime (Cordesman, 1999, 2018; Delmonte, 2001; Falk, 2002; Gause III 1999; Ismael and Ismael, 2005). This proved to be one of the more controversial aspects of the scheme because it prevented the Iraq people from getting relief from the harsh conditions that had been created by the sanctions in the first place. In other words, the living conditions that had worsened under the sanction's regime were exacerbated by the sanctions themselves (Cordesman, 2018; Delmonte, 2001; Falk, 2002; Gause III 1999; Ismael and Ismael, 2005; Joyner, 2003; Karsh and Rautsi, 1991).

The process itself was too bureaucratic and designed to make it incredibly difficult to do any business with Iraq or in Iraq for that matter (Clawson, 1993; Cordesman, 1999, 2018; Delmonte, 2001; Falk, 2002; Gause III, 1999). For example, when an application was made for an export license, the member state sent the application to the Sanctions Committee. There were no time guarantees and the committee could use its discretion in any way it saw fit (Byman, Pollack, and Waxman, 1998; Clawson, 1993; Cordesman, 1999, 2018; Delmonte, 2001; Falk, 2002). The committee made its decision in secret, raising questions about the transparency of the entire process. Given the fact that many members of this committee were already hostile to the Iraq regime, it was doubtful that its decision could be impartial in any meaningful sense (Bolton, 1997; Byman, Pollack, and Waxman, 1998; Clawson, 1993; Cordesman, 1999, 2018; Delmonte, 2001). Moreover, any Committee member could veto a permission without giving any reason, which opened up the possibility of very arbitrary decision-making (Al-Ali, 2005; Bolton, 1997; Byman, Pollack, and Waxman, 1998; Clawson, 1993; Cordesman, 1999, 2018; Delmonte, 2001). As a rule of thumb, anything that could have a conceivable military use was banned, no matter how innocuous the initial application seemed. The implication was the de-militarization of Iraq through the backdoor and under the guise of the UN (Abunimah, 2002; Al-Ali, 2005; Bolton, 1997; Byman, Pollack, and Waxman, 1998; Clawson, 1993; Cordesman, 1999). Hence there were items such as computers and tractors which were banned despite them being useful in other non-military spheres of life. All in all, these restrictions made life incredibly and unnecessarily difficult for ordinary Iraq citizens who had very little to do with the ongoing dictatorship (Delmonte, 2001; Falk, 2002; Gause III 1999; Ismael and Ismael, 2005; Joyner, 2003; Karsh and Rautsi, 1991; Lopez, 1998).

The powers that were given to the committee were draconian and could conceivably be abused to settle old scores or issues that were not related to the Iraq invasion of Kuwait. This situation was akin to a victor's court trying to find justice for their defeated enemy (Falk, 2002; Gause III 1999; Ismael and Ismael, 2005; Joyner, 2003; Karsh and Rautsi, 1991; Lopez, 1998; Lopez and Cortright, 2004). For example, the committee asserted its sole discretion in determining what is essential for every Iraqi. Not only were such assertions based on ignorance of the situation on the ground, but they were also profoundly humiliating for the Iraq people and state (Gause III 1999; Ismael and Ismael, 2005; Joyner, 2003; Karsh and Rautsi, 1991; Lopez, 1998; Lopez and Cortright, 2004). This practice continued even though some of the people on that committee were not intimately engaged in the lives of ordinary Iraq people (Ismael and Ismael, 2005; Joyner, 2003; Karsh and Rautsi, 1991; Lopez, 1998; Lopez and Cortright, 2004; Mackey, 2003). The discretion for either permitting or denying anything to the Iraqi population seemed like an excessive imposition on their freedom and sovereignty (Joyner, 2003; Karsh and Rautsi, 1991; Lopez, 1998; Lopez and Cortright, 2004; Mackey, 2003; Nagy, 2001).

The same bureaucratic barriers continued throughout the process (Karsh and Rautsi, 1991; Lopez, 1998; Lopez and Cortright, 2004; Mackey, 2003; Nagy, 2001). For example, If the committee granted approval, it notified the country where the application came from. A transaction that involved one supply chain would then be extended to multiple countries with no certain response or timescale (Abunimah, 2002; Al-Ali, 2005; Bolton, 1997; Byman, Pollack, and Waxman, 1998; Clawson, 1993). All this involved a lot of time and expense, which many businesses were just not prepared to shoulder. The country that had received an application then informed the applicant about the decision (Cordesman, 1999, 2018; Delmonte, 2001; Falk, 2002; Gause III, 1999). However, there were no strict time limits, and this process could also be delayed indefinitely at the discretion of the decision-makers (Ismael and Ismael, 2005; Joyner, 2003; Karsh and Rautsi, 1991; Lopez, 1998; Lopez and Cortright, 2004; Mackey, 2003; Nagy, 2001). When everything was in order, the applicant then finally shipped the items. By this time, the cost of application and shipping were much higher than in other comparative industries and that meant that Iraq was less of an attractive business opportunity (Abunimah, 2002; Al-Ali, 2005; Bolton, 1997; Byman, Pollack, and Waxman, 1998; Clawson, 1993; Cordesman, 1999). Moreover, all the items remained subject to inspection and risk of impoundment (Al-Ali, 2005; Bolton, 1997; Byman, Pollack, and Waxman, 1998; Clawson, 1993; Cordesman, 1999, 2018; Delmonte, 2001). Given these harsh conditions, it is not surprising that many businesses simply gave up on Iraq. Quite simply, the international community was collectively making Iraq less competitive on the international stage (Bolton, 1997; Byman, Pollack, and Waxman, 1998; Clawson, 1993; Cordesman, 1999, 2018; Delmonte, 2001). This caused untold suffering to the local communities that could no longer commercially access essential items (Byman, Pollack, and Waxman, 1998; Clawson, 1993; Cordesman, 1999, 2018; Delmonte, 2001; Falk, 2002).

There were efforts to correct some of the errors that had been made in the initial implementation of the sanction's regime (Clawson, 1993; Cordesman, 1999, 2018; Delmonte, 2001; Falk, 2002; Gause III 1999). For example, in 2002, the process was streamlined whereby a sanctions committee established a 'Goods Review List' for certain items. This was meant to bring some much-needed objectivity in the process (Cordesman, 1999, 2018; Delmonte, 2001; Falk, 2002; Gause III 1999; Ismael and Ismael,

2005). In practice, it meant that anything not on the Goods Review list could be imported without restriction (Cordesman, 2018; Delmonte, 2001; Falk, 2002; Gause III 1999; Ismael and Ismael, 2005; Joyner, 2003; Karsh and Rautsi, 1991). At the same time, items with dual-purpose would be reviewed on a case-by-case basis (Karsh and Rautsi, 1991; Lopez, 1998; Lopez and Cortright, 2004; Mackey, 2003; Nagy, 2001).

Limitations on Iraqi exports (particularly crude oil and related products) made it difficult to fund the import of goods into Iraq (Joyner, 2003; Karsh and Rautsi, 1991; Lopez, 1998; Lopez and Cortright, 2004; Mackey, 2003; Nagy, 2001). Following the 1991 Gulf War, a United Nations inter-agency mission suggested that there was an imminent catastrophe of disease epidemics and famines (Ismael and Ismael, 2005; Joyner, 2003; Karsh and Rautsi, 1991; Lopez, 1998; Lopez and Cortright, 2004; Mackey, 2003). It also suggested that the only way to address the problem was to ensure that massive life-supporting needs are rapidly met through the modification of some of the terms of the sanctions (Gause III 1999; Ismael and Ismael, 2005; Joyner, 2003; Karsh and Rautsi, 1991; Lopez, 1998; Lopez and Cortright, 2004).

Despite the considerable suffering that the sanctions had created among its population, the Iraq government at times seemed unwilling to relent to the great powers and UN (Falk, 2002; Gause III 1999; Ismael and Ismael, 2005; Joyner, 2003; Karsh and Rautsi, 1991; Lopez, 1998; Lopez and Cortright, 2004). For example, the Government of Iraq declined offers of assistance and modified terms under the UNSRC resolutions 706 and 712 (Delmonte, 2001; Falk, 2002; Gause III 1999; Ismael and Ismael, 2005; Joyner, 2003; Karsh and Rautsi, 1991; Lopez, 1998). These had been designed in such a way as to enable Iraq to sell limited quantities of oil to meet its people's needs (Cordesman, 1999, 2018; Delmonte, 2001; Falk, 2002; Gause III 1999; Ismael and Ismael, 2005). Under the auspices of Chapter VII of the United Nations Charter, the Security Council established the "Oil for Food Program" using resolution 986 which was issued on the 14th of April 1995 (Cordesman, 2018; Delmonte, 2001; Falk, 2002; Gause III 1999; Ismael and Ismael, 2005; Joyner, 2003; Karsh and Rautsi, 1991).

The oil for food program ended up becoming a symbol of the possibilities for corruption and abuse in international institutions (Clawson, 1993; Cordesman, 1999, 2018; Delmonte, 2001; Falk, 2002; Gause III 1999). This was intended as a temporary measure to provide for the humanitarian needs of the Iraqi people (Byman, Pollack, and Waxman, 1998; Clawson,

1993; Cordesman, 1999, 2018; Delmonte, 2001; Falk, 2002). The program was conditioned on the fulfillment by Iraq of the relevant Security Council resolutions (Bolton, 1997; Byman, Pollack, and Waxman, 1998; Clawson, 1993; Cordesman, 1999, 2018; Delmonte, 2001). Implementation of the program started in December 1996 and its first shipment of supplies arrived in March 1997 (Al-Ali, 2005; Bolton, 1997; Byman, Pollack, and Waxman, 1998; Clawson, 1993; Cordesman, 1999, 2018; Delmonte, 2001).

It is notable that the program was funded exclusively with the proceeds from Iraqi oil exports, meaning that the international community was in no way supporting Iraq (Abunimah, 2002; Al-Ali, 2005; Bolton, 1997; Byman, Pollack, and Waxman, 1998; Clawson, 1993; Cordesman, 1999). Initially, Iraq was permitted to sell up to $2 billion worth of oil every six months (Delmonte, 2001; Falk, 2002; Gause III 1999; Ismael and Ismael, 2005; Joyner, 2003; Karsh and Rautsi, 1991; Lopez, 1998). According to the terms of the program, two-thirds of the proceeds from the sale of oil to be used to meet Iraq's humanitarian needs (Falk, 2002; Gause III 1999; Ismael and Ismael, 2005; Joyner, 2003; Karsh and Rautsi, 1991; Lopez, 1998; Lopez and Cortright, 2004). In 1998, the limit was raised to $5.26 billion every six months (Gause III 1999; Ismael and Ismael, 2005; Joyner, 2003; Karsh and Rautsi, 1991; Lopez, 1998; Lopez and Cortright, 2004). In December 1999, Security Council resolution 1284 removed the limit on the amount of oil exported but did not significantly change the expenditure mandates (Ismael and Ismael, 2005; Joyner, 2003; Karsh and Rautsi, 1991; Lopez, 1998; Lopez and Cortright, 2004; Mackey, 2003). Once again, it appeared that the world powers were trying to ensure that Iraq could not resurrect its military capabilities through the program (Joyner, 2003; Karsh and Rautsi, 1991; Lopez, 1998; Lopez and Cortright, 2004; Mackey, 2003; Nagy, 2001).

This was not a purely diplomatic offensive, but one that called for military solutions to ensure that the sanctions were not violated (Karsh and Rautsi, 1991; Lopez, 1998; Lopez and Cortright, 2004; Mackey, 2003; Nagy, 2001). For example, the enforcement of the sanctions was primarily by means of military force and legal redress (Abunimah, 2002; Al-Ali, 2005; Bolton, 1997; Byman, Pollack, and Waxman, 1998; Clawson, 1993). In line with Security Council Resolution 665, a Multinational Interception Force was organized and led by the United States (Cordesman, 1999, 2018; Delmonte, 2001; Falk, 2002; Gause III 1999). The stated role of this force was to intercept, inspect, and possibly impound vessels, cargoes, and crews suspected of carrying freight to or from Iraq (Ismael and Ismael, 2005; Joyner, 2003; Karsh and Rautsi, 1991; Lopez, 1998; Lopez and Cortright, 2004; Mackey, 2003; Nagy,

2001). The legal side of sanctions included enforcement through actions brought by individual governments (Abunimah, 2002; Al-Ali, 2005; Bolton, 1997; Byman, Pollack, and Waxman, 1998; Clawson, 1993; Cordesman, 1999). In the United States, legal enforcement was handled by the Office of Foreign Assets Control or OFAC (Al-Ali, 2005; Bolton, 1997; Byman, Pollack, and Waxman, 1998; Clawson, 1993; Cordesman, 1999, 2018; Delmonte, 2001). This demonstrates the nature of international sanctions, which sometimes have to have the power of a military force behind them in order to work effectively (Bolton, 1997; Byman, Pollack, and Waxman, 1998; Clawson, 1993; Cordesman, 1999, 2018; Delmonte, 2001). In fact, for some time, Iraq was really under the control of foreign powers through the strategic use of sanctions (Byman, Pollack, and Waxman, 1998; Clawson, 1993; Cordesman, 1999, 2018; Delmonte, 2001; Falk, 2002). Much later on, this approach to Iraq affairs led to uprisings and a generalized resentment against the USA and its allies (Clawson, 1993; Cordesman, 1999, 2018; Delmonte, 2001; Falk, 2002; Gause III 1999).

Some of the enforcement measures appeared to be ethically dubious, despite the reassurances that were provided to the contrary (Cordesman, 1999, 2018; Delmonte, 2001; Falk, 2002; Gause III 1999; Ismael and Ismael, 2005). For example, in 2005 OFAC fined Voices in the Wilderness $20,000 for gifting medicine and other humanitarian supplies to Iraqis without prior acquisition of an export license as required by law (Cordesman, 2018; Delmonte, 2001; Falk, 2002; Gause III 1999; Ismael and Ismael, 2005; Joyner, 2003; Karsh and Rautsi, 1991). Similarly, OFAC attempted to impose a $10,000 fine, plus interest, against Bert Sacks for bringing medicine to residents of Basra (Karsh and Rautsi, 1991; Lopez, 1998; Lopez and Cortright, 2004; Mackey, 2003; Nagy, 2001). The Iraqi people were being inadvertently (and sometimes deliberately) punished for the actions of Saddam Hussein on the one hand; and the (sometimes unfounded) suspicions of the USA and its allies (Joyner, 2003; Karsh and Rautsi, 1991; Lopez, 1998; Lopez and Cortright, 2004; Mackey, 2003; Nagy, 2001).

There is a consensus that the sanctions achieved the express goals of limiting Iraqi arms (Ismael and Ismael, 2005; Joyner, 2003; Karsh and Rautsi, 1991; Lopez, 1998; Lopez and Cortright, 2004; Mackey, 2003) (Ismael and Ismael, 2005; Joyner, 2003; Karsh and Rautsi, 1991; Lopez, 1998; Lopez and Cortright, 2004; Mackey, 2003). For example, the sanctions diminished Iraq militarily and compelled the country to accept inspections and monitoring (Gause III 1999; Ismael and Ismael, 2005; Joyner, 2003; Karsh and Rautsi, 1991; Lopez, 1998; Lopez and Cortright, 2004). Another effect was winning concessions from Baghdad on political issue such as the border dispute with Kuwait (Falk, 2002; Gause III 1999; Ismael and Ismael, 2005; Joyner, 2003; Karsh and Rautsi, 1991; Lopez, 1998; Lopez and Cortright, 2004). The sanctions helped in preventing the rebuilding of Iraqi defenses after the Persian Gulf War. More specifically, the sanctions were effective in blocking the import of materials and technologies for producing weapons of mass destruction (Delmonte, 2001; Falk, 2002; Gause III 1999; Ismael and Ismael, 2005; Joyner, 2003; Karsh and Rautsi, 1991; Lopez, 1998). However, that later became an goal for the USA when it was discovered that a second Iraq iwar had been justified on the dubious grounds that Saddam Hussein was amassing weapons of mass destruction (Cordesman, 1999, 2018; Delmonte, 2001; Falk, 2002; Gause III 1999; Ismael and Ismael, 2005).

However, there were significant costs that have inspired some to completely rethink the role that the USA played in Iraq (Cordesman, 2018; Delmonte, 2001; Falk, 2002; Gause III 1999; Ismael and Ismael, 2005; Joyner, 2003; Karsh and Rautsi, 1991). For example, there is evidence indicating high rates of malnutrition, lack of medical supplies, and diseases from lack of clean water during the sanctions (Clawson, 1993; Cordesman, 1999, 2018; Delmonte, 2001; Falk, 2002; Gause III 1999). Consequently, the chairman of the Iraqi Medical Association's scientific committee sent a plea to the BMJ to help it raise awareness of the disastrous effects the sanctions were having on the Iraqi healthcare system (Byman, Pollack, and Waxman, 1998; Clawson, 1993; Cordesman, 1999, 2018; Delmonte, 2001; Falk, 2002). The modern Iraqi economy had been highly dependent on oil exports (Bolton, 1997; Byman, Pollack, and Waxman, 1998; Clawson, 1993; Cordesman, 1999, 2018; Delmonte, 2001). For example, in 1989, the oil sector comprised 61% of the GNP (Al-Ali, 2005; Bolton, 1997; Byman, Pollack, and Waxman, 1998; Clawson, 1993; Cordesman, 1999, 2018; Delmonte, 2001). A drawback of this dependence was the narrowing of the economic base, with the agricultural sector rapidly declining in the 1970s (Abunimah, 2002; Al-Ali, 2005; Bolton, 1997; Byman, Pollack, and Waxman, 1998; Clawson, 1993; Cordesman, 1999). Some claim that, as a result, the post-1990 sanctions had a particularly devastating effect on Iraq's economy and food security levels of the population (Delmonte, 2001; Falk, 2002; Gause III 1999; Ismael and Ismael, 2005; Joyner, 2003; Karsh and Rautsi, 1991; Lopez, 1998).

Whereas the Iraq government mounted some response to the humanitarian crisis facing it, quite often its efforts were inadequate to the task (Falk, 2002; Gause III 1999; Ismael and Ismael, 2005; Joyner, 2003; Karsh and Rautsi,

1991; Lopez, 1998; Lopez and Cortright, 2004). For example, shortly after the sanctions were imposed, the Iraqi government developed a system of free food rations consisting of 1000 calories per person per day (Gause III 1999; Ismael and Ismael, 2005; Joyner, 2003; Karsh and Rautsi, 1991; Lopez, 1998; Lopez and Cortright, 2004). This roughly translates into about 40% of the daily requirements. It is estimated that 60% of the population relied on this program for a vital part of their sustenance (Ismael and Ismael, 2005; Joyner, 2003; Karsh and Rautsi, 1991; Lopez, 1998; Lopez and Cortright, 2004; Mackey, 2003). With the introduction of the Oil-for-Food Program in 1997, this situation gradually improved. In May 2000, a United Nations Children's Fund (UNICEF) survey noted that almost half the children under 5 years suffered from diarrhea (Joyner, 2003; Karsh and Rautsi, 1991; Lopez, 1998; Lopez and Cortright, 2004; Mackey, 2003; Nagy, 2001). This is a significant statistic in a country where about 45% of the population was under 14 years of age (Karsh and Rautsi, 1991; Lopez, 1998; Lopez and Cortright, 2004; Mackey, 2003; Nagy, 2001).

There were other negative impositions on the ordinary lives of Iraq residents. For example, power shortages, lack of spare parts and insufficient technical know-how led to the breakdown of many modern facilities during and after the sanctions (Abunimah, 2002; Al-Ali, 2005; Bolton, 1997; Byman, Pollack, and Waxman, 1998; Clawson, 1993). The per capita income in Iraq dropped from $3510 in 1989 to $450 in 1996 (Cordesman, 1999, 2018; Delmonte, 2001; Falk, 2002; Gause III 1999). This was heavily influenced by the rapid devaluation of the Iraqi dinar. There were other unintended consequences that set the country back from its relatively prosperous path. For example, Iraq had been one of the few countries in the Middle East that invested in women's education (Ismael and Ismael, 2005; Joyner, 2003; Karsh and Rautsi, 1991; Lopez, 1998; Lopez and Cortright, 2004; Mackey, 2003; Nagy, 2001). However, that distinction was largely erased from the late 1980s which were blighted by increasing militarization and a declining economy (Abunimah, 2002; Al-Ali, 2005; Bolton, 1997; Byman, Pollack, and Waxman, 1998; Clawson, 1993; Cordesman, 1999). Consequently, the economic hardships and war casualties in the last decades have increased the number of women-headed households and working women (Al-Ali, 2005; Bolton, 1997; Byman, Pollack, and Waxman, 1998; Clawson, 1993; Cordesman, 1999, 2018; Delmonte, 2001).

There were also questions about the ostensibly humanitarian and internationalist credentials of those that were imposing sanctions on Iraq (Bolton, 1997; Byman, Pollack, and Waxman, 1998; Clawson, 1993;

Cordesman, 1999, 2018; Delmonte, 2001). For example, some have argued that the US government intelligence and actions in the previous 10 years demonstrates that the USA acted to intentionally destroy Iraq's water supply (Byman, Pollack, and Waxman, 1998; Clawson, 1993; Cordesman, 1999, 2018; Delmonte, 2001; Falk, 2002). Others see things differently in terms of the humanitarian aid that has flowed into Iraq to deal with some of the negative impact of the sanctions (Clawson, 1993; Cordesman, 1999, 2018; Delmonte, 2001; Falk, 2002; Gause III 1999). Estimates of excess deaths during the sanctions vary widely, use different methodologies and cover different timeframes (Cordesman, 1999, 2018; Delmonte, 2001; Falk, 2002; Gause III 1999; Ismael and Ismael, 2005). The figure of 500,000 child deaths was for a long period widely cited (Cordesman, 2018; Delmonte, 2001; Falk, 2002; Gause III 1999; Ismael and Ismael, 2005; Joyner, 2003; Karsh and Rautsi, 1991). However, recent research has shown that that figure was the result of survey data manipulated by the Saddam Hussein regime (Karsh and Rautsi, 1991; Lopez, 1998; Lopez and Cortright, 2004; Mackey, 2003; Nagy, 2001). The next section examines the onset of the US embargo on Cuba, another similarly controversial use of international sanctions.

2.2. US EMBARGO AGAINST CUBA

For nearly half a century, the United States has had an ongoing embargo against Cuba, one of the longest in the world (Barry, 2000; Boas, 2000; Cain 1994; Copeland, Jolly, and Thompson, 2011; Drain and Barry, 2010; Falk, 1996). In various ways and through various means, this embargo prevents American businesses (as well as businesses with commercial activities in the USA) from conducting trade with Cuban companies or companies with Cuban interests (Boas, 2000; Cain, 1994; Copeland, Jolly, and Thompson, 2011; Drain and Barry, 2010; Falk, 1996; Fandl, 2017). This has been described as one of the most enduring trade embargoes in modern history (Cain, 1994; Copeland, Jolly, and Thompson, 2011; Drain and Barry, 2010; Falk, 1996; Fandl, 2017; Fisk, 2000). The USA first imposed an embargo on the sale of arms to Cuba on the 14th of March 1958 (Copeland, Jolly, and Thompson, 2011; Drain and Barry, 2010; Falk, 1996; Fandl, 2017; Fisk, 2000; Garfield and Santana, 1997). This was during the Fulgencio Batista regime at a time when relations with the USA were not on the best of terms (Drain and Barry, 2010; Falk, 1996; Fandl, 2017; Fisk, 2000; Garfield and Santana, 1997; Gordon, 2012; Kirkpatrick, 1996). Further action was taken on the 19th of October 1960 (Falk, 1996; Fandl, 2017; Fisk, 2000; Garfield and Santana,

1997; Gordon, 2012; Kirkpatrick, 1996). Because this second wave was almost two years after the Cuban Revolution had led to the deposition of the Batista regime. It became apparent that the sanctions were not just against the government but also the nation of Cuba (Fandl, 2017; Fisk, 2000; Garfield and Santana, 1997; Gordon, 2012; Kirkpatrick, 1996; Kuntz and Jackson, 1994). In due course, the USA placed an embargo on exports to Cuba except for food and medicine (Fisk, 2000; Garfield and Santana, 1997; Gordon, 2012; Kirkpatrick, 1996; Kuntz and Jackson, 1994; LeoGrande, 1997). One of the triggers for these aggressions occurred after Cuba nationalized American-owned Cuban oil refineries without compensation (Garfield and Santana, 1997; Gordon, 2012; Kirkpatrick, 1996; Kuntz and Jackson, 1994; LeoGrande, 1997; Osieja, 2006). This was seen as an attack on property rights that could have international repercussions for other international businesses if left unpunished (Gordon, 2012; Kirkpatrick, 1996; Kuntz and Jackson, 1994; LeoGrande, 1997; Osieja, 2006; Purcell and Rothkopf, 2000). On the 7th of February 1962, the embargo was extended to include almost all exports (Kirkpatrick, 1996; Kuntz and Jackson, 1994; LeoGrande, 1997; Osieja, 2006; Purcell and Rothkopf, 2000; Reinisch, 1996).

The USA administrations have consistently tried to explain that their intention was not to harm the Cuban people per say, but rather their leaders (Kuntz and Jackson, 1994; LeoGrande, 1997; Osieja, 2006; Purcell and Rothkopf, 2000; Reinisch, 1996). For example, the embargo does not prohibit the trade of food and humanitarian supplies (LeoGrande, 1997; Osieja, 2006; Purcell and Rothkopf, 2000; Reinisch, 1996; Roman, 1995; Smugula, 1995; Spadoni, 2010). In reality, this has been subject to very loose interpretations that sometimes render the exemptions a moot point (Osieja, 2006; Purcell and Rothkopf, 2000; Reinisch, 1996; Roman, 1995; Smugula, 1995; Spadoni, 2010; Zimbalist, 1993). The small Cuban nation is undeniably suffering under the weight of the ongoing embargo, to the extent that even some in Washington have questioned the moral justification for its continuance (Purcell and Rothkopf, 2000; Reinisch, 1996; Roman, 1995; Smugula, 1995; Spadoni, 2010; Zimbalist, 1993). As Figure 2.2 demonstrates, this is an embargo that is not popular across the globe (Biersteker, Eckert, and Tourinho, 2016; Cleveland, 2001; Eriksson, 2016; Hiraide and Chakraborty, 2012).

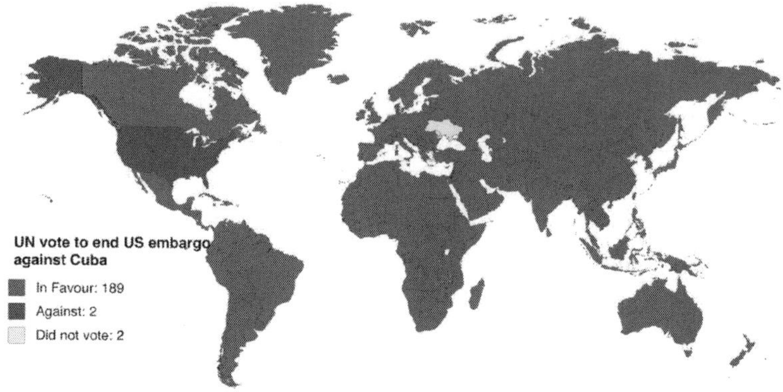

Figure 2.2. Global approval for ending US embargo on Cuba.

Source: Reddit.

Currently, the embargo is enforced mainly through six statutes (Barry, 2000; Boas, 2000; Cain, 1994; Copeland, Jolly, and Thompson, 2011; Drain and Barry, 2010). The first of these is the Trading with the Enemy Act of 1917 (Falk, 1996; Fandl, 2017; Fisk, 2000; Garfield and Santana, 1997; Gordon, 2012). The second is the Foreign Assistance Act of 1961 (Kirkpatrick, 1996; Kuntz and Jackson, 1994; LeoGrande, 1997; Osieja, 2006). The third is the Cuban Assets Control Regulations of 1963 (Purcell and Rothkopf, 2000; Reinisch, 1996; Roman, 1995; Smugula, 1995; Spadoni, 2010; Zimbalist, 1993). The fourth is the Cuban Democracy Act of 1992 (Barry, 2000; Boas, 2000; Cain, 1994; Fandl, 2017; Fisk, 2000; Garfield and Santana, 1997; Osieja, 2006; Purcell and Rothkopf, 2000). The fifth is the Helms-Burton Act of 1996 (Copeland, Jolly, and Thompson, 2011; Gordon, 2012; Kirkpatrick, 1996; Reinisch, 1996; Roman, 1995). The 6th instrument is the Trade Sanctions Reform and Export Enhancement Act of 2000 (Drain and Barry, 2010; Falk, 1996; Kuntz and Jackson, 1994; LeoGrande, 1997; Smugula, 1995; Spadoni, 2010; Zimbalist, 1993). Many of these acts have been modified to reflect the changes in the US administration as well as its relationships with the Cuban government (Purcell and Rothkopf, 2000; Reinisch, 1996; Roman, 1995; Smugula, 1995; Spadoni, 2010; Zimbalist, 1993).

Often there has been a mismatch between the intention of a legal instrument and the actuality of the trade embargo (Osieja, 2006; Purcell and Rothkopf, 2000; Reinisch, 1996; Roman, 1995; Smugula, 1995; Spadoni,

2010; Zimbalist, 1993). For example, the stated purpose of the Cuban Democracy Act of 1992 is to maintain sanctions on Cuba if the Cuban government refuses to move toward "democratization and greater respect for human rights" (LeoGrande, 1997; Osieja, 2006; Purcell and Rothkopf, 2000; Reinisch, 1996; Roman, 1995; Smugula, 1995; Spadoni, 2010). However, sanctions have been tightened even when the Cuban administration has made some small concessions (Kuntz and Jackson, 1994; LeoGrande, 1997; Osieja, 2006; Purcell and Rothkopf, 2000; Reinisch, 1996). For example, the Helms-Burton Act further restricted United States citizens from doing business in or with Cuba (Kirkpatrick, 1996; Kuntz and Jackson, 1994; LeoGrande, 1997; Osieja, 2006; Purcell and Rothkopf, 2000; Reinisch, 1996). This became a very onerous conditions for those that had friends, family, and business interests in the country (Gordon, 2012; Kirkpatrick, 1996; Kuntz and Jackson, 1994; LeoGrande, 1997; Osieja, 2006; Purcell and Rothkopf, 2000). It also meant that Cuba was isolated more than ever before (Garfield and Santana, 1997; Gordon, 2012; Kirkpatrick, 1996; Kuntz and Jackson, 1994; LeoGrande, 1997; Osieja, 2006).

The embargo on Cuba has very far-reaching restrictions on a range of matters such as giving public or private assistance to any successor government in Havana (Fisk, 2000; Garfield and Santana, 1997; Gordon, 2012; Kirkpatrick, 1996; Kuntz and Jackson, 1994; LeoGrande, 1997). Often these terms are premised with a condition that they can be eased if certain claims against the Cuban government were met (Fandl, 2017; Fisk, 2000; Garfield and Santana, 1997; Gordon, 2012; Kirkpatrick, 1996; Kuntz and Jackson, 1994). These claims primarily stem from the nationalization program that did not offer any compensation to those that had lost their stake in Cuban industry (Falk, 1996; Fandl, 2017; Fisk, 2000; Garfield and Santana, 1997; Gordon, 2012; Kirkpatrick, 1996).

Successive US governments have continued to strengthen the sanctions, regardless of any overtures from Cuba (Drain and Barry, 2010; Falk, 1996; Fandl, 2017; Fisk, 2000; Garfield and Santana, 1997; Gordon, 2012; Kirkpatrick, 1996). For example, in 1999 President Bill Clinton expanded the trade embargo by also disallowing foreign subsidiaries of US companies to trade with Cuba (Copeland, Jolly, and Thompson, 2011; Drain and Barry, 2010; Falk, 1996; Fandl, 2017; Fisk, 2000; Garfield and Santana, 1997). At the same time, the US administration sometimes adopted a "carrot and stick" approach which was meant to signal that the sanctions could be eased if the Cuban government were much more cooperative (Cain, 1994; Copeland, Jolly, and Thompson, 2011; Drain and Barry, 2010; Falk, 1996; Fandl, 2017;

Fisk, 2000). For example, in 2000, Clinton authorized the sale of food and "humanitarian" products to Cuba (Boas, 2000; Cain, 1994; Copeland, Jolly, and Thompson, 2011; Drain and Barry, 2010; Falk, 1996; Fandl, 2017). This was partly in response to the public outcry on the human cost that the embargo elicited on the Cuban people (Barry, 2000; Boas, 2000; Cain, 1994; Copeland, Jolly, and Thompson, 2011; Drain and Barry, 2010; Falk, 1996).

Cuba has often engaged its local population against some of the worst effects of the sanctions (Barry, 2000; Boas, 2000; Cain, 1994; Copeland, Jolly, and Thompson, 2011; Drain and Barry, 2010; Falk, 1996). This is often couched in the language of patriotism and victimhood against a wealthier and bigger nation trying to bully Cuba (Boas, 2000; Cain, 1994; Copeland, Jolly, and Thompson, 2011; Drain and Barry, 2010; Falk, 1996; Fandl, 2017). For example, the embargo is called 'the blockade' in Cuba to emphasize the notion that this is an illegal aggressive act on the part of the USA (Cain, 1994; Copeland, Jolly, and Thompson, 2011; Drain and Barry, 2010; Falk, 1996; Fandl, 2017; Fisk, 2000). The term is used in Cuba despite there being no naval blockade (Copeland, Jolly, and Thompson, 2011; Drain and Barry, 2010; Falk, 1996; Fandl, 2017; Fisk, 2000; Garfield and Santana, 1997). The Cuban government frequently blames the US "blockade" for the economic problems of Cuba (Drain and Barry, 2010; Falk, 1996; Fandl, 2017; Fisk, 2000; Garfield and Santana, 1997; Gordon, 2012; Kirkpatrick, 1996). Hence, some have argued that contrary to the stated aim of removing the Cuban administration; the embargo has effectively entrenched the government by turning the USA into a "bogeyman" of sorts (Falk, 1996; Fandl, 2017; Fisk, 2000; Garfield and Santana, 1997; Gordon, 2012; Kirkpatrick, 1996).

Not only is the USA engaged in conflict with Cuba, but it has also required other countries to comply with the embargo (Fisk, 2000; Garfield and Santana, 1997; Gordon, 2012; Kirkpatrick, 1996; Kuntz and Jackson, 1994; LeoGrande, 1997). For example, the United States has threatened to stop financial aid to other countries if they trade non-food items with Cuba (Garfield and Santana, 1997; Gordon, 2012; Kirkpatrick, 1996; Kuntz and Jackson, 1994; LeoGrande, 1997; Osieja, 2006). However, the embargo is not popularly supported internationally, and other countries are not under the jurisdiction of US law (Gordon, 2012; Kirkpatrick, 1996; Kuntz and Jackson, 1994; LeoGrande, 1997; Osieja, 2006; Purcell and Rothkopf, 2000). This means that American attempts to discourage its allies from trading with Cuba have not been successful (Kirkpatrick, 1996; Kuntz and Jackson, 1994; LeoGrande, 1997; Osieja, 2006; Purcell and Rothkopf, 2000; Reinisch, 1996). America's attempts to do so have been vocally condemned by the

United Nations General Assembly (Kuntz and Jackson, 1994; LeoGrande, 1997; Osieja, 2006; Purcell and Rothkopf, 2000; Reinisch, 1996). Many have labeled this as nothing more than an extraterritorial measure (LeoGrande, 1997; Osieja, 2006; Purcell and Rothkopf, 2000; Reinisch, 1996; Roman, 1995; Smugula, 1995; Spadoni, 2010). They argue that the actions of the USA are in effect a contravention of "the sovereign equality of States, non-intervention in their internal affairs and freedom of trade and navigation as paramount to the conduct of international affairs" (Osieja, 2006; Purcell and Rothkopf, 2000; Reinisch, 1996; Roman, 1995; Smugula, 1995; Spadoni, 2010; Zimbalist, 1993).

The USA has not been entirely successful in isolating the Cuban government internationally since there are many international relationships (IRs) that have persisted throughout the duration of the sanctions (Purcell and Rothkopf, 2000; Reinisch, 1996; Roman, 1995; Smugula, 1995; Spadoni, 2010; Zimbalist, 1993). For example, Cuba has been able to conduct international trade with many countries, including many US allies (Barry, 2000; Boas, 2000; Cain, 1994; Copeland, Jolly, and Thompson, 2011; Drain and Barry, 2010). This calls into question whether the embargo is effective in the first place (Falk, 1996; Fandl, 2017; Fisk, 2000; Garfield and Santana, 1997; Gordon, 2012). However, US based companies which trade in Cuba do so at the risk of US sanctions, and many have chosen the easier route of not doing trade with the nation at all (Kirkpatrick, 1996; Kuntz and Jackson, 1994; LeoGrande, 1997; Osieja, 2006).

Nevertheless, Cuba has continued to build relationships internationally which are beneficial to its survival in the face of US agreement (Purcell and Rothkopf, 2000; Reinisch, 1996; Roman, 1995; Smugula, 1995; Spadoni, 2010; Zimbalist, 1993). For example, Cuba has been a member of the World Trade Organization since 1995 (Barry, 2000; Boas, 2000; Cain, 1994; Fandl, 2017; Fisk, 2000; Garfield and Santana, 1997; Osieja, 2006; Purcell and Rothkopf, 2000). Perhaps this indicates a willingness on the part of Cuba to explore alternative avenues for trade in the absence of US cooperation (Copeland, Jolly, and Thompson, 2011; Gordon, 2012; Kirkpatrick, 1996; Reinisch, 1996; Roman, 1995).

There are already signs that other large trading partners are increasingly looking to Cuba as an addition or even alternative to their current trading arrangements (Drain and Barry, 2010; Falk, 1996; Kuntz and Jackson, 1994; LeoGrande, 1997; Smugula, 1995; Spadoni, 2010; Zimbalist, 1993). For example, the European Union (EU) remains Cuba's largest trading partner

(Purcell and Rothkopf, 2000; Reinisch, 1996; Roman, 1995; Smugula, 1995; Spadoni, 2010; Zimbalist, 1993). Indeed, even the United States itself is the fifth largest exporter to Cuba despite the embargo (Osieja, 2006; Purcell and Rothkopf, 2000; Reinisch, 1996; Roman, 1995; Smugula, 1995; Spadoni, 2010; Zimbalist, 1993). It has been estimated that about 6.6% of Cuba's imports come from the USA, a statistic that is surprising given how bad the relationships between the two countries have been in the recent past (LeoGrande, 1997; Osieja, 2006; Purcell and Rothkopf, 2000; Reinisch, 1996; Roman, 1995; Smugula, 1995; Spadoni, 2010).

Despite these efforts at trade outside the embargo, Cuba must contend with very serious restrictions (Kuntz and Jackson, 1994; LeoGrande, 1997; Osieja, 2006; Purcell and Rothkopf, 2000; Reinisch, 1996). For example, Cuba is required to pay cash for all imports (Kirkpatrick, 1996; Kuntz and Jackson, 1994; LeoGrande, 1997; Osieja, 2006; Purcell and Rothkopf, 2000; Reinisch, 1996). This is because credit is not allowed under the terms of the embargo (Gordon, 2012; Kirkpatrick, 1996; Kuntz and Jackson, 1994; LeoGrande, 1997; Osieja, 2006; Purcell and Rothkopf, 2000). Beyond criticisms of human rights in Cuba, the United States holds $6 billion worth of financial claims against the Cuban government (Garfield and Santana, 1997; Gordon, 2012; Kirkpatrick, 1996; Kuntz and Jackson, 1994; LeoGrande, 1997; Osieja, 2006). This demonstrates the often complex and contradictory relationship between the two countries (Fisk, 2000; Garfield and Santana, 1997; Gordon, 2012; Kirkpatrick, 1996; Kuntz and Jackson, 1994; LeoGrande, 1997).

Many who still support the embargo in the USA argue that Cuba owes compensation to those who lost their stake in the nationalized companies (Fandl, 2017; Fisk, 2000; Garfield and Santana, 1997; Gordon, 2012; Kirkpatrick, 1996; Kuntz and Jackson, 1994). For example, the Latin America Working Group argues that pro-embargo Cuban-American exiles have swayed many politicians to adopt views similar to their own (Falk, 1996; Fandl, 2017; Fisk, 2000; Garfield and Santana, 1997; Gordon, 2012; Kirkpatrick, 1996). This is particularly true in Florida, where they play an increasingly important electoral role (Drain and Barry, 2010; Falk, 1996; Fandl, 2017; Fisk, 2000; Garfield and Santana, 1997; Gordon, 2012; Kirkpatrick, 1996). Some business leaders (e.g., James Perrella, Dwayne Andreas, and Peter Blyth) have opposed the embargo on the basis that free trade would be mutually beneficial to the USA and Cuba (Copeland, Jolly, and Thompson, 2011; Drain and Barry, 2010; Falk, 1996; Fandl, 2017; Fisk, 2000; Garfield and Santana, 1997).

In response to pressure from some American farmers and agribusiness, the embargo was relaxed by the Trade Sanctions Reform and Export Enhancement Act, which was passed by the Congress in October 2000 and signed by President Bill Clinton (Cain, 1994; Copeland, Jolly, and Thompson, 2011; Drain and Barry, 2010; Falk, 1996; Fandl, 2017; Fisk, 2000). The relaxation allowed the sale of agricultural goods and medicine to Cuba for humanitarian reasons (Boas, 2000; Cain, 1994; Copeland, Jolly, and Thompson, 2011; Drain and Barry, 2010; Falk, 1996; Fandl, 2017). Although Cuba initially declined to engage in such trade, the Cuban government eventually began to allow the purchase of food from the US because of Hurricane Michelle in November 2001 (Barry, 2000; Boas, 2000; Cain, 1994; Copeland, Jolly, and Thompson, 2011; Drain and Barry, 2010; Falk, 1996). These purchases have grown since then, even though all sales are made in cash, which can be inconvenient for traders (Barry, 2000; Boas, 2000; Cain, 1994; Copeland, Jolly, and Thompson, 2011; Drain and Barry, 2010; Falk, 1996). In 2007, the US was the largest food supplier of Cuba as a case in point in the progress on this front (Boas, 2000; Cain, 1994; Copeland, Jolly, and Thompson, 2011; Drain and Barry, 2010; Falk, 1996; Fandl, 2017).

In some tourist spots across the island, American brands such as Coca-Cola can be purchased hence reflected the reducing isolation of the Cuban communities (Cain, 1994; Copeland, Jolly, and Thompson, 2011; Drain and Barry, 2010; Falk, 1996; Fandl, 2017; Fisk, 2000). Additionally, Ford tankers refuel planes in airports and some computers use Microsoft software. The origin of the financing behind such goods is not always clear (Copeland, Jolly, and Thompson, 2011; Drain and Barry, 2010; Falk, 1996; Fandl, 2017; Fisk, 2000; Garfield and Santana, 1997). The goods often come from third parties based in countries outside the USA, even if the product being dealt originally has US shareholders or investors (Drain and Barry, 2010; Falk, 1996; Fandl, 2017; Fisk, 2000; Garfield and Santana, 1997; Gordon, 2012; Kirkpatrick, 1996). This can be seen, for example, with Nestlé products (10% US ownership) that can be bought in Cuba with Cuban convertible pesos or CUCs (Falk, 1996; Fandl, 2017; Fisk, 2000; Garfield and Santana, 1997; Gordon, 2012; Kirkpatrick, 1996). These CUC pesos are hard currency that are traded in foreign exchange against the US dollar, Euro, and other currencies (Fandl, 2017; Fisk, 2000; Garfield and Santana, 1997; Gordon, 2012; Kirkpatrick, 1996; Kuntz and Jackson, 1994).

On the 16th of July 2012, the Ana Cecilia became the first officially sanctioned direct ship to sail from Miami to (Fisk, 2000; Garfield and

Santana, 1997; Gordon, 2012; Kirkpatrick, 1996; Kuntz and Jackson, 1994; LeoGrande, 1997). It carried food, medicine, and personal hygiene goods sent by Cuban Americans to family members. In 2014, the Obama administration announced its intention to re-establish relations with Cuba. In January 2015, the Administration lightened restrictions on US citizen travel to Cuba. While restrictions on travel for missionary work and education have been loosened, visits for tourism remain banned (Garfield and Santana, 1997; Gordon, 2012; Kirkpatrick, 1996; Kuntz and Jackson, 1994; LeoGrande, 1997; Osieja, 2006). President Obama and President Raúl Castro of Cuba met on the 11th of April 2015. This was the first meeting between distinct leaders of the two countries in over 50 years (Gordon, 2012; Kirkpatrick, 1996; Kuntz and Jackson, 1994; LeoGrande, 1997; Osieja, 2006; Purcell and Rothkopf, 2000). In May 2015, several American companies reported they had been granted licenses to establish ferry travel between Florida and Cuba. This raised hopes that the notoriously bad relationships between the US and Cuban government would eventually improve. However, that hope was once again dashed by the entrance of a new administration led by Donald Trump which reversed many of the gains.

So far, the general ban on travel to Cuba remains in effect for Americans, so the ferry service will not be accessible to Americans who have not received special approval for travel to Cuba. (Kirkpatrick, 1996; Kuntz and Jackson, 1994; LeoGrande, 1997; Osieja, 2006; Purcell and Rothkopf, 2000; Reinisch, 1996). On the 8th of November 2017, it was announced that US President Donald Trump's Administration had enacted new rules which would re-enforce the business and travel restrictions that were loosened by the Obama Administration. There had been no marked change in Cuba's behavior to elicit this response, but ultimately the politics of the USA were impacting on the embargo. Some of the objections against Cuba are ideological while others stem from the need to ensure electoral success with exiled Cuban Americans who remain an important voting bloc in Florida (Kuntz and Jackson, 1994; LeoGrande, 1997; Osieja, 2006; Purcell and Rothkopf, 2000; Reinisch, 1996). The next section will closely look at the impact and responses to the embargo on Cuba.

2.3. MIXED REACTIONS TO US EMBARGO OF CUBA

The USA embargo on Cuba is one of the least popular sanctions in history and many nations have expressed discomfort with their rationale and actual implementation (Hanushek and Woessmann, 2010; Haugh and Kitson,

2007; Hinds, 1997; Hiraide and Chakraborty, 2012; Ho-Chuan, Yi-Chen, and Chih-Chuan, 2012). In November 1991, the Cuban ambassador, Ricardo Alarcón, in a speech to the UN General Assembly, cited 27 recent cases of trade contracts interrupted by US pressure (Daviron and Ponte, 2007; De Visscher, 2015; De Vos, 2010; Defourny, 2013; Denzin, 2008; Devarajan and Mottaghi, 2015; Dobler, 2008). The British journal Cuba Business claimed that British Petroleum was seemingly dissuaded by US authorities from investing in offshore oil exploration in Cuba despite being initially keenly interested (Kirshner, 1997; Klotz, 1995; Koskenniemi, 2014; Kunz, 1960; Laub, 2015; Lee, 2018) (Saeidnia and Abdollahi, 2013; Tridimas and Guiterrex-Fons, 2008). The Petroleum economist claimed, in September 1992, that the US State Department vigorously discouraged firms like Royal Dutch Shell and Clyde Petroleum from investing in Cuba (Choi and Luo, 2013; Dunoff, Ratner, and Wippman, 2015; Haugh and Kitson, 2007; Kaempfer and Lowenberg, 2000).

This pressure did not work in all cases. According to the Mexican newspaper El Financiero, the US ambassador to Mexico, John Negroponte traveled to meet two Mexican businessmen who had signed a textile deal with Cuba on October 17, 1992. Despite the representation, the deal went ahead and was eventually worth $500 million in foreign capital. All of this happened before the signing of the Cuban Democracy Act (Lutz and Lux, 1995; Meyer and Thein, 2014; Mueller and Mueller, 1999; Ryngaert, 2015). As Figure 2.3 shows, there is a mixed reaction to the restrictions that have been placed on Cuba by the USA.

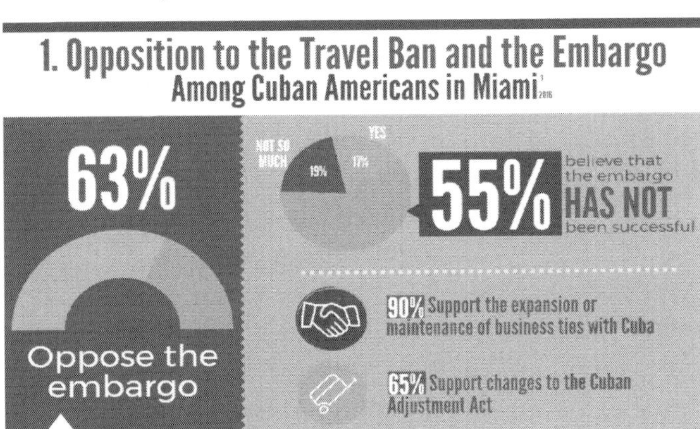

Figure 2.3. Mixed reactions to US embargo of Cuba.

Source: Latin America Working Group.

The sanctions on Cuba and their economic impacts can be traced back to their onset in the 1960s, as well as the ongoing hostilities against the country (LeoGrande, 1997; Osieja, 2006; Purcell and Rothkopf, 2000; Reinisch, 1996; Roman, 1995; Smugula, 1995; Spadoni, 2010). It has been estimated that the embargo costs the United States economy $1.2 billion per year in lost trade, investment, tourism, and raw materials (Osieja, 2006; Purcell and Rothkopf, 2000; Reinisch, 1996; Roman, 1995; Smugula, 1995; Spadoni, 2010; Zimbalist, 1993). This is a direct consequence of because of the legal structures that prevented American exporters from entering Cuban markets and hence closing off the potential of that market (Purcell and Rothkopf, 2000; Reinisch, 1996; Roman, 1995; Smugula, 1995; Spadoni, 2010; Zimbalist, 1993). The Cuba Policy Foundation (CPF) estimates put the cost of the embargo at $4.84 billion per year (Barry, 2000; Boas, 2000; Cain, 1994; Copeland, Jolly, and Thompson, 2011; Drain and Barry, 2010). At the same time, this embargo is costing Cuba close to $685 million per year overall, which is substantially less than what the USA loses. However, the relative weaknesses of Cuba in economic, social, and political terms means that it is in fact paying dearly for the embargo (Falk, 1996; Fandl, 2017; Fisk, 2000; Garfield and Santana, 1997; Gordon, 2012). More specifically, Cuba is estimated to have lost over $28.6 billion in trade, an income source that the country desperately needs (Kirkpatrick, 1996; Kuntz and Jackson, 1994; LeoGrande, 1997; Osieja, 2006). These are hindrances that have direct impact on people and communities that are living in both the USA and Cuba (Purcell and Rothkopf, 2000; Reinisch, 1996; Roman, 1995; Smugula, 1995; Spadoni, 2010; Zimbalist, 1993).

Interestingly, Cuba was once a trading partner to the USA (Barry, 2000; Boas, 2000; Cain, 1994; Fandl, 2017; Fisk, 2000; Garfield and Santana, 1997; Osieja, 2006; Purcell and Rothkopf, 2000). For example, between 1954 and 1959, trade between Cuba and the United States was at a higher level than what it is today (Copeland, Jolly, and Thompson, 2011; Gordon, 2012; Kirkpatrick, 1996; Reinisch, 1996; Roman, 1995). At the time, 65% of Cuba's total exports went to the United States (Drain and Barry, 2010; Falk, 1996; Kuntz and Jackson, 1994; LeoGrande, 1997; Smugula, 1995; Spadoni, 2010; Zimbalist, 1993). Simultaneously American imports totaled 74% of Cuba's international purchases (Purcell and Rothkopf, 2000; Reinisch, 1996; Roman, 1995; Smugula, 1995; Spadoni, 2010; Zimbalist, 1993). After the formal implementation of the embargo and the passage of Proclamation 3355, there was a 95% decrease in Cuba's sugar quota (Osieja, 2006; Purcell and Rothkopf, 2000; Reinisch, 1996; Roman, 1995; Smugula,

1995; Spadoni, 2010; Zimbalist, 1993). This translates into a cancellation of about 700,000 tons of the 3,119,655 tons previously allotted to the United States (LeoGrande, 1997; Osieja, 2006; Purcell and Rothkopf, 2000; Reinisch, 1996; Roman, 1995; Smugula, 1995; Spadoni, 2010). A year later, Cuba's sugar quota was reduced to zero when President Eisenhower issued Proclamation 3383 (Kuntz and Jackson, 1994; LeoGrande, 1997; Osieja, 2006; Purcell and Rothkopf, 2000; Reinisch, 1996). This substantially affected Cuba's total exports, as Cuba was one of the world's leading sugar exporters at the time (Kirkpatrick, 1996; Kuntz and Jackson, 1994; LeoGrande, 1997; Osieja, 2006; Purcell and Rothkopf, 2000; Reinisch, 1996).

In 1989, and partly due to the collapse of the Soviet bloc; Cuba witnessed its most devastating economic crises (Gordon, 2012; Kirkpatrick, 1996; Kuntz and Jackson, 1994; LeoGrande, 1997; Osieja, 2006; Purcell and Rothkopf, 2000). For example, Cuba's GDP plummeted 34% and trade between the countries declined by 56% (Garfield and Santana, 1997; Gordon, 2012; Kirkpatrick, 1996; Kuntz and Jackson, 1994; LeoGrande, 1997; Osieja, 2006). Between 1989 and 1992, the termination of traditional trade partnerships with the Soviet bloc caused the total value of Cuba's exports to fall by 61% (Fisk, 2000; Garfield and Santana, 1997; Gordon, 2012; Kirkpatrick, 1996; Kuntz and Jackson, 1994; LeoGrande, 1997). Subsequently, imports fell by approximately 72% (Fandl, 2017; Fisk, 2000; Garfield and Santana, 1997; Gordon, 2012; Kirkpatrick, 1996; Kuntz and Jackson, 1994). This period is known as the '*Special Period*' in Cuban history and is associated with significant suffering (Falk, 1996; Fandl, 2017; Fisk, 2000; Garfield and Santana, 1997; Gordon, 2012; Kirkpatrick, 1996). Supporters of the embargo and many international economists mistakenly assumed that the dissolution of the Soviet Union and the resultant economic crisis would lead to the downfall of Fidel Castro's government (Drain and Barry, 2010; Falk, 1996; Fandl, 2017; Fisk, 2000; Garfield and Santana, 1997; Gordon, 2012; Kirkpatrick, 1996). Instead, Cuba's government instituted a campaign of macroeconomic adjustment and liberalization, which helped significant economic recovery (Copeland, Jolly, and Thompson, 2011; Drain and Barry, 2010; Falk, 1996; Fandl, 2017; Fisk, 2000; Garfield and Santana, 1997). This is an example of a nation under sanctions finding coping mechanism to sustain itself despite overwhelming US aggression (Cain, 1994; Copeland, Jolly, and Thompson, 2011; Drain and Barry, 2010; Falk, 1996; Fandl, 2017; Fisk, 2000). According to critics, one of the major problems with the embargo is that the United States is the only major country that has such an embargo against Cuba in place (Boas, 2000; Cain, 1994; Copeland, Jolly, and Thompson, 2011; Drain and Barry, 2010; Falk, 1996; Fandl, 2017). Others have been either lukewarm or even outwardly critical of the embargo (Barry, 2000; Boas, 2000; Cain, 1994; Copeland, Jolly, and Thompson, 2011; Drain and Barry, 2010; Falk, 1996). For example, Cuba still receives tourists and trade from other countries (Barry, 2000; Boas, 2000; Cain, 1994; Copeland, Jolly, and Thompson, 2011; Drain and Barry, 2010; Falk, 1996). Spurred by a burgeoning interest in the assumed untapped product demand in Cuba; a growing number of free marketers in Congress, backed by Western and Great Plains lawmakers who represent agribusiness, have lobbied against the embargo (Boas, 2000; Cain, 1994; Copeland, Jolly, and Thompson, 2011; Drain and Barry, 2010; Falk, 1996; Fandl, 2017). Four times over that time, the United States House of Representatives has adopted language lifting the travel ban (Cain, 1994; Copeland, Jolly, and Thompson, 2011; Drain and Barry, 2010; Falk, 1996; Fandl, 2017; Fisk, 2000). Moreover, in 2003 the US Senate followed suit for the first time (Copeland, Jolly, and Thompson, 2011; Drain and Barry, 2010; Falk, 1996; Fandl, 2017; Fisk, 2000; Garfield and Santana, 1997). Each time President George W. Bush threatened to veto the bill. Faced with a veto threat, each year Congress dropped its attempt to lift the travel ban before sending legislation to the president.

Some United States nationals circumvent the ban by traveling to Cuba from a different country, such as Mexico, The Bahamas, Canada, or Costa Rica (Drain and Barry, 2010; Falk, 1996; Fandl, 2017; Fisk, 2000; Garfield and Santana, 1997; Gordon, 2012; Kirkpatrick, 1996). Cuban immigration authorities do not routinely stamp passports to prevent detection of unauthorized travel to the country (Falk, 1996; Fandl, 2017; Fisk, 2000; Garfield and Santana, 1997; Gordon, 2012; Kirkpatrick, 1996). Instead, the Cuban authorities stamp a visa page which is provided and not permanently affixed to the passport to circumvent US authorities. However, the practice still opens US citizens to a risk of prosecution and fines by the US government if discovered (Fandl, 2017; Fisk, 2000; Garfield and Santana, 1997; Gordon, 2012; Kirkpatrick, 1996; Kuntz and Jackson, 1994).

Until the 20th of July 2015, there was no US Embassy or consulate in Cuba and the United States representation was limited to a United States Interests Section (Fisk, 2000; Garfield and Santana, 1997; Gordon, 2012; Kirkpatrick, 1996; Kuntz and Jackson, 1994; LeoGrande, 1997). This made it very difficult to engage in legal travel to Cuba from the USA, certainly for tourists and other ordinary travelers (Garfield and Santana, 1997; Gordon,

2012; Kirkpatrick, 1996; Kuntz and Jackson, 1994; LeoGrande, 1997; Osieja, 2006). The United States Treasury Department's OFAC considers any visit of more than one day to be prima facie proof of violation (Gordon, 2012; Kirkpatrick, 1996; Kuntz and Jackson, 1994; LeoGrande, 1997; Osieja, 2006; Purcell and Rothkopf, 2000). US citizens may not receive goods or services for free from any Cuban national (Kirkpatrick, 1996; Kuntz and Jackson, 1994; LeoGrande, 1997; Osieja, 2006; Purcell and Rothkopf, 2000; Reinisch, 1996). This measure is designed to prevent any attempts to circumvent the regulation, albeit causing considerable hardship for Cubans that have family in the USA (Kuntz and Jackson, 1994; LeoGrande, 1997; Osieja, 2006; Purcell and Rothkopf, 2000; Reinisch, 1996).

The embargo has been criticized for its effects on food, clean water, medicine, and other economic needs of the Cuban population (LeoGrande, 1997; Osieja, 2006; Purcell and Rothkopf, 2000; Reinisch, 1996; Roman, 1995; Smugula, 1995; Spadoni, 2010). Criticism have come from both Fidel Castro and Raúl Castro, citizens, and groups from within Cuba, and international organizations and international leaders (Osieja, 2006; Purcell and Rothkopf, 2000; Reinisch, 1996; Roman, 1995; Smugula, 1995; Spadoni, 2010; Zimbalist, 1993). Some have linked the embargo to shortages of medical supplies and soap which have resulted in a series of medical crises and heightened levels of infectious (Purcell and Rothkopf, 2000; Reinisch, 1996; Roman, 1995; Smugula, 1995; Spadoni, 2010; Zimbalist, 1993). Others have linked the embargo to specific diseases epidemics, including neurological disorders and blindness resulting from poor nutrition (Barry, 2000; Boas, 2000; Cain, 1994; Copeland, Jolly, and Thompson, 2011; Drain and Barry, 2010).

Travel restrictions embedded in the embargo have also been shown to limit the amount of medical information that flows into Cuba from the United States (Falk, 1996; Fandl, 2017; Fisk, 2000; Garfield and Santana, 1997; Gordon, 2012). Research suggests that malnutrition and disease resulting from increased food and medicine prices have affected men and the elderly as specifically vulnerable groups (Kirkpatrick, 1996; Kuntz and Jackson, 1994; LeoGrande, 1997; Osieja, 2006). This is due to Cuba's rationing system which gives preferential treatment to women and children (Purcell and Rothkopf, 2000; Reinisch, 1996; Roman, 1995; Smugula, 1995; Spadoni, 2010; Zimbalist, 1993). Cuban Foreign Minister Felipe Pérez Roque called the embargo "an act of genocide." He also referenced a classified State Department memo dated the 6th of April 1960 which called on the USA to bring down Fidel Castro through hunger and disease

(Barry, 2000; Boas, 2000; Cain, 1994; Fandl, 2017; Fisk, 2000; Garfield and Santana, 1997; Osieja, 2006; Purcell and Rothkopf, 2000).

The Helms-Burton Act has been the target of criticism from Canadian and European governments (Copeland, Jolly, and Thompson, 2011; Gordon, 2012; Kirkpatrick, 1996; Reinisch, 1996; Roman, 1995). These governments individually and collectively object to what they say is the extraterritorial pretensions of a piece of legislation aimed at punishing non-US corporations and non-US investors who have economic interests in Cuba (Drain and Barry, 2010; Falk, 1996; Kuntz and Jackson, 1994; LeoGrande, 1997; Smugula, 1995; Spadoni, 2010; Zimbalist, 1993). The European Council has stated that it reaffirms its concern to promote democratic reform in Cuba (Purcell and Rothkopf, 2000; Reinisch, 1996; Roman, 1995; Smugula, 1995; Spadoni, 2010; Zimbalist, 1993). However, it also recalled the deep concern expressed by the European Council over the extraterritorial effects of the "Cuban Liberty and Democratic Solidarity (Libertad) Act" (Osieja, 2006; Purcell and Rothkopf, 2000; Reinisch, 1996; Roman, 1995; Smugula, 1995; Spadoni, 2010; Zimbalist, 1993). The EU has noted the widespread international objections to this. Based on those objections, the EU requested President Clinton to waive the provisions of Title III (LeoGrande, 1997; Osieja, 2006; Purcell and Rothkopf, 2000; Reinisch, 1996; Roman, 1995; Smugula, 1995; Spadoni, 2010). Europe also expressed serious concern at the measures already taken to implement Title IV of the Act (Kuntz and Jackson, 1994; LeoGrande, 1997; Osieja, 2006; Purcell and Rothkopf, 2000; Reinisch, 1996).

The embargo has attracted diverse criticism for expected and unexpected quarters (Kirkpatrick, 1996; Kuntz and Jackson, 1994; LeoGrande, 1997; Osieja, 2006; Purcell and Rothkopf, 2000; Reinisch, 1996). For example, some critics say that the embargo helps the regime more than it hurts it (Gordon, 2012; Kirkpatrick, 1996; Kuntz and Jackson, 1994; LeoGrande, 1997; Osieja, 2006; Purcell and Rothkopf, 2000). The rationale for this is that by providing the Cuban administration with a bogeyman for all of Cuba's misfortunes in the form of the oppressive USA, the embargo ultimately suppresses dissent (Garfield and Santana, 1997; Gordon, 2012; Kirkpatrick, 1996; Kuntz and Jackson, 1994; LeoGrande, 1997; Osieja, 2006). This is the same problem that has arisen in other areas under sanction such as Iraq, Iran, and North Korea (Fisk, 2000; Garfield and Santana, 1997; Gordon, 2012; Kirkpatrick, 1996; Kuntz and Jackson, 1994; LeoGrande, 1997). There are American business leaders who openly call for an end to the embargo based on its negative impact on their business interests (Fandl, 2017; Fisk, 2000;

Garfield and Santana, 1997; Gordon, 2012; Kirkpatrick, 1996; Kuntz and Jackson, 1994). For example, non-US foreign businesses in Cuba that violate the embargo do not have to compete with US businesses (Falk, 1996; Fandl, 2017; Fisk, 2000; Garfield and Santana, 1997; Gordon, 2012; Kirkpatrick, 1996). This means that such businesses will have a head start when and if the embargo is lifted (Drain and Barry, 2010; Falk, 1996; Fandl, 2017; Fisk, 2000; Garfield and Santana, 1997; Gordon, 2012; Kirkpatrick, 1996).

Some religious leaders oppose the embargo for a variety of reasons, including humanitarian and economic restrictions the embargo imposes on Cubans (Copeland, Jolly, and Thompson, 2011; Drain and Barry, 2010; Falk, 1996; Fandl, 2017; Fisk, 2000; Garfield and Santana, 1997). Pope John Paul II, for example, called for the end to the embargo during his 1979 pastoral visit to Mexico. Patriarch Bartholomew I called the embargo a "historic mistake" while visiting the island on the 25th of January 2004. Rev. Jesse Jackson, Rev. Al Sharpton, and Minister Louis Farrakhan have also publicly opposed the embargo because of its social injustice implication. On the 15th of May 2002, former President Jimmy Carter spoke in Havana, calling for an end to the embargo. The assembly of US bishops also called for an end to the embargo on Cuba, following Pope Benedict XVI's 2012 visit to the island.

The United Nations General Assembly has condemned the embargo as a violation of international law every year since 1992 (Cain, 1994; Copeland, Jolly, and Thompson, 2011; Drain and Barry, 2010; Falk, 1996; Fandl, 2017; Fisk, 2000). Israel is the only country that routinely joins the US in voting against the resolution (Boas, 2000; Cain, 1994; Copeland, Jolly, and Thompson, 2011; Drain and Barry, 2010; Falk, 1996; Fandl, 2017). Additionally, Palau has expressed tacit support for the embargo every year from 2004 to 2008 (Barry, 2000; Boas, 2000; Cain, 1994; Copeland, Jolly, and Thompson, 2011; Drain and Barry, 2010; Falk, 1996). On the 26th of October 2010, the General Assembly condemned the embargo, 187 to 2 with 3 abstentions. This was for the 19th time that such an action had taken place on this issue (Boas, 2000; Cain, 1994; Copeland, Jolly, and Thompson, 2011; Drain and Barry, 2010; Falk, 1996; Fandl, 2017). Israel sided with the USA while Marshall Islands, Palau, and Micronesia abstained. There have been other overt and covert demonstrations against the embargo. For example, film director Michael Moore challenged the embargo by bringing 9/11 rescue workers in need of health care to Cuba to obtain subsidized health care. In June 2011, former Democratic presidential candidate George McGovern blamed "embittered Cuban exiles in Miami" for keeping the embargo alive. Proponents of the embargo argue that the Cubans have done much to antagonize the United States (Cain, 1994; Copeland, Jolly, and Thompson, 2011; Drain and Barry, 2010; Falk, 1996; Fandl, 2017; Fisk, 2000). Indeed, the Cubans backed, armed, and fought with militant movements that attempted to overthrow US allies and targeted US interests throughout Latin America and Africa for significant periods of time (Copeland, Jolly, and Thompson, 2011; Drain and Barry, 2010; Falk, 1996; Fandl, 2017; Fisk, 2000; Garfield and Santana, 1997). One example of this was Cuba's assistance to FARC in their operations through several South American countries, especially Colombia (Drain and Barry, 2010; Falk, 1996; Fandl, 2017; Fisk, 2000; Garfield and Santana, 1997; Gordon, 2012; Kirkpatrick, 1996). Another example is Cuba's shooting down of unarmed American civilian aircraft (Falk, 1996; Fandl, 2017; Fisk, 2000; Garfield and Santana, 1997; Gordon, 2012; Kirkpatrick, 1996). Furthermore, proponents argue that Cuba has little to offer the United States economically (Fandl, 2017; Fisk, 2000; Garfield and Santana, 1997; Gordon, 2012; Kirkpatrick, 1996; Kuntz and Jackson, 1994). Other's objective to Cuba's one-party semi-dictatorial form of government which is tainted by crackdowns on religious freedom, repression of the press, and repression of almost all criticism of the government (Fisk, 2000; Garfield and Santana, 1997; Gordon, 2012; Kirkpatrick, 1996; Kuntz and Jackson, 1994; LeoGrande, 1997).

Supporters of the embargo argue that these policies in Cuba are designed to ensure one-party, dictatorial rule for as long as possible (Garfield and Santana, 1997; Gordon, 2012; Kirkpatrick, 1996; Kuntz and Jackson, 1994; LeoGrande, 1997; Osieja, 2006). Many in the United States profoundly disagree with Cuba's historical policies of severely limiting private property ownership and property rights to attain a more communistic society (Gordon, 2012; Kirkpatrick, 1996; Kuntz and Jackson, 1994; LeoGrande, 1997; Osieja, 2006; Purcell and Rothkopf, 2000). Then there is the purported argument that Cuba may export its repressive and backward form of government, especially into the United States (Kirkpatrick, 1996; Kuntz and Jackson, 1994; LeoGrande, 1997; Osieja, 2006; Purcell and Rothkopf, 2000; Reinisch, 1996). Some see this as a national security threat due to Cuba's proximity to the United States (Kuntz and Jackson, 1994; LeoGrande, 1997; Osieja, 2006; Purcell and Rothkopf, 2000; Reinisch, 1996). Indeed, Cuba has launched several military campaigns, by itself and with other usually hostile nations

(LeoGrande, 1997; Osieja, 2006; Purcell and Rothkopf, 2000; Reinisch, 1996; Roman, 1995; Smugula, 1995; Spadoni, 2010). These aggressions are primarily designed to export its undesirable form of government to other parts of the world to create a socialist majority across the globe (Osieja, 2006; Purcell and Rothkopf, 2000; Reinisch, 1996; Roman, 1995; Smugula, 1995; Spadoni, 2010; Zimbalist, 1993).

In reality, the USA would not gain much economically from removing the embargo (Purcell and Rothkopf, 2000; Reinisch, 1996; Roman, 1995; Smugula, 1995; Spadoni, 2010; Zimbalist, 1993). For example, Cuba does not have an advanced industrial base and manufactures little of value that could be traded with the United States if the embargo were lifted (Drain and Barry, 2010; Falk, 1996; Kuntz and Jackson, 1994; LeoGrande, 1997; Smugula, 1995; Spadoni, 2010; Zimbalist, 1993). American demand for products that Cuba does export are generally easily covered by domestic production or trade relations with more economically reliable and friendlier nations (Copeland, Jolly, and Thompson, 2011; Gordon, 2012; Kirkpatrick, 1996; Reinisch, 1996; Roman, 1995). Cuban benefits would include the easing of the frequent shortages of goods the island experiences (Barry, 2000; Boas, 2000; Cain, 1994; Fandl, 2017; Fisk, 2000; Garfield and Santana, 1997; Osieja, 2006; Purcell and Rothkopf, 2000). Removing the embargo might also help Cuba by giving it access to additional low-cost services not readily available in Cuba (Purcell and Rothkopf, 2000; Reinisch, 1996; Roman, 1995; Smugula, 1995; Spadoni, 2010; Zimbalist, 1993). Eventually, Cuba may be able to access to new and better technology for personal consumption and economic development (Kirkpatrick, 1996; Kuntz and Jackson, 1994; LeoGrande, 1997; Osieja, 2006). For these reasons, proponents argue that lifting the embargo is not advantageous to the United States or Cuba's population until economic or political reforms are enacted by the Cubans (Falk, 1996; Fandl, 2017; Fisk, 2000; Garfield and Santana, 1997; Gordon, 2012).

A majority of poll respondents have repeatedly expressed unease with the embargo, with many calling for its cancellation altogether (Barry, 2000; Boas, 2000; Cain, 1994; Copeland, Jolly, and Thompson, 2011; Drain and Barry, 2010). For example, a 2008 USA Today/Gallup Poll indicated that Americans believed that diplomatic relations "should" be re-established with Cuba with 61% in favor, 31% opposed. In January 2012, an Angus

Reid Public Opinion poll showed that 57% of Americans called for ending the travel ban that prevented most Americans from visiting Cuba, with 27% disagreeing and 16% not sure. Polls also show declining support for sanctions among Cuban Americans. A June 2014 poll showed 52% of Cuban Americans in Miami-Dade County, Florida, opposed the embargo and 48% supported it. This compares with the 56% of Cuban Americans in Miami-Dade County who had supported the embargo in 2011, while 87% had supported it in 1991. Lobbying groups such as Engage Cuba advocate for the end of the embargo (Purcell and Rothkopf, 2000; Reinisch, 1996; Roman, 1995; Smugula, 1995; Spadoni, 2010; Zimbalist, 1993). It remains to be seen whether the new Joe Biden administration in the USA will reverse Donald Trump's policy of putting more restrictions on Cuba. The next section examines the use of psychological warfare to subdue nations, a goal that might otherwise be achieved through international sanctions.

2.4. PSYCHOLOGICAL WARFARE AND SANCTIONS

Psychological warfare (or PSYWAR) remains one of the most basic aspects of modern psychological operations or PSYOP (Bechtel, 1991; Bhatt, 2015; Brennen and Cadwalladr, 2018; Cheng, 2003; Cheng, 2012; Cortright, Lopez, and Gerber-Stellingwerf, 2007). This type of combat or tactic has been known by many other names or terms including MISO, PSYOPs, political warfare, "Hearts and Minds," and propaganda (Bhatt, 2015; Brennen and Cadwalladr, 2018; Cheng, 2003; Cheng, 2012; Cortright, Lopez, and Gerber-Stellingwerf, 2007). It is distinguished from traditional military warfare in as far as it attacks the minds and thoughts of the victim community, rather than inflicting bodily harm (Brennen and Cadwalladr, 2018; Cheng, 2003; Cheng, 2012; Cortright, Lopez, and Gerber-Stellingwerf, 2007; Crawshaw, 1989). Nevertheless, psychological warfare can be as devastating as any military skirmishes because it negatively impacts on the morale of the community when it most needs to be upbeat (Cheng, 2003; Cheng, 2012; Cortright, Lopez, and Gerber-Stellingwerf, 2007; Crawshaw, 1989; Galtung, 1966).

The term psychological warfare is used to denote any action which is practiced mainly by psychological methods (Cheng, 2012; Cortright, Lopez, and Gerber-Stellingwerf, 2007; Crawshaw, 1989; Galtung, 1966;

Gilmore, 2000). In most cases, the main aim of psychological warfare involves evoking a planned psychological reaction in other people to their detriment (Cortright, Lopez, and Gerber-Stellingwerf, 2007; Crawshaw, 1989; Galtung, 1966; Gilmore, 2000; Iftimie, 2019). Over time, various techniques of psychological warfare have been developed, perfected, and used in a range of situations of conflict (Crawshaw, 1989; Galtung, 1966; Gilmore, 2000; Iftimie, 2019; Jacobson, 2005; Lerner and Crossman, 1949; Long, 2020). In these cases, psychological warfare is aimed at influencing a target audience's value system, belief system, emotions, motives, reasoning, or behavior (Galtung, 1966; Gilmore, 2000; Iftimie, 2019; Jacobson, 2005; Lerner and Crossman, 1949; Long, 2020).

There have been occasions when psychological warfare is used to induce confessions or reinforce attitudes (Gilmore, 2000; Iftimie, 2019; Jacobson, 2005; Lerner and Crossman, 1949; Long, 2020; Mathew and Boyd, 2011). At other times, the techniques of psychological warfare are used to elicit behaviors favorable to the originator's objectives (Iftimie, 2019; Jacobson, 2005; Lerner and Crossman, 1949; Long, 2020; Mathew and Boyd, 2011; Radvanyi, 1990). At other times, psychological warfare is combined with black operations or false flag tactics. The use of psychological warfare has been very effective when trying to destroy the morale of enemies (Jacobson, 2005; Lerner and Crossman, 1949; Long, 2020; Mathew and Boyd, 2011; Radvanyi, 1990; Reisman, 2009). These tactics have the effect of depressing the opponent's troops' psychological states hence rendering them less effective fighters (Lerner and Crossman, 1949; Long, 2020; Mathew and Boyd, 2011; Radvanyi, 1990; Reisman, 2009; Speier, 1951). Often psychological warfare is used at a national and international level (Long, 2020; Mathew and Boyd, 2011; Radvanyi, 1990; Reisman, 2009; Speier, 1951; Thomas, 2005; Wook, 2004). For example, the USA has attempted to break Iran using a combination of sanctions and psychological warfare (see Figure 2.4 for examples).

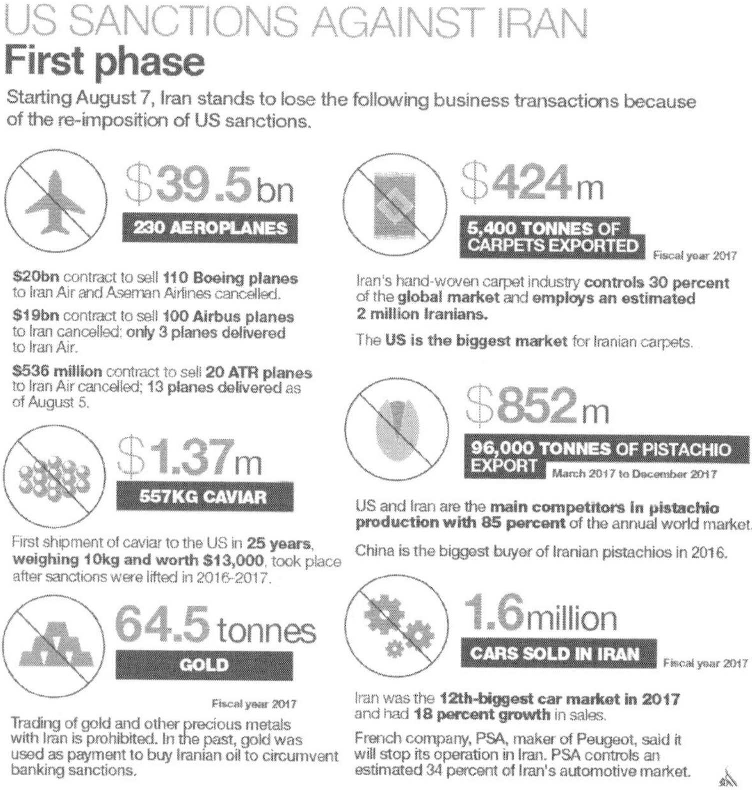

Figure 2.4. Psychological warfare and sanctions against Iran.

Source: Al Jazeera with references to OPEC, Forbes, Financial Tribune and Bloomberg.

The target audiences of psychological warfare can be governments, organizations, groups, and individuals (Mathew and Boyd, 2011; Radvanyi, 1990; Reisman, 2009; Speier, 1951; Thomas, 2005; Wook, 2004). However, it is important to note that psychological warfare is not just limited to soldiers. Civilians of foreign territories can also be targeted by technology and media (Bechtel, 1991; Bhatt, 2015; Brennen and Cadwalladr, 2018; Cheng, 2003; Cheng, 2012; Cortright, Lopez, and Gerber-Stellingwerf, 2007). The reason why psychological warfare is used in this way is to cause an effect in the government of their country (Crawshaw, 1989; Galtung, 1966; Gilmore, 2000; Iftimie, 2019; Jacobson, 2005; Lerner and Crossman, 1949). Some authors such as Jacques Ellul discuss psychological warfare as a common peace policy practice between nations as a form of indirect confrontation

(Long, 2020; Mathew and Boyd, 2011; Radvanyi, 1990; Reisman, 2009; Speier, 1951; Thomas, 2005; Wook, 2004). One advantage of this type of confrontation is that it is less costly than conventional methods (Bechtel, 1991; Bhatt, 2015; Crawshaw, 1989; Galtung, 1966; Mathew and Boyd, 2011).

The control of information is an important facet of psychological warfare, and often, there are instances in which the local populace is deliberately misled (Brennen and Cadwalladr, 2018; Cheng, 2003; Gilmore, 2000; Iftimie, 2019; Radvanyi, 1990; Reisman, 2009). This type of propaganda drains the public opinion of an opposing regime by stripping away its power on public opinion (Cheng, 2012; Cortright, Lopez, and Gerber-Stellingwerf, 2007; Jacobson, 2005). Indeed, there could be occasions when the nation may turn against its leaders (Lerner and Crossman, 1949; Long, 2020; Speier, 1951; Thomas, 2005; Wook, 2004). This form of aggression is hard to defend against because no International Court of Justice (ICJ) can protect against psychological aggression (Mathew and Boyd, 2011; Radvanyi, 1990; Reisman, 2009; Speier, 1951; Thomas, 2005; Wook, 2004). This is because in most jurisdictions, psychological warfare cannot be legally adjudicated (Long, 2020; Mathew and Boyd, 2011; Radvanyi, 1990; Reisman, 2009; Speier, 1951; Thomas, 2005; Wook, 2004). Even the international courts are reluctant to get involved in the form of conflict that is so nebulous (Lerner and Crossman, 1949; Long, 2020; Mathew and Boyd, 2011; Radvanyi, 1990; Reisman, 2009; Speier, 1951). In this case, the propagandists are dealing with a foreign adversary whose morale he seeks to destroy by psychological means (Jacobson, 2005; Lerner and Crossman, 1949; Long, 2020; Mathew and Boyd, 2011; Radvanyi, 1990; Reisman, 2009). The end effect is that the opponent begins to doubt the validity of his beliefs and actions (Iftimie, 2019; Jacobson, 2005; Lerner and Crossman, 1949; Long, 2020; Mathew and Boyd, 2011; Radvanyi, 1990).

There is evidence of psychological warfare throughout history and some of those ancient techniques have been adopted for our contemporary age (Gilmore, 2000; Iftimie, 2019; Jacobson, 2005; Lerner and Crossman, 1949; Long, 2020; Mathew and Boyd, 2011). In modern times, psychological warfare efforts have been used extensively +to confuse and subjugate the enemy (Galtung, 1966; Gilmore, 2000; Iftimie, 2019; Jacobson, 2005; Lerner and Crossman, 1949; Long, 2020). For example, mass communication allows for direct communication with an enemy populace to the detriment of its leaders (Crawshaw, 1989; Galtung, 1966; Gilmore, 2000; Iftimie, 2019; Jacobson, 2005; Lerner and Crossman, 1949; Long,

2020). In recent times, the internet allows for campaigns of disinformation and misinformation which are extensively performed by agents anywhere in the world (Cortright, Lopez, and Gerber-Stellingwerf, 2007; Crawshaw, 1989; Galtung, 1966; Gilmore, 2000; Iftimie, 2019).

When it comes to psychological warfare, the old is as good as new in terms of recycling techniques (Cheng, 2012; Cortright, Lopez, and Gerber-Stellingwerf, 2007; Crawshaw, 1989; Galtung, 1966; Gilmore, 2000). For example, we now speak of troll farms as sources of significant psychological warfare (Cheng, 2003; Cheng, 2012; Cortright, Lopez, and Gerber-Stellingwerf, 2007; Crawshaw, 1989; Galtung, 1966). However, many of the techniques that were used in the historical context are now being adapted so that they can serve modern audiences and conflicts (Brennen and Cadwalladr, 2018; Cheng, 2003; Cheng, 2012; Cortright, Lopez, and Gerber-Stellingwerf, 2007; Crawshaw, 1989). Since prehistoric times, warlords, and chiefs have recognized the importance of weakening the morale of opponents (Bhatt, 2015; Brennen and Cadwalladr, 2018; Cheng, 2003; Cheng, 2012; Cortright, Lopez, and Gerber-Stellingwerf, 2007). For example, during the Battle of Pelusium (525 BC) between the Persian Empire and ancient Egypt; the Persian forces used cats and other animals as a psychological tactic against the Egyptians (Bechtel, 1991; Bhatt, 2015; Brennen and Cadwalladr, 2018; Cheng, 2003; Cheng, 2012; Cortright, Lopez, and Gerber-Stellingwerf, 2007). This was because the Egyptians were known to avoid harming cats due to religious belief and spells.

The Operations Fortitude and Titanic in World War II is a modern example of very effective psychological warfare (Bechtel, 1991; Bhatt, 2015; Brennen and Cadwalladr, 2018; Cheng, 2003; Cheng, 2012; Cortright, Lopez, and Gerber-Stellingwerf, 2007). However, the start of modern PSYOP in war is generally dated to World War I (Bhatt, 2015; Brennen and Cadwalladr, 2018; Cheng, 2003; Cheng, 2012; Cortright, Lopez, and Gerber-Stellingwerf, 2007). By that point, Western societies were increasingly educated and urbanized (Brennen and Cadwalladr, 2018; Cheng, 2003; Cheng, 2012; Cortright, Lopez, and Gerber-Stellingwerf, 2007; Crawshaw, 1989). There was also the additional advantage of mass media which was available in the form of large-circulation newspapers and posters (Cheng, 2003; Cheng, 2012; Cortright, Lopez, and Gerber-Stellingwerf, 2007; Crawshaw, 1989; Galtung, 1966).

That meant that a propagandist could very easily reach a large audience in a very short period (Cheng, 2012; Cortright, Lopez, and Gerber-

Stellingwerf, 2007; Crawshaw, 1989; Galtung, 1966; Gilmore, 2000). It was also possible to transmit propaganda to the enemy via the use of airborne leaflets (Cortright, Lopez, and Gerber-Stellingwerf, 2007; Crawshaw, 1989; Galtung, 1966; Gilmore, 2000; Iftimie, 2019). Others would work through explosive delivery systems like modified artillery or mortar rounds (Crawshaw, 1989; Galtung, 1966; Gilmore, 2000; Iftimie, 2019; Jacobson, 2005; Lerner and Crossman, 1949; Long, 2020). The negative impact on the victimized populations was incalculable, and the effects would sometimes occur for a long period after the initial messages were sent (Galtung, 1966; Gilmore, 2000; Iftimie, 2019; Jacobson, 2005; Lerner and Crossman, 1949; Long, 2020).

The use of psychological warfare during both major world wars was profound and, in many cases, quite effective (Gilmore, 2000; Iftimie, 2019; Jacobson, 2005; Lerner and Crossman, 1949; Long, 2020; Mathew and Boyd, 2011). For example, at the start of the war, the belligerents (particularly British and Germans officer) began distributing propaganda (Iftimie, 2019; Jacobson, 2005; Lerner and Crossman, 1949; Long, 2020; Mathew and Boyd, 2011; Radvanyi, 1990). This propaganda was distributed both domestically and on the Western front in order to ensure that not only were war efforts broadly supported at home; but also, that the enemy would be demoralized (Jacobson, 2005; Lerner and Crossman, 1949; Long, 2020; Mathew and Boyd, 2011; Radvanyi, 1990; Reisman, 2009). This raises a very important aspect of psychological warfare in as far as it is sometimes used to manipulate a friendly population in order get it to support a war effort or even to ignore the mistakes that the government is making (Lerner and Crossman, 1949; Long, 2020; Mathew and Boyd, 2011; Radvanyi, 1990; Reisman, 2009; Speier, 1951).

Many countries will leverage their own inherent advantages when using psychological warfare so that they are even more effective than any opponent (Long, 2020; Mathew and Boyd, 2011; Radvanyi, 1990; Reisman, 2009; Speier, 1951; Thomas, 2005; Wook, 2004). For instance, the British had several advantages that allowed them to succeed in the battle for world opinion during the world wars (Mathew and Boyd, 2011; Radvanyi, 1990; Reisman, 2009; Speier, 1951; Thomas, 2005; Wook, 2004). First, they had one of the world's most reputable news systems which could easily be used to reach the breadth of the earth (Bechtel, 1991; Bhatt, 2015; Brennen and Cadwalladr, 2018; Cheng, 2003; Cheng, 2012; Cortright, Lopez, and Gerber-Stellingwerf, 2007). Secondly, the British forces possessed significant experience in international and cross-cultural communication (Crawshaw,

1989; Galtung, 1966; Gilmore, 2000; Iftimie, 2019; Jacobson, 2005; Lerner and Crossman, 1949). This was a colonial heritage as well as a legacy of the ongoing dominance of the British on the seas (Long, 2020; Mathew and Boyd, 2011; Radvanyi, 1990; Reisman, 2009; Speier, 1951; Thomas, 2005; Wook, 2004). Third, Britain controlled much of the undersea cable system then in operation, mainly due to the naval capabilities of the empire (Bechtel, 1991; Bhatt, 2015; Crawshaw, 1989; Galtung, 1966; Mathew and Boyd, 2011). These capabilities were easily transitioned to the task of warfare (Brennen and Cadwalladr, 2018; Cheng, 2003; Gilmore, 2000; Iftimie, 2019; Radvanyi, 1990; Reisman, 2009).

Other subtle tools were used to give the British an advantage in the psychological warfare that was taking place (Cheng, 2012; Cortright, Lopez, and Gerber-Stellingwerf, 2007; Jacobson, 2005). For example, the British benefited from a well-oiled diplomatic service that maintained good relations with many nations around the world (Lerner and Crossman, 1949; Long, 2020; Speier, 1951; Thomas, 2005; Wook, 2004). This team could easily persuade and manipulate countries into joining the alliance or even refusing to ally with German (Mathew and Boyd, 2011; Radvanyi, 1990; Reisman, 2009; Speier, 1951; Thomas, 2005; Wook, 2004). In contrast the German services had merely developed a reputation for brutality and rather awkward diplomacy, which did not help their cause when it came to persuading the undecided nations to join them (Long, 2020; Mathew and Boyd, 2011; Radvanyi, 1990; Reisman, 2009; Speier, 1951; Thomas, 2005; Wook, 2004). The German attempts to foment revolution in parts of the British Empire (including Ireland and India) came to very little (Lerner and Crossman, 1949; Long, 2020; Mathew and Boyd, 2011; Radvanyi, 1990; Reisman, 2009; Speier, 1951). The British used their experience in the Middle East to induce the Arabs to revolt against the Ottoman Empire, hence taking away an important potential ally for Germany (Jacobson, 2005; Lerner and Crossman, 1949; Long, 2020; Mathew and Boyd, 2011; Radvanyi, 1990; Reisman, 2009). In this instance, psychological warfare was being used to isolate the target internationally (Iftimie, 2019; Jacobson, 2005; Lerner and Crossman, 1949; Long, 2020; Mathew and Boyd, 2011; Radvanyi, 1990).

Although the actual operations of the propaganda war were basic, they had far reaching consequences (Gilmore, 2000; Iftimie, 2019; Jacobson, 2005; Lerner and Crossman, 1949; Long, 2020; Mathew and Boyd, 2011). For example, aerial leaflets were dropped over German trenches containing postcards from prisoners of war detailing their humane conditions (Galtung, 1966; Gilmore, 2000; Iftimie, 2019; Jacobson, 2005; Lerner and Crossman,

1949; Long, 2020). Some contained surrender notices while others spread general propaganda against the Kaiser and the German generals (Crawshaw, 1989; Galtung, 1966; Gilmore, 2000; Iftimie, 2019; Jacobson, 2005; Lerner and Crossman, 1949; Long, 2020). This emphasized the notion that the allied nations were on the right side of the law while the Germans were cast as brutes who were intent on dominating the world (Cortright, Lopez, and Gerber-Stellingwerf, 2007; Crawshaw, 1989; Galtung, 1966; Gilmore, 2000; Iftimie, 2019). By the end of the war, MI7b had distributed almost 26 million leaflets (Cheng, 2012; Cortright, Lopez, and Gerber-Stellingwerf, 2007; Crawshaw, 1989; Galtung, 1966; Gilmore, 2000).

The other side was not letting things to chance. For example, the Germans began shooting the leaflet-dropping pilots (Cheng, 2003; Cheng, 2012; Cortright, Lopez, and Gerber-Stellingwerf, 2007; Crawshaw, 1989; Galtung, 1966). This retaliatory move helped in prompting the British to develop unmanned leaflet balloons that drifted across no-man's land (Brennen and Cadwalladr, 2018; Cheng, 2003; Cheng, 2012; Cortright, Lopez, and Gerber-Stellingwerf, 2007; Crawshaw, 1989). At the same time, the attentions of the German officers were now being diverted towards dealing with the propaganda war (Bhatt, 2015; Brennen and Cadwalladr, 2018; Cheng, 2003; Cheng, 2012; Cortright, Lopez, and Gerber-Stellingwerf, 2007). This meant that the German army was at risk of betrayal and subterfuge (Bhatt, 2015; Brennen and Cadwalladr, 2018; Cheng, 2003; Cheng, 2012; Cortright, Lopez, and Gerber-Stellingwerf, 2007). For example, at least one in seven of these leaflets were not handed in by the soldiers to their superiors, despite severe penalties for that offense (Brennen and Cadwalladr, 2018; Cheng, 2003; Cheng, 2012; Cortright, Lopez, and Gerber-Stellingwerf, 2007; Crawshaw, 1989). As the cases above demonstrate, psychological warfare has been used to subdue opponents where international sanctions are readily available (Cheng, 2003; Cheng, 2012; Cortright, Lopez, and Gerber-Stellingwerf, 2007; Crawshaw, 1989; Galtung, 1966). To a great extent, the propaganda war that the USA has waged on Iran, North Korea, and Cuba have not been effective because these have in effect become closed paranoid societies that see foreign influence as an attempt to trample on their sovereignty (Cheng, 2012; Cortright, Lopez, and Gerber-Stellingwerf, 2007; Crawshaw, 1989; Galtung, 1966; Gilmore, 2000). This chapter will close by addressing the links and diversions between war and deceptive actions.

2.5. WAR AND DECEPTION

War and international sanctions are sometimes used interchangeably to achieve the same objective of subduing or incapacitating an enemy (Grauvogel, Licht, and von Soest, 2017; Gui, 1991; Hafner-Burton and Montgomery, 2008). World War II was particularly noted for its use of psychological tactics for both the military and civilian communities (Devarajan and Mottaghi, 2015; Dobler, 2008; Doxey, 1972, 1983).

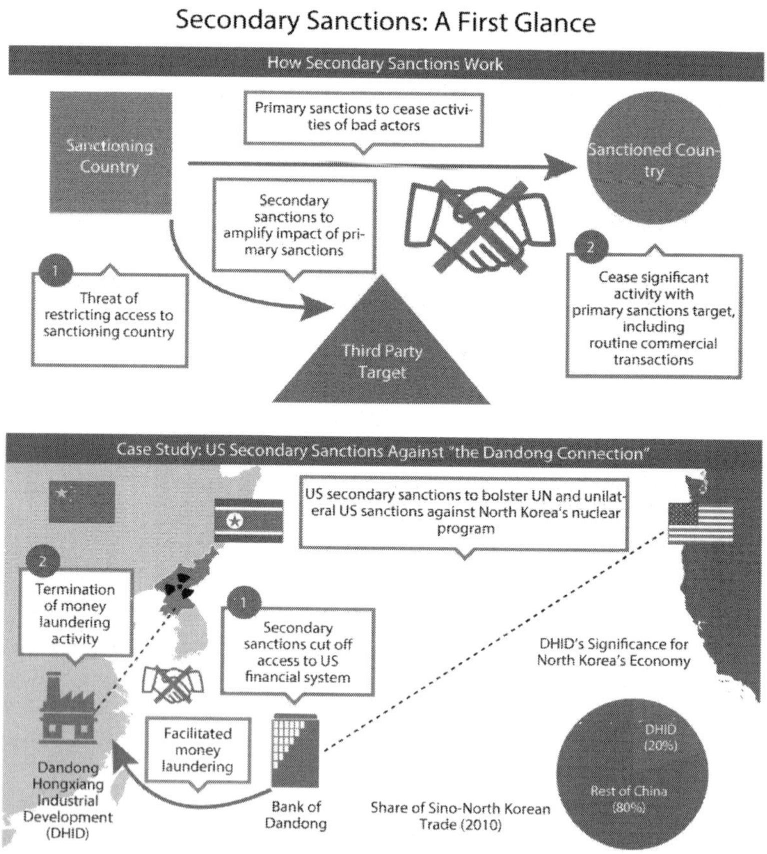

Figure 2.5. Overview of secondary sanctions.

Source: Atlantic Council.

Adolf Hitler was greatly influenced by the psychological tactics of warfare the British had employed during World War I and attributed the defeat of Germany to the effects this propaganda had on the soldiers (Pape,

1998; Ponte, 2004; Reilly, 2012; Reisman and Stevick, 1998; Richard and Raimo, 1999). Similar effects can be achieved through secondary sanctions that demoralize the local populace by significantly reducing their standards of living (see Figure 2.5 for an example). Hitler became committed to the use of mass propaganda to influence the minds of the German population in the decades to come (Eliat and Einav, 2004; Eriksson, 2016; Escribà-Folch, 2010, 2012; Escribà-Folch and Wright, 2010; Farzanegan, 2013; Farzanegan and Hayo, 2019). By calling his movement The Third Reich, he was able to convince many civilians that his cause was not just a fad, but the way of their future (Mikhaylova, Babich, and Smirnova, 2017; Morgan and Schwebach, 1997). Joseph Goebbels was appointed as Propaganda Minister when Hitler came to power in 1933, and he portrayed Hitler as a messianic figure for the redemption of Germany (Ozawa and Castello, 2001; Pape, 1997, 1998). Hitler also coupled this with the resonating projections of his orations for effect (Drezner, 2000, 2011, 2015; Drezner and Drezner, 1999; Drury and Peksen, 2014; Dunn and Shaw, 2001; Dunoff, Ratner, and Wippman, 2015).

Germany's Fall Grün plan of invasion of Czechoslovakia had a large part dealing with psychological warfare aimed both at the Czechoslovak civilians and government as well as, crucially, at Czechoslovak allies (Ponte, 2004; Reilly, 2012; Reisman and Stevick, 1998; Richard and Raimo, 1999; Ross, 1989). It became successful to the point that Germany gained support of UK and France through appeasement to occupy Czechoslovakia without having to fight an all-out war, sustaining only minimum losses in covert war before the Munich Agreement (Solingen, 2012; Stephanides et al., 2002; Strack and Strack, 1978; Takian, Raoofi, and Kazempour-Ardebili, 2020). At the start of the Second World War, the British set up the Political Warfare Executive to produce and distribute propaganda (Biersteker, Eckert, and Tourinho, 2016; Blyton, 2004; Bolander, 2011; Borszik, 2014, 2016). Using powerful transmitters, broadcasts could be made across Europe (Ivanov, Sypchenko, and Webster, 2017; James, 2013). Sefton Delmer managed a successful black propaganda campaign through several radio stations which were designed to be popular with German troops while at the same time introducing news material that would weaken their morale under a veneer of authenticity (Seyfi and Hall, 2019; Solingen, 2012; Stephanides et al., 2002). British Prime Minister Winston Churchill made use of radio broadcasts for propaganda against the Germans (Drury and Peksen, 2014; Dunn and Shaw, 2001; Dunoff, Ratner, and Wippman, 2015; Eliat and Einav, 2004; Eriksson, 2016; Escribà-Folch, 2010). During World War II, the British made extensive use of deception and developing many new techniques and theories in the process (Chiquiar, 2008; Dunn and Shaw, 2001; Hanushek and Woessmann, 2010; Kaempfer and Lowenberg, 1999). The main protagonists at this time were 'A' Force, set up in 1940 under Dudley Clarke, and the London Controlling Section (LCS), chartered in 1942 under the control of John Bevan (Alam, 2008; Buck, Gallant, and Nossal, 1998; Devarajan and Mottaghi, 2015; Fridell, 2014; Hultman and Peksen, 2017). Clarke pioneered many of the strategies of military deception. His ideas for combining fictional orders of battle, visual deception and double agents helped define Allied deception strategy during the war, for which he has been referred to as "the greatest British deceiver of WW2" (Bosco, 2012; Bradley and Galbraith, 2016; Brzoska, 2015; Buck, Gallant, and Nossal, 1998; Caron, 1989).

During the lead up to the Allied invasion of Normandy, many new tactics in psychological warfare were devised (Al-Jawaheri, 2008; Dobler, 2008; Fu et al., 2020; Hurd, 2017; Laub, 2015). The plan for Operation Bodyguard set out a general strategy to mislead German high command as to the exact date and location of the invasion (Reilly, 2012; Reisman and Stevick, 1998; Richard and Raimo, 1999; Ross, 1989; Rothwell and Stephens, 2016). Planning began in 1943 under the auspices of the LCS. A draft strategy, referred to as Plan Jael, was presented to Allied high command at the Tehran Conference (Matsushita et al., 2015; McCorkell and Gillard, 2010; Meyer and Thein, 2014; Mikhaylova, Babich, and Smirnova, 2017). Operation Fortitude was intended to convince the Germans of a greater Allied military strength than existed, through fictional field armies, faked operations to prepare the ground for invasion and leaked information about the Allied order of battle and war plans (Hiraide and Chakraborty, 2012; Ho-Chuan, Yi-Chen, and Chih-Chuan, 2012; Hovdenak, 2009; Huang, Xu, and Lu, 2011).

The United States ran an extensive program of psychological warfare during the Vietnam War (Askari et al., 2003; Caruso, 2003; Doxey, 1983; Igami, 2015). The Phoenix Program had the dual aim of assassinating National Liberation Front (NLF) of South Vietnam (NLF or Viet Cong) personnel and terrorizing any potential sympathizers or passive supporters (Frick, Humphreys, and Scheel, 2015; Fridell, 2014; Fu et al., 2020; Genzberger et al., 1994). The Chieu Hoi program of the South Vietnam government promoted NLF defections (Caron, 1989; Carter, 1987; Caruso, 2003; Chachavalpongpun, 2014; Chan, 2000; Chan and Drury, 2000). The CIA made extensive use of Contra soldiers to destabilize the Sandinista government in Nicaragua (Jiang, Chen, and Liu, 2010; Jing, Kaempfer, and Lowenberg, 2003; Kaempfer and Lowenberg, 1999). The CIA used psychological warfare techniques against the Panamanians by delivering unlicensed TV broadcasts (Reilly, 2012; Reisman and Stevick, 1998; Richard and Raimo, 1999; Ross, 1989; Rothwell and Stephens, 2016).

In the Iraq War, the United States used the shock and awe campaign to psychologically maim and break the will of the Iraqi Army to fight (Pape, 1998; Ponte, 2004; Reilly, 2012; Reisman and Stevick, 1998; Richard and Raimo, 1999). In cyberspace, social media has enabled the use of disinformation on a wide scale (Buck, Gallant, and Nossal, 1998; Caron, 1989; Carter, 1987; Caruso, 2003; Chachavalpongpun, 2014). Analysts have found evidence of doctored or misleading photographs spread by social media in the Syrian Civil War and 2014 Russian military intervention in Ukraine, possibly with state involvement (Jiang, Chen, and Liu, 2010; Jing, Kaempfer, and Lowenberg, 2003; Kaempfer and Lowenberg, 1999). Military and governments have engaged in PSYOP and informational warfare on social networking platforms to regulate foreign propaganda, which includes countries like the US, Russia, and China (Strack and Strack, 1978; Takian, Raoofi, and Kazempour-Ardebili, 2020; Taylor, 2012; Thaver and Ekanayake, 2010). One of the effects of what is deception is that there is a generalized mistrust of state agencies. This has sometimes had the unintended consequence of creating paranoid states such as North Korea, where the external world is completely excluded (Askari et al., 2003; Attia, Grauvogel, and von Soest, 2020). As ordinary people learn more about the psychological tactics used in war, they become less effective in their deception (Biersteker, Eckert, and Tourinho, 2016; Blyton, 2004).

CHAPTER 2 SUMMARY

There is an ongoing debate as to whether international sanctions are effective in any case. Moreover, this chapter has shown that the harm caused by these sanctions may prove to be ethically too high. The case of the USA embargo on Cuba shows that sanctions can continue and be largely effective despite the disavowal by most of the world's nations. The chapter has also highlighted psychological warfare as an alternative way of subduing people. However, the costs of each of these methods cannot be escaped. In the next section, we consider the uneven distribution of international sanctions and enforcement.

Chapter 3

Uneven Distribution and Enforcement of Sanctions

CONTENTS

There is hardly equality or fairness in the distribution of international sanctions. The victors and superpowers have all the leverage, and they strategically deploy it against weaker or smaller nations. In this chapter, we consider the example of the sanctions against Yugoslavia while at the same time contrast similar sanctions with the right to development. We critically appraise the role of the International Progress Organization (IPO) and its relevance to the Democratic Peace Theory. The chapter will close by examining how provocations such as sanctions can stimulate and sustain violence. By the end of this chapter, the reader should have a view of how sanctions are selectively imposed and managed depending on the whims, goals, and objectives of powerful nations.

3.1. SANCTIONS AGAINST YUGOSLAVIA

As a starting point, we might consider the sanctions that were imposed on Yugoslavia from the 8th of November 1991 to the 19th of January 2001 (Andreas, 2005; Babic and Jokic, 2000; Babić and Jokić, 2002; Barber, 1979; Braha, 1999; Brooks, 2002; Canor, 1998). During the Yugoslav Wars of the 1990s and early 2000s, several rounds of international sanctions were imposed against the Federal Republic of Yugoslavia (Babic and Jokic, 2000; Babić and Jokić, 2002; Barber, 1979; Braha, 1999; Brooks, 2002; Canor, 1998; Delevic, 1998). The area that was affected by the international sanctions consisted of the Yugoslav republics of Serbia and Montenegro (Babić and Jokić, 2002; Barber, 1979; Braha, 1999; Brooks, 2002; Canor, 1998; Delevic, 1998; Dimitrijevic and Pejic, 1995). The Bosnian War triggered the first round of sanctions from April 1992 to October 1995 (Barber, 1979; Braha, 1999; Brooks, 2002; Canor, 1998; Delevic, 1998; Dimitrijevic and Pejic, 1995; Elliott, 1998; Garfield, 2001).

During this time Yugoslavia was under a United Nations embargo (Brooks, 2002; Canor, 1998; Delevic, 1998; Dimitrijevic and Pejic, 1995; Elliott, 1998; Garfield, 2001; Garfield, Devin, and Fausey, 1995). The embargo was lifted after the Dayton Agreement was signed to effectively end the conflict (Braha, 1999; Brooks, 2002; Canor, 1998; Delevic, 1998; Dimitrijevic and Pejic, 1995; Elliott, 1998; Garfield, 2001). In this instance, the example shows how international sanctions can be used to secure peace (Canor, 1998; Delevic, 1998; Dimitrijevic and Pejic, 1995; Elliott, 1998; Garfield, 2001; Garfield, Devin, and Fausey, 1995). This is particularly true of situations in which military options are either undesirable or have otherwise been ineffective in achieving peace (Delevic, 1998; Dimitrijevic and Pejic, 1995; Elliott, 1998; Garfield, 2001; Garfield, Devin, and Fausey, 1995; Gottstein, 1999).

The second wave of sanctions occurred during the Kosovo War, which took place between 1998 and 1999 (Dimitrijevic and Pejic, 1995; Elliott, 1998; Garfield, 2001; Garfield, Devin, and Fausey, 1995; Gottstein, 1999; Hajdinjak, 2002). This time the sanctions were mainly led by the UN, European Union (EU) and the United States (Elliott, 1998; Garfield, 2001; Garfield, Devin, and Fausey, 1995; Gottstein, 1999; Hajdinjak, 2002; Hejsek, 2012). However, there were attempts to win the approval and participation of other smaller actors to give the sanctions the necessary legitimacy (Garfield, 2001; Garfield, Devin, and Fausey, 1995; Gottstein, 1999; Hajdinjak, 2002; Hejsek, 2012; Hufbauer, Schott, and Elliott, 1990). When President Slobodan Milošević was removed from power in October 2000, the sanctions were withdrawn (Garfield, Devin, and Fausey, 1995; Gottstein, 1999; Hajdinjak, 2002; Hejsek, 2012; Hufbauer, Schott, and Elliott, 1990; Klip, 1997). Indeed, most of the existing sanctions against Yugoslavia were lifted by the 19th of January (Gottstein, 1999; Hajdinjak, 2002; Hejsek, 2012; Hufbauer, Schott, and Elliott, 1990; Klip, 1997; Knudsen, 2008; Lamotte, 2012). This is a situation in which the sanctions were conditional on the behavioral change of the rogue state at the time (Hajdinjak, 2002; Hejsek, 2012; Hufbauer, Schott, and Elliott, 1990; Klip, 1997; Knudsen, 2008; Lamotte, 2012; Licht, 2018).

It is notable, that the ethnic tensions and complexities of the region (see Figure 3.1) were never really given sufficient credence or treated with sensitivity during the Balkan crisis (Hejsek, 2012; Hufbauer, Schott, and Elliott, 1990; Klip, 1997; Knudsen, 2008; Lamotte, 2012; Licht, 2018; Rogers, 1996). Sanctions appeared to be a blunt instrument of achieving the policy objectives of the Western powers and the international community at large (Hufbauer, Schott, and Elliott, 1990; Klip, 1997; Knudsen, 2008; Lamotte, 2012; Licht, 2018; Rogers, 1996; Scharf and Dorosin, 1993). This has often been the Achilles Heel of international sanctions because they are often imposed in situations that are more complex than the simplistic "punishment frameworks" or even the "axis of evil" approach (Klip, 1997; Knudsen, 2008; Lamotte, 2012; Licht, 2018; Rogers, 1996; Scharf and Dorosin, 1993; Selden, 1999). In order for international sanctions to be effective, they have to remain cognizant of the complex dynamics of the local situations as well as the people that are affected (Knudsen, 2008; Lamotte, 2012; Licht, 2018; Rogers, 1996; Scharf and Dorosin, 1993; Selden, 1999; Stephanides et al., 2002).

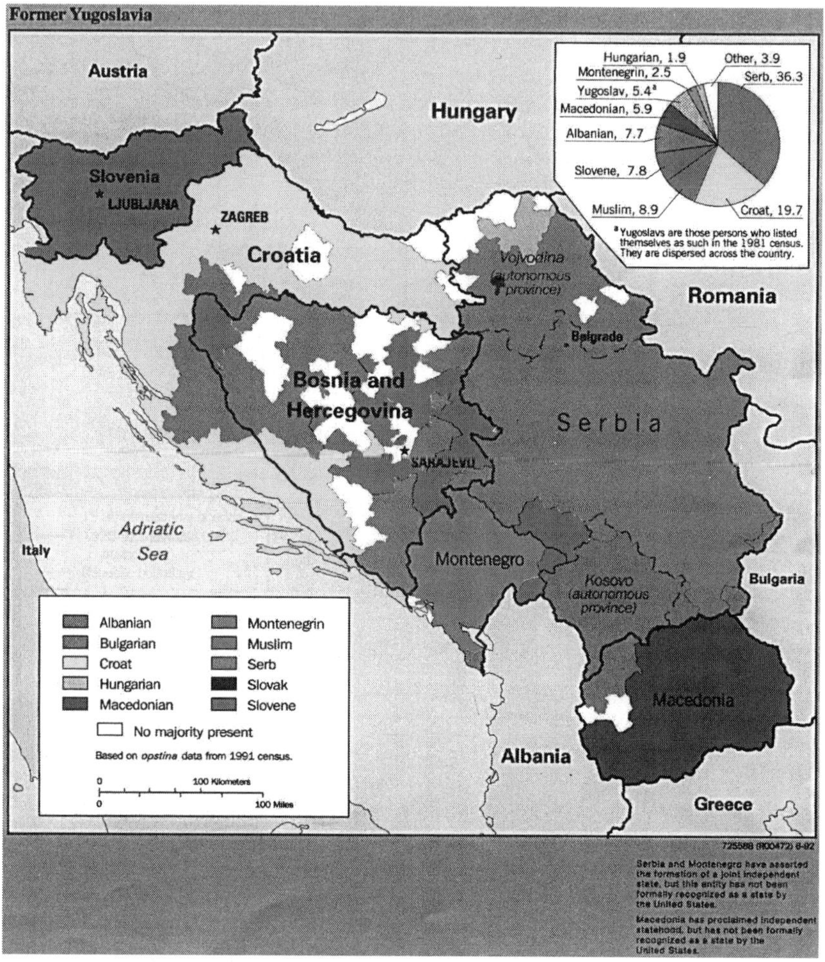

Figure 3.1. Ethnic diversity in Yugoslavia and surrounding areas.

Source: Academic Home Page.

As anticipated by their creators, the sanctions had a major impact on the Yugoslav economy (Lamotte, 2012; Licht, 2018; Rogers, 1996; Scharf and Dorosin, 1993; Selden, 1999; Stephanides et al., 2002; Weiss, 1999). They also had other unintended and sometimes unforeseen negative effects on Yugoslav society (Licht, 2018; Rogers, 1996; Scharf and Dorosin, 1993; Selden, 1999; Stephanides et al., 2002; Weiss, 1999; Woodward, 1993). Existing research has shown that the hardest-hit area was modern day Serbia (Rogers, 1996; Scharf and Dorosin, 1993; Selden, 1999; Stephanides et al., 2002; Weiss, 1999; Woodward, 1993; Woodward, 2018). For example,

Serbia's GDP dropped from $24 billion in 1990 to below $10 billion in 1993 (Scharf and Dorosin, 1993; Selden, 1999; Stephanides et al., 2002; Weiss, 1999; Woodward, 1993; Woodward, 2018; Žilović, 2011). The drop in GDP continued until it was only $8.66 billion by 2000 (Selden, 1999; Stephanides et al., 2002; Weiss, 1999; Woodward, 1993; Woodward, 2018; Žilović, 2011).

The combined weight of sanctions imposed on the state had a negative effect on local communities of Serbians who had to deal with high levels of unemployment and runaway inflation (Andreas, 2005; Babic and Jokic, 2000; Babić and Jokić, 2002; Barber, 1979; Braha, 1999; Brooks, 2002; Canor, 1998). The sanctions also had a devastating impact on Yugoslavian industry since they were so widespread and comprehensive in their nature (Delevic, 1998; Dimitrijevic and Pejic, 1995; Elliott, 1998; Garfield, 2001; Garfield, Devin, and Fausey, 1995; Gottstein, 1999). For example, poverty was at its highest in 1993 where national statistics revealed that close to 39% of the Serbian population was living on less than $2 per day (Hajdinjak, 2002; Hejsek, 2012; Hufbauer, Schott, and Elliott, 1990; Klip, 1997; Knudsen, 2008; Lamotte, 2012; Licht, 2018). These were more akin to the ones in developing parts of Africa and Asia than in the heart of modern Europe (Rogers, 1996; Scharf and Dorosin, 1993; Selden, 1999; Stephanides et al., 2002; Weiss, 1999; Woodward, 1993; Woodward, 2018; Žilović, 2011).

The incremental nature of the sanctions meant that local communities did not get much relief from the onslaught (Andreas, 2005; Babic and Jokic, 2000; Elliott, 1998; Garfield, 2001; Knudsen, 2008; Lamotte, 2012). For example, poverty levels rose again when international sanctions were re-imposed in 1998 (Babić and Jokić, 2002; Barber, 1979; Garfield, Devin, and Fausey, 1995; Gottstein, 1999; Licht, 2018; Rogers, 1996). This was a calculus that was either ignored or underestimated when the decision was made to re-impose sanctions for covertly political reasons and overtly humanitarian ones (Braha, 1999; Brooks, 2002; Hajdinjak, 2002; Hejsek, 2012; Scharf and Dorosin, 1993; Selden, 1999).

There was a significant loss of skilled manpower and expertise during the height of the sanctions and long afterwards (Canor, 1998; Delevic, 1998; Hufbauer, Schott, and Elliott, 1990; Stephanides et al., 2002; Weiss, 1999). For instance, an estimated 300,000 people emigrated from Serbia in the 1990s (Dimitrijevic and Pejic, 1995; Klip, 1997; Woodward, 1993; Woodward, 2018; Žilović, 2011). This represented a significant brain drain which ended up benefitting the more developed Western European powers (Selden, 1999; Stephanides et al., 2002; Weiss, 1999; Woodward,

1993; Woodward, 2018; Žilović, 2011). It is significant that about 20% of Serbian emigrees at the time had a higher education, a lot of which had been sponsored by the Serbian people (Scharf and Dorosin, 1993; Selden, 1999; Stephanides et al., 2002; Weiss, 1999; Woodward, 1993; Woodward, 2018; Žilović, 2011). The loss of the investment in human capital set the country back significantly (Rogers, 1996; Scharf and Dorosin, 1993; Selden, 1999; Stephanides et al., 2002; Weiss, 1999; Woodward, 1993; Woodward, 2018). It is not uncommon for international sanctions to lead to social-economic deprivation in the targeted countries, such that the educated elite migrate to the very same countries that imposed the sanctions in the first place (Licht, 2018; Rogers, 1996; Scharf and Dorosin, 1993; Selden, 1999; Stephanides et al., 2002; Weiss, 1999; Woodward, 1993). This is the type of brain drain that makes international sanctions so devasting to their targets, particularly if those countries are still developing and do not have alternative sources of income (Lamotte, 2012; Licht, 2018; Rogers, 1996; Scharf and Dorosin, 1993; Selden, 1999; Stephanides et al., 2002; Weiss, 1999).

Although Serbia is now a member of the wider European community, the EU was instrumental in the sanctions against Yugoslavia (Knudsen, 2008; Lamotte, 2012; Licht, 2018; Rogers, 1996; Scharf and Dorosin, 1993; Selden, 1999; Stephanides et al., 2002). For example, on the 8th of November 1991, the European Economic Community imposed the first economic sanctions against Yugoslavia (Klip, 1997; Knudsen, 2008; Lamotte, 2012; Licht, 2018; Rogers, 1996; Scharf and Dorosin, 1993; Selden, 1999). These sanctions forbade the EEC's members from importing textiles from Yugoslavia (Hufbauer, Schott, and Elliott, 1990; Klip, 1997; Knudsen, 2008; Lamotte, 2012; Licht, 2018; Rogers, 1996; Scharf and Dorosin, 1993). The impact on the local textile industry was devastating since this had been one of the mainstays of the economy (Hejsek, 2012; Hufbauer, Schott, and Elliott, 1990; Klip, 1997; Knudsen, 2008; Lamotte, 2012; Licht, 2018; Rogers, 1996).

As is often the case with these sanctions, the prevention of trade is also linked to the refusal to provide aid to the targeted country to maximize the pressure on it (Hajdinjak, 2002; Hejsek, 2012; Hufbauer, Schott, and Elliott, 1990; Klip, 1997; Knudsen, 2008; Lamotte, 2012; Licht, 2018). In the case of Yugoslavia, the EU also suspended an aggregate total of $1.9 billion in EEC aid packages (Gottstein, 1999; Hajdinjak, 2002; Hejsek, 2012; Hufbauer, Schott, and Elliott, 1990; Klip, 1997; Knudsen, 2008; Lamotte, 2012). The lack of aid created a humanitarian crisis that belied the overt goals of the sanctions in the first place (Garfield, Devin, and Fausey, 1995; Gottstein,

1999; Hajdinjak, 2002; Hejsek, 2012; Hufbauer, Schott, and Elliott, 1990; Klip, 1997). Moreover, this held back aid had been promised to Yugoslavia before 12 cease-fires failed to materialize in the Croatian war zone (Garfield, 2001; Garfield, Devin, and Fausey, 1995; Gottstein, 1999; Hajdinjak, 2002; Hejsek, 2012; Hufbauer, Schott, and Elliott, 1990). That meant that the government was not well-prepared for the subsequent hardship when the promised aid was not forwarded (Elliott, 1998; Garfield, 2001; Garfield, Devin, and Fausey, 1995; Gottstein, 1999; Hajdinjak, 2002; Hejsek, 2012).

Although the powers that imposed the sanctions did not explicitly talk about destroying the Yugoslav economy, that is what exactly happened (Dimitrijevic and Pejic, 1995; Elliott, 1998; Garfield, 2001; Garfield, Devin, and Fausey, 1995; Gottstein, 1999; Hajdinjak, 2002). For example, starting from 1992, the Yugoslav dinar experienced an episode of significant and sustained hyperinflation (Delevic, 1998; Dimitrijevic and Pejic, 1995; Elliott, 1998; Garfield, 2001; Garfield, Devin, and Fausey, 1995; Gottstein, 1999). This period of hyperinflation lasted for a total of 25 months and had severe effects on other parts of the economy (Canor, 1998; Delevic, 1998; Dimitrijevic and Pejic, 1995; Elliott, 1998; Garfield, 2001; Garfield, Devin, and Fausey, 1995). In 1993, the dinar recorded a monthly inflation rate of 313 million percent which was unprecedented at the time and left the economy in freefall (Brooks, 2002; Canor, 1998; Delevic, 1998; Dimitrijevic and Pejic, 1995; Elliott, 1998; Garfield, 2001; Garfield, Devin, and Fausey, 1995). The hyperinflation reached its climax when the dinar's monthly inflation reached 5.578 quintillion percent (Braha, 1999; Brooks, 2002; Canor, 1998; Delevic, 1998; Dimitrijevic and Pejic, 1995; Elliott, 1998; Garfield, 2001).

The implementation of sanctions corresponded with the emergence of an underground economy (Barber, 1979; Braha, 1999; Brooks, 2002; Canor, 1998; Delevic, 1998; Dimitrijevic and Pejic, 1995; Elliott, 1998; Garfield, 2001). For example, although there was no legal import of cigarettes during the sanctions; there existed a thriving market of low-quality and fake cigarettes (Babić and Jokić, 2002; Barber, 1979; Braha, 1999; Brooks, 2002; Canor, 1998; Delevic, 1998; Dimitrijevic and Pejic, 1995). This was also associated with the illicit in other products such as alcohol (Babic and Jokic, 2000; Babić and Jokić, 2002; Barber, 1979; Braha, 1999; Brooks, 2002; Canor, 1998; Delevic, 1998). There was a general decline in societal cohesion and lawfulness as exemplified by the various street drugs industries that took hold of the country (Andreas, 2005; Babic and Jokic, 2000; Babić and Jokić, 2002; Barber, 1979; Braha, 1999; Brooks, 2002; Canor, 1998). Even though the sanctions included restrictions on gasoline, there were smugglers who tried to profit by purchasing gas from across the Yugoslav border (Andreas, 2005; Babic and Jokic, 2000; Babić and Jokić, 2002; Barber, 1979; Braha, 1999; Brooks, 2002; Canor, 1998).

The formal economy declined as people tried to circumvent the restrictions that the powers had placed on Yugoslavia (Babic and Jokic, 2000; Babić and Jokić, 2002; Barber, 1979; Braha, 1999; Brooks, 2002; Canor, 1998; Delevic, 1998). Many smugglers made abnormal profits from their illicit activities which meant that underground business became an attractive option for the struggling populace (Babić and Jokić, 2002; Barber, 1979; Braha, 1999; Brooks, 2002; Canor, 1998; Delevic, 1998; Dimitrijevic and Pejic, 1995). However, this type of business was very risky. A case in point is how purchases were always made in hard cash (Barber, 1979; Braha, 1999; Brooks, 2002; Canor, 1998; Delevic, 1998; Dimitrijevic and Pejic, 1995; Elliott, 1998; Garfield, 2001). It is not surprising that certain parts of Yugoslavia became an ideal target for various mafia groups (Braha, 1999; Brooks, 2002; Canor, 1998; Delevic, 1998; Dimitrijevic and Pejic, 1995; Elliott, 1998; Garfield, 2001). These criminal enterprises could profit from killing smugglers and taking their cash intended to import gas into Yugoslavia (Brooks, 2002; Canor, 1998; Delevic, 1998; Dimitrijevic and Pejic, 1995; Elliott, 1998; Garfield, 2001; Garfield, Devin, and Fausey, 1995). The financial sector was severely impacted by the sanctions on Yugoslavia, and this led to the emergence of unethical practices (Canor, 1998; Delevic, 1998; Dimitrijevic and Pejic, 1995; Elliott, 1998; Garfield, 2001; Garfield, Devin, and Fausey, 1995). For example, many existing banks closed (Delevic, 1998; Dimitrijevic and Pejic, 1995; Elliott, 1998; Garfield, 2001; Garfield, Devin, and Fausey, 1995; Gottstein, 1999). This led to the emergence of several pyramid schemes. Specific cases include fraudulent banks such as Jugoskandik and the Darfiment Bank (Dimitrijevic and Pejic, 1995; Elliott, 1998; Garfield, 2001; Garfield, Devin, and Fausey, 1995; Gottstein, 1999; Hajdinjak, 2002). These criminal institutions were set up by opportunistic exploiters to lure local people while charging them extraordinary interest rates (Elliott, 1998; Garfield, 2001; Garfield, Devin, and Fausey, 1995; Gottstein, 1999; Hajdinjak, 2002; Hejsek, 2012). Many people who fell for the pyramid banks were left homeless, hence compounding the already catastrophic deprivation in Yugoslavia (Garfield, 2001; Garfield, Devin, and Fausey, 1995; Gottstein, 1999; Hajdinjak, 2002; Hejsek, 2012; Hufbauer, Schott, and Elliott, 1990). Some might argue that such devastating sanctions regimes go against the right to development which we will explore in the next section.

3.2. THE RIGHT TO DEVELOPMENT

The right to development was first recognized in 1981 in Article 22 of the African Charter on Human and Peoples' Rights as a definitive individual and collective right. Article 22(122) provides that: "All peoples shall have the right to their economic, social, and cultural development with due regard to their freedom and identity and in the equal enjoyment of the common heritage of mankind" (Kaempfer, Lowenberg, and Mertens, 2004; Kendall, 2000; Kiriya, 2017; Kirshner, 1997). The right to development was subsequently proclaimed by the United Nations in 1986 in the "Declaration on the Right to Development," which was adopted by the United Nations General Assembly resolution 41/128 (Baldwin and Pape, 1998; Barber, 1979; Bederman and Keitner, 2016). The right to development is a group right of peoples as opposed to an individual right and was reaffirmed by the 1993 Vienna Declaration and Program of Action (Choi and Luo, 2013; Clegg and Palmer, 1996; Cleveland, 2001; Cortright et al., 2000; Cranmer, Heinrich, and Desmarais, 2014). Figure 3.2 summarizes the premises of the right to development.

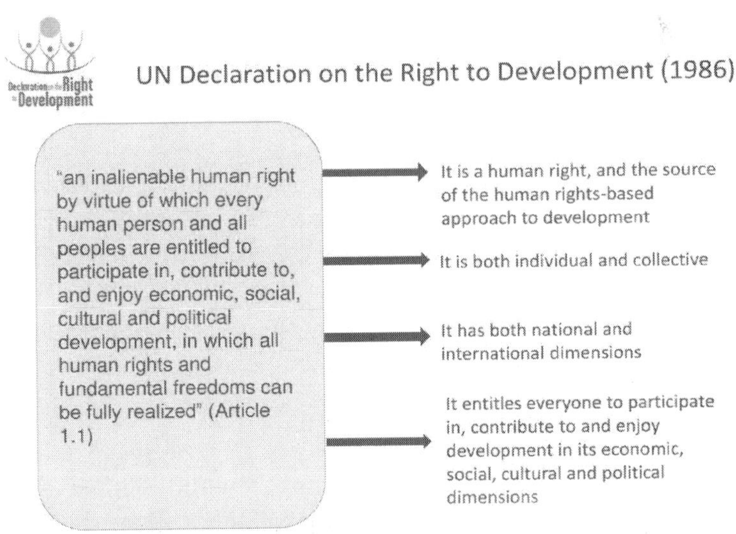

Figure 3.2. The right to development.

Source: OCHR via Slide Player.

The right to development is now included in the mandate of several UN institutions and offices (Taylor, 2012; Thaver and Ekanayake, 2010; Tridimas and Guiterrex-Fons, 2008). The Preamble of the Declaration on the Right to Development states "development is a comprehensive economic, social, cultural, and political process, which aims at the constant improvement of the well-being of the entire population and of all individuals on the basis of their active, free, and meaningful participation in development and in the fair distribution of benefits resulting therefrom" (Von Glahn and Taulbee, 2015; Wallensteen and Staibano, 2005). The Vienna Declaration and Program of Action states in Article 10 "The World Conference on Human Rights reaffirms the "right to development," as established in the Declaration on the Right to Development, as a universal and inalienable right and an integral part of fundamental human rights (Gui, 1991; Hafner-Burton and Montgomery, 2008; Hanushek and Woessmann, 2010).

As stated in the Declaration on the Right to Development, the human person is the central subject of development (Mueller and Mueller, 1999; Nossal, 1989; Ogden, 2008). While development facilitates the enjoyment of all human rights, the lack of development may not be invoked to justify the abridgement of internationally recognized human rights (Ho-Chuan, Yi-Chen, and Chih-Chuan, 2012; Hovdenak, 2009; Huang, Xu, and Lu, 2011; Huebner, 2009; Hultman and Peksen, 2017). States should cooperate with each other in ensuring development and eliminating obstacles to development (Mahmud, 2001; Matsushita et al., 2015; McCorkell and Gillard, 2010; Meyer and Thein, 2014). The international community should promote an effective international cooperation for the realization of the right to development and the elimination of obstacles to development (Hovdenak, 2009; Huang, Xu, and Lu, 2011; Huebner, 2009; Hultman and Peksen, 2017; Hurd, 2017). Lasting progress towards the implementation of the right to development requires effective development policies at the national level, as well as equitable economic relations and a favorable economic environment at the international level" (Igami, 2015; Ivanov, Sypchenko, and Webster, 2017; James, 2013).

The Rio Declaration on Environment and Development, also known as Rio Declaration or the G.R.E.G, recognizes the right to development as one of its 27 principles (Stephanides et al., 2002; Strack and Strack, 1978; Takian, Raoofi, and Kazempour-Ardebili, 2020). Principle 3 of the Declaration states, "The right to development" must be fulfilled so as to equitably meet developmental and environmental needs of present and future generations" (Bederman and Keitner, 2016; Biersteker, Eckert, and Tourinho, 2016). The Declaration on the Rights of Indigenous Peoples recognizes the right to development as an indigenous people's right (Hinds, 1997; Hiraide and

Chakraborty, 2012; Ho-Chuan, Yi-Chen, and Chih-Chuan, 2012; Hovdenak, 2009; Huang, Xu, and Lu, 2011). The declaration states in its preamble that the General Assembly is "Concerned that indigenous peoples have suffered from historic injustices as a result of, inter alia, their colonization and dispossession of their lands, territories, and resources, thus preventing them from exercising, in particular, their right to development in accordance with their own needs and interests" (David and Holliday, 2012; Daviron and Ponte, 2007; De Visscher, 2015; De Vos, 2010; Defourny, 2013; Denzin, 2008; Devarajan and Mottaghi, 2015). Ironically, in imposing pernicious sanctions against weaker states, the developed world has been accused of stifling development or deliberately sabotaging it (Doxey, 1987; Grauvogel and Von Soest, 2014; James, 2013). Institutions such as the International Progress Organization (IPO) have helped in reducing the risk of war and sanctions (Grauvogel and Von Soest, 2014; Grauvogel, Licht, and von Soest, 2017). However, their work is not entirely effective or clear, as we shall see in the next section.

3.3. ROLE OF THE INTERNATIONAL PROGRESS ORGANIZATION (IPO)

The development of the IPO is linked to the right to self-defense which is often quoted by those that are imposing sanctions and other pernicious measures on an international scale (Kiriya, 2017; Kirshner, 1997; Klotz, 1995; Koskenniemi, 2014; Kunz, 1960; Laub, 2015; Lee, 2018). The right of self-defense (also called, when it applies to the defense of another, alter ego defense, defense of others, defense of a third person) is the right for people to use reasonable force or defensive force, for the purpose of defending one's own life (self-defense) or the lives of others (Morgan and Schwebach, 1997; Mueller and Mueller, 1999). This may include, in certain circumstances, the use of deadly force. If a defendant uses defensive force because of a threat of deadly or grievous harm by the other person, or a reasonable perception of such harm, the defendant is said to have a "perfect self-defense" justification (Biersteker, Eckert, and Tourinho, 2016). If defendant uses defensive force because of such a perception, and the perception is not reasonable, the defendant may have an "imperfect self-defense" as an excuse (Huang, Xu, and Lu, 2011; Huebner, 2009; Hultman and Peksen, 2017; Hurd, 2017; Igami, 2015). Similar principles are used at the international level but with much more serious consequences, and this is a concern for IPO (Kiriya, 2017; Kirshner, 1997; Klotz, 1995; Koskenniemi, 2014; Kunz, 1960; Laub,

2015; Lee, 2018). Figure 3.3 shows a rather optimistic view of the UN as a driver of peace, yet there is ample evidence of the organization being rendered ineffective by virtue of its own rules and regulations (Cortright et al., 2000; Cranmer, Heinrich, and Desmarais, 2014; Crawford and Klotz, 1999; Crook, 2013; David and Holliday, 2012).

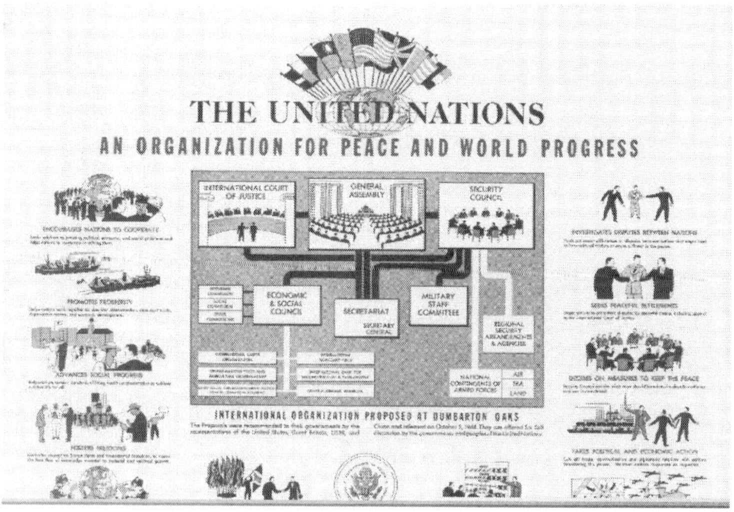

Figure 3.3. The UN cast as a driver of international peace.

Source: UNT Digital Library.

The IPO is a Vienna-based think tank dealing with world affairs (Bosco, 2012; Bradley and Galbraith, 2016; Brzoska, 2015; Buck, Gallant, and Nossal, 1998; Caron, 1989). As an international non-governmental organization (NGO) it enjoys consultative status with the Economic and Social Council of the United Nations and is associated with the United Nations Department of Public Information (Askari et al., 2003; Attia, Grauvogel, and von Soest, 2020; Bacchiega and Borzaga, 2003). The organization aims at promoting peaceful co-existence among all nations, in particular the dialog among civilizations; a just international economic order; global respect for human rights; and the international rule of law (Thaver and Ekanayake, 2010; Tridimas and Guiterrex-Fons, 2008). The IPO has members in more than 70 countries on all continents and organizes conferences and expert meetings on issues of conflict resolution, civilizational dialog, international law, and United Nations reform (Doxey, 1980, 1987; Drezner, 2000, 2011, 2015; Drezner and Drezner, 1999; Drury and Peksen, 2014; Dunn and Shaw, 2001). The organization publishes the series Studies in international relations (IRs) (since, 1978) and monographs in the field of IRs theory (Borszik, 2016; Crook, 2013; Farzanegan, 2013; Kirshner, 1997; Pape, 1997; Takian, Raoofi, and Kazempour-Ardebili, 2020).

Since 1974 the IPO has organized a series of lectures and conferences on the cultural dimension of international affairs including at Amman in, 1974; Innsbruck in, 1974; Vienna in, 1979; Rome in, 1981; and Nicosia in 1984 (Doxey, 1987; Grauvogel and Von Soest, 2014; James, 2013). These activities preceded the current global discourse on the dialog of civilizations in which the I.P.O. has participated through the organization of expert meetings in Europe and the Muslim world (Ponte, 2004; Reilly, 2012; Reisman and Stevick, 1998; Richard and Raimo, 1999; Ross, 1989). In 1987 the IPO initiated (in co-operation with Nobel Laureate Seán MacBride) the Lawyers' Appeal Against Nuclear War which led to a worldwide civil society campaign for a resolution by the UN General Assembly calling for an Advisory Opinion from the International Court of Justice (ICJ) on the question of the legality of nuclear arms (Von Glahn and Taulbee, 2015).

In September 1991 the IPO convened the Second International Conference on a More Democratic United Nations (CAMDUN-2) at the United Nations Office at Vienna (Ozawa and Castello, 2001; Pape, 1997, 1998; Ponte, 2004; Reilly, 2012). In 2000 the Secretary-General of the United Nations nominated two officials of the organization as international observers at the Lockerbie trial in the Netherlands. Since 1985, the IPO has been calling for a democratization of the United Nations Organization, in particular. the UN Security Council (Biersteker, Eckert, and Tourinho, 2016; Blyton, 2004; Bolander, 2011). Since 1987, the organization has been dealing with the problem of international terrorism, repeatedly suggesting a legal definition of terrorism by the UN General Assembly (Blyton, 2004; Cortright et al., 2000; Escribà-Folch, 2010; Ho-Chuan, Yi-Chen, and Chih-Chuan, 2012; Kendall, 2000). The various initiatives and proposals are documented in the IPO conference proceedings (Hafner-Burton and Montgomery, 2008; Hanushek and Woessmann, 2010; Haugh and Kitson, 2007; Hinds, 1997). In addition to the organization of lectures and international conferences, the IPO has undertaken (since, 1980) monitoring missions in the fields of human rights and the rule of law (Farzanegan, 2013; Farzanegan and Hayo, 2019; Franzway and Fonow, 2011; Frick, Humphreys, and Scheel, 2015). The challenge for IPO and similar organizations is the tendency for powerful nations to selectively quote the law in their own interests (Tridimas and Guiterrex-Fons, 2008). The next section provides a philosophical basis for this in the form of the democratic peace theory.

3.4. DEMOCRATIC PEACE THEORY

The democratic peace theory posits that democracies are hesitant to engage in armed conflict with other identified democracies (Leyton-Brown, 2017; Li and Saghaian, 2013; Lutz and Lux, 1995; Mahmud, 2001). Among proponents of the democratic peace theory, several factors are held as motivating peace between democratic states (Askari et al., 2003; Attia, Grauvogel, and von Soest, 2020; Bacchiega and Borzaga, 2003). First, democratic leaders are forced to accept responsibility for war losses to a voting public (Bederman and Keitner, 2016; Biersteker, Eckert, and Tourinho, 2016). Secondly, publicly accountable states people are inclined to establish diplomatic institutions for resolving international tensions (Hovdenak, 2009; Huang, Xu, and Lu, 2011; Huebner, 2009; Hultman and Peksen, 2017; Hurd, 2017).

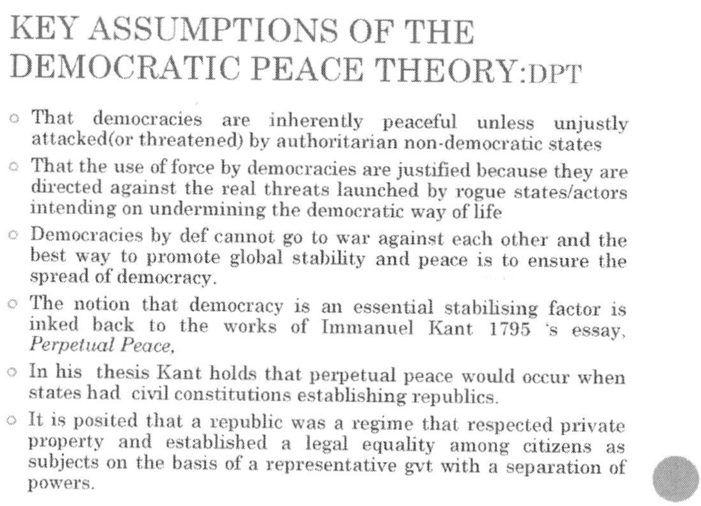

Figure 3.4. Key assumptions of the democratic peace theory.

Source: Slide Player.

Third, democracies are not inclined to view countries with adjacent policy and governing doctrine as hostile (Fridell, 2014; Fu et al., 2020; Genzberger et al., 1994; Gharehgozli, 2017; Goodhart, 2016). Fourth, democracies tend to possess greater public wealth than other states, and therefore eschew war to preserve infrastructure and resources (McCorkell and Gillard, 2010; Meyer and Thein, 2014; Mikhaylova, Babich, and Smirnova, 2017). Those who dispute this theory often do so on grounds that it conflates correlation with causation (Daviron and Ponte, 2007; De Visscher, 2015; De Vos, 2010; Defourny, 2013; Denzin, 2008; Devarajan and Mottaghi, 2015; Dobler). Moreover, it is argued that the academic definitions of 'democracy' and 'war' can be manipulated to manufacture an artificial trend (Bacchiega and Borzaga, 2003; Baldwin and Pape, 1998; Barber, 1979; Bederman and Keitner, 2016). The key assumptions of the Democratic Peach Theory are summarized in Figure 3.4. The democratic peace theory was not rigorously or scientifically studied until the 1960s (Gui, 1991; Hafner-Burton and Montgomery, 2008). However, the basic principles of the concept had been argued as early as the 1700s in the works of philosopher Immanuel Kant and political theorist Thomas Paine (Farzanegan and Hayo, 2019; Franzway and Fonow, 2011; Frick, Humphreys, and Scheel, 2015; Fridell, 2014). Kant foreshadowed the theory in his essay "*Perpetual Peace: A Philosophical Sketch*" written in 1795 (Koskenniemi, 2014; Kunz, 1960; Laub, 2015; Lee, 2018; Levy, 1999; Leyton-Brown, 2017). However, Kant thought that a world with only constitutional republics was only one of several necessary conditions for a perpetual peace (Afesorgbor, 2019; Alam, 2008; Al-Jawaheri, 2008). Kant's theory was that most of the people would never vote to go to war, unless in self-defense (Tridimas and Guiterrex-Fons, 2008). Therefore, if all nations were republics, it would end war, because there would be no aggressors (Clegg and Palmer, 1996; Eliat and Einav, 2004; Hinds, 1997; Kaempfer, Lowenberg, and Mertens, 2004). In earlier but less cited works, Thomas Paine made similar or stronger claims about the peaceful nature of republics. Paine wrote in "*Common Sense*" in 1776 that "the Republics of Europe are all (and we may say always) in peace." Paine argued that kings would go to war out of pride in situations where republics would not. French historian and social scientist Alexis de Tocqueville also argued, in "*Democracy in America*" (1835–1840), that democratic nations were less likely to wage war.

Dean Babst, a criminologist, was the first to do statistical research on this topic. Melvin Small and J. David Singer (1976, pp. 50–69) responded that they found an absence of wars between democratic states with two "marginal exceptions." However, they denied that this pattern had statistical significance. This chapter was published in the Jerusalem Journal of IRs which finally brought more widespread attention to the theory, and started the academic debate (Saeidnia and Abdollahi, 2013; Seyfi and Hall, 2019). A 1983 paper by political scientist Michael W. Doyle contributed further to popularizing the theory (Lutz and Lux, 1995; Mahmud, 2001; Matsushita et al., 2015). Rudolph J. Rummel was another early researcher and drew considerable lay attention to the subject in his later works (Chan, 2000; Chan and Drury, 2000; Chen et al., 2019; Cheraghali, 2013; Chiquiar, 2008; Choi and Luo, 2013). There is literature that extended the research to lesser conflicts than wars (Drezner, 2015; Drezner and Drezner, 1999; Drury and Peksen, 2014; Dunn and Shaw, 2001; Dunoff, Ratner, and Wippman, 2015; Eliat and Einav, 2004). Some researchers found the correlation between democracy and peacefulness remained significant after controlling for many possible confounding variables (Nossal, 1989; Ogden, 2008; Ozawa and Castello, 2001). This moved the theory into the mainstream of social science (Genzberger et al., 1994; Gharehgozli, 2017; Goodhart, 2016; Grauvogel and Von Soest, 2014). Supporters of realism in IRs and others responded by raising many new objections (Haugh and Kitson, 2007; Hinds, 1997; Hiraide and Chakraborty, 2012; Ho-Chuan, Yi-Chen, and Chih-Chuan, 2012; Hovdenak, 2009). Other researchers attempted more systematic explanations of how democracy might cause peace (Doxey, 1972, 1980, 1983, 1987; Drezner, 2000, 2011). There are also researchers who sought to explain how democracy might also affect other aspects of foreign relations such as alliances and collaboration (Biersteker, Eckert, and Tourinho, 2016; Cleveland, 2001; Eriksson, 2016; Hiraide and Chakraborty, 2012).

Democracies have been defined differently by different theorists and researchers depending on their philosophical prism. This accounts for some of the variations in their findings and research approaches with regards to democracies generally (Drezner, 2015; Drezner and Drezner, 1999; Drury and Peksen, 2014; Dunn and Shaw, 2001; Dunoff, Ratner, and Wippman, 2015; Eliat and Einav, 2004). A democracy is a nation that fulfills three key conditions. First, the democracy holds periodic elections in which the oppositing parties run as government parties (De Vos, 2010; Reisman and Stevick 1998; Seyfi and Hall, 2019). Second, the democracy allows at least 10% of the adult population to vote (Levy, 1999; Leyton-Brown, 2017; Li and Saghaian, 2013). Third, the democracy has a parliament that either controls or enjoys parity with the executive branch of the government (Seyfi and Hall, 2019; Solingen, 2012; Stephanides et al., 2002).

Other researchers have extended the list to four criteria. First, that "liberal regimes" have market or private property economics (De Vos, 2010; Defourny, 2013; Denzin, 2008; Devarajan and Mottaghi, 2015; Dobler, 2008). Second, that they have policies that are internally sovereign (Dunoff, Ratner, and Wippman, 2015; Eliat and Einav, 2004; Eriksson, 2016; Escribà-Folch, 2010, 2012; Escribà-Folch and Wright, 2010; Farzanegan, 2013).

Third, that they have citizens with juridical rights (Bolander, 2011; Borszik, 2014, 2016; Bosco, 2012; Bradley and Galbraith, 2016; Brzoska, 2015; Buck, Gallant, and Nossal, 1998). Fourth, that they have representative governments (Li and Saghaian, 2013; Lutz and Lux, 1995; Mahmud, 2001; Matsushita et al., 2015). Either 30% of the adult males were able to vote, or it was possible for every man to acquire voting rights as by attaining enough property (Matsushita et al., 2015; Nossal, 1989; Reilly, 2012; Strack and Strack, 1978). These researchers allow greater power to hereditary monarchs, a case in point being Louis-Philippe (Goodhart, 2016; Grauvogel and Von Soest, 2014; Grauvogel, Licht, and von Soest, 2017).

A significant portion of literature has only considered who is involved in the conflicts and ignored the question of who initiated the conflict. In many conflicts, both sides argue that the other side was initiator (Chan, 2000; Chan and Drury, 2000; Chen et al., 2019; Cheraghali, 2013; Chiquiar, 2008; Choi and Luo, 2013; Clegg and Palmer, 1996). Hence, some have argued that studying conflict initiation is of limited value, because existing data about conflict initiation may be especially unreliable (Solingen, 2012; Stephanides et al., 2002; Strack and Strack, 1978; Takian, Raoofi, and Kazempour-Ardebili, 2020). Given the nebulous definitions of war and democracy, it is not clear that democracy prevents war or other forms of government cause those wars (Hafner-Burton and Montgomery, 2008; Hanushek and Woessmann, 2010; Haugh and Kitson, 2007; Hinds, 1997). Nevertheless, the democratic peace theory has been used to advocate for regime change or even regime form (Lutz and Lux, 1995; Mahmud, 2001; Matsushita et al., 2015; McCorkell and Gillard, 2010). Often this mirrors the Western model and some nations have complained about being bullied by powerful Western nations like the USA (Solingen, 2012; Stephanides et al., 2002; Strack and Strack, 1978; Takian, Raoofi, and Kazempour-Ardebili, 2020). The final section in this chapter will explore some of these provocations and how they can lead to war.

3.5. PROVOCATION THROUGH INTERNATIONAL VIOLENCE

International violence is often manifested in outright wars (Reilly, 2012; Reisman and Stevick, 1998; Richard and Raimo, 1999; Ross, 1989; Rothwell and Stephens, 2016). However, there are other subtle but equally damaging forms of violence such as the crippling sanctions that are often levied on nations that are perceived to be vulnerable or outside the norm (Lutz and

Lux, 1995; Meyer and Thein, 2014; Mueller and Mueller, 1999; Ryngaert, 2015). Some have argued that Hitler and World War II would not have arisen had the victorious powers in World War I not written such an oppressive and unjust peace settlement (Saeidnia and Abdollahi, 2013; Seyfi and Hall, 2019). This final section considers how international provocations can lead to international war and the resultant violence. A significant amount of research focuses on relations between states and how that can descend into violent conflict (Barber, 1979; Drezner, 2015; Jiang, Chen, and Liu, 2010; Leyton-Brown, 2017). However, there is also evidence that democracies have less internal systematic violence (Hurd, 2017; Igami, 2015; Ivanov, Sypchenko, and Webster, 2017; James, 2013). Hence, most democratic and the most authoritarian states have few civil wars, and intermediate regimes the most (Attia, Grauvogel, and von Soest, 2020; Chachavalpongpun, 2014; Doxey, 1980; Goodhart, 2016; Ivanov, Sypchenko, and Webster, 2017). It is also worth noting that often it is often the vulnerable, such as women, who end up bearing the brunt of violence (see Figure 3.5 for an illustration of violence against women in Bangladesh).

Figure 3.5. Forms of violence against women in Bangladesh.

Source: Share-Net Bangladesh.

The probability for a civil war is also increased by political change, regardless of whether there is greater democracy or greater autocracy (Kunz, 1960; Laub, 2015; Lee, 2018; Levy, 1999; Leyton-Brown, 2017; Li and Saghaian, 2013). Intermediate regimes continue to be the most prone to civil war, regardless of the time since the political change (Reilly, 2012; Reisman and Stevick, 1998; Richard and Raimo, 1999; Ross, 1989; Rothwell and Stephens, 2016). In the long run, since intermediate regimes are less stable than autocracies, which in turn are less stable than democracies, durable democracy is the most probable endpoint of the process of democratization (Caruso, 2003; Chachavalpongpun, 2014; Chan, 2000; Chan and Drury, 2000; Chen et al., 2019; Cheraghali, 2013). There is evidence to suggest that the most democratic nations have the least levels of terrorism (Takian, Raoofi, and Kazempour-Ardebili, 2020; Taylor, 2012; Thaver and Ekanayake, 2010). Indeed, some argue that genocide and politicide are rare in democracies (Doxey, 1972, 1980, 1983, 1987; Drezner, 2000, 2011, 2015; Drezner and Drezner, 1999; Drury and Peksen, 2014). Then there are those that call for consideration to be given to external forces that have an interest in maintaining violence to destabilize the country before robbing it of its resources (Crawford and Klotz, 1999; Crook, 2013; David and Holliday, 2012; Daviron and Ponte, 2007; De Visscher, 2015). A case in point is the Democratic Republic of Congo in which the perpetual presence of international agencies and organizations has never completely eradicated civil war (Ozawa and Castello, 2001; Pape, 1997, 1998; Ponte, 2004). Hence, one of the wealthiest countries in terms of natural resources is also one of the poorest today (Mueller and Mueller, 1999; Nossal, 1989; Ogden, 2008).

Countries that are undemocratic tend to suffer from and inflict international violence (Nossal, 1989; Ogden, 2008; Ozawa and Castello, 2001). For example, there are studies which show that the more democratic a regime, the less its democide (McCorkell and Gillard, 2010; Ogden, 2008; Richard and Raimo, 1999). Some have argued that old colonial powers have an interest in maintaining a status quo in which old colonies are in perpetual conflict with themselves and with the rest of the world (Afesorgbor, 2019; Brzoska, 2015; Denzin, 2008; Frick, Humphreys, and Scheel, 2015; Huebner, 2009; Kunz, 1960). The Iranian government certainly believes that many of its conflicts stem from British duplicity and American support of Israel (Jiang, Chen, and Liu, 2010; Jing, Kaempfer, and Lowenberg, 2003; Kaempfer and Lowenberg, 1999).

When recovering from war, it is often the case that there is a call for reconciliation and containment of violence (Hanushek and Woessmann, 2010; Haugh and Kitson, 2007; Hinds, 1997; Hiraide and Chakraborty, 2012; Ho-Chuan, Yi-Chen, and Chih-Chuan, 2012). However, less attention is given to the underlying causes of war (Farzanegan, 2013; Farzanegan and Hayo, 2019; Franzway and Fonow, 2011; Frick, Humphreys, and Scheel, 2015). This could be a particularly important factor in preventing future wars, given the fact that many of the key actors engage with the conflict in a covert way which may not even be immediately noticed by the warring parties (Borszik, 2014; Crawford and Klotz, 1999; Escribà-Folch and

Wright, 2010; Li and Saghaian, 2013). Then there are countries which are always wary of international intervention which often leaves the country in a worse state than it was in before the conflict in the first place (Drezner and Drezner, 1999; Drury and Peksen, 2014; Dunn and Shaw, 2001; Dunoff, Ratner, and Wippman, 2015; Eliat and Einav, 2004; Eriksson, 2016).

American actions in the Iraq wars have called into question the very neutrality of international institutions and actors that give lip service to the concerns of those that are being targeted (McCorkell and Gillard, 2010; Ogden, 2008; Richard and Raimo, 1999). Having bombed the country and caused the death of many, the allied powers (particularly the USA as supported by the UK) later acknowledged that the premise of the war against Saddam Hussein was misleading (Bederman and Keitner, 2016; Chen et al., 2019; Drezner and Drezner, 1999; Gui, 1991; Jing, Kaempfer, and Lowenberg, 2003). There were really no weapons of mass destruction (Huebner, 2009; Hultman and Peksen, 2017; Hurd, 2017; Igami, 2015; Ivanov, Sypchenko, and Webster, 2017). However, the aggressors also argued that it was a good idea to get rid of Saddam Hussein since he was a dictator who was oppressing his people and potentially threatening weaker neighbors (Solingen, 2012; Stephanides et al., 2002; Strack and Strack, 1978; Takian, Raoofi, and Kazempour-Ardebili, 2020).

Public confidence in the political class and their ability to wage "just wars" has meant that many are now reluctant to get involved in international conflicts unless there is a very clear national interest associated with doing so (Attia, Grauvogel, and von Soest, 2020; Chachavalpongpun, 2014; Doxey, 1980; Goodhart, 2016; Ivanov, Sypchenko, and Webster, 2017). Recently, the USA irrationally canceled an agreement with Iran even though Iran had complied with all the terms of that agreement (Buck, Gallant, and Nossal, 1998; Caron, 1989; Carter, 1987; Caruso, 2003; Chachavalpongpun, 2014). The reason for the cancellation was the policy of a new United States, President, Donald Trump, edged on by Israel and Conservative voices in the USA (Doxey, 1972, 1980, 1983, 1987; Drezner, 2000, 2011, 2015; Drezner and Drezner, 1999). To the Iranians, it seemed like international agreements meant very little and that the EU could do little but wring its hands when the Americans decided to unilaterally break agreements (Drury and Peksen, 2014; Dunn and Shaw, 2001; Dunoff, Ratner, and Wippman, 2015; Eliat and Einav, 2004; Eriksson, 2016).

At that moment, the big powers are protected by their might and therefore do not anticipate retaliatory measures by the smaller countries that they attack (Kendall, 2000; Kiriya, 2017; Kirshner, 1997; Klotz, 1995; Koskenniemi, 2014; Kunz, 1960). However, that is not to say that there will never come a time when the provocations are so egregious that the attacked nations rise into even more armed conflict (Franzway and Fonow, 2011; Frick, Humphreys, and Scheel, 2015; Fridell, 2014). That is exactly the situation that provoked Germany following World War I and a peace that was written in favor of the victors in its entirety (Carter, 1987; Doxey, 1972; Gharehgozli, 2017; Lee, 2018; Ozawa and Castello, 2001). In the absence of a strong legal framework, international conflict can turn into mercantilism in which countries seek to attain an advantage by oppressing and cheating their neighbors (Laub, 2015; Lee, 2018; Levy, 1999; Leyton-Brown, 2017; Li and Saghaian, 2013).

CHAPTER 3 SUMMARY

This chapter has shown that conflict, war, and even sanctions rarely create or sustain justice. Instead, they lead to simmering tensions that might yet lead to more violence. The example of Yugoslavia shows that even where sanctions are justified by the egregious behavior of a rogue government, their impact unevenly and unfairly falls on the most vulnerable populations. This goes against the dictates of the right to development. Institutions such as the International Progress Organization (IPO) are no more than think tanks which cannot always alter the violent policies of those in power. According to the Democratic Peace Theory, countries that are liberalized, inclusive, and participatory are less likely to engage in war than those that are led by autocratic regimes. However, there is also evidence of democracies behaving in decidedly undemocratic ways. This can lead to provocations which heighten the risk of international violence. The next chapter closely examines some of the reasons that are given for triggering international sanctions.

Chapter 4

Reasons for Triggering International Sanctions

CONTENTS

There are many reasons that are given for starting and sustaining international sanctions. It is rare that these reasons are the entirety of the story. This chapter considers the overt and covert reasons for using this tool of international aggression. Some of the key issues that will be discussed include political similarity, economic factors, realist explanations, deterrence, the international relations (IRs) theory, and the role of Liberalism as an ideology. By the end of this chapter, the reader should be able to distinguish between the manifest and latent justifications for international sanctions.

4.1. POLITICAL SIMILARITY AND ECONOMIC FACTORS

Political similarity and certain economic factors have been associated with international conflict, or even the lack of it (Blyton, 2004; Cortright et al., 2000; Escribà-Folch, 2010; Ho-Chuan, Yi-Chen, and Chih-Chuan, 2012; Kendall, 2000). It is argued that countries with similar economic and political systems are less likely to engage in conflict (at least violent ones) than those that are very diverse (Austin, 1966; Boczek, 1968; Cohen, 2011; Curtin, 1969; Fenwick, 1967; Galtung, 1967; Harris, 1968; Hintz, 1972). That perhaps explains some of the antipathy towards countries that are not conforming to what is accepted as the best practice in the world (Boczek, 1968; Cohen, 2011; Curtin, 1969; Fenwick, 1967; Galtung, 1967; Harris, 1968; Hintz, 1972; Kreczko, 1980; Kuyper, 1975). The problem with such an approach is that it is too deterministic and does not consider the innate ability that countries must forge and break alliances depending on their strategic interests at a given moment in time (Cohen, 2011; Curtin, 1969; Fenwick, 1967; Galtung, 1967; Harris, 1968; Hintz, 1972; Kreczko, 1980; Kuyper, 1975).

One general criticism motivating research of different explanations is that actually the theory cannot claim that "democracy causes peace" (Chan, 2000; Chan and Drury, 2000; Chen et al., 2019; Cheraghali, 2013; Chiquiar, 2008; Choi and Luo, 2013; Clegg and Palmer, 1996). We have already seen in history that countries which claim to be democratic are often the ones that are at the forefront of creating aggression against others (Curtin, 1969; Fenwick, 1967; Galtung, 1967; Harris, 1968; Hintz, 1972; Kreczko, 1980; Kuyper, 1975; McDougal and Reisman, 1968). In the arms race, the winners are almost always the industrialized and apparently "civilized" nations of the world (Fenwick, 1967; Galtung, 1967; Harris, 1968; Hintz, 1972; Kreczko, 1980; Kuyper, 1975; McDougal and Reisman, 1968). These have then created a hegemony of sorts in which any country that is different from them is attacked using sanctions and other measures (Galtung, 1967; Harris, 1968; Hintz, 1972; Kreczko, 1980; Kuyper, 1975; McDougal and Reisman, 1968; McKinnell, 1968). The international institutions such as the United Nations have often been co-opted in this endeavor (Harris, 1968; Hintz, 1972; Kreczko, 1980; Kuyper, 1975; McDougal and Reisman, 1968; McKinnell, 1968; Minter and Schmidt, 1988). This is because the evidence for democracies being, in general, more peaceful, is very slight or nonexistent it only can support the claim that "joint democracy causes peace" (Fu et al., 2020; Genzberger et al., 1994; Gharehgozli, 2017; Goodhart, 2016; Grauvogel and Von Soest, 2014).

Some researchers doubt whether democracy is a cause of peace (Barber, 1979; Bederman and Keitner, 2016). In that sense, we go back to the ongoing debate between association and causation (Hintz, 1972; Kreczko, 1980; Kuyper, 1975; McDougal and Reisman, 1968; McKinnell, 1968; Minter and Schmidt, 1988). Just because a democracy is peaceful does not necessarily mean that it is peaceful because of democracy (Kreczko, 1980; Kuyper, 1975; McDougal and Reisman, 1968; McKinnell, 1968; Minter and Schmidt, 1988; Mlambo, 2005). Indeed, there may be other factors that impact on a country's predilection for peace including its culture and economic strength (Kuyper, 1975; McDougal and Reisman, 1968; McKinnell, 1968; Minter and Schmidt, 1988; Mlambo, 2005; Mobley, 2002). On the other hand, repressive regimes do not always want to invade or aggress against other nations (McDougal and Reisman, 1968; McKinnell, 1968; Minter and Schmidt, 1988; Mlambo, 2005; Mobley, 2002; Porter, 1978). Some of these countries are merely looking for the time and space to be able to develop their own unique systems of government (McKinnell, 1968; Minter and Schmidt, 1988; Mlambo, 2005; Mobley, 2002; Porter, 1978; Rowe, 1999, 2001).

Researchers are skeptical about any attempt to establish causation between democracy and peace, even where most of the countries that are subject to international sanctions cannot be described as being "democratic" in the full sense of that word (Minter and Schmidt, 1988; Mlambo, 2005; Mobley, 2002; Porter, 1978; Rowe, 1999, 2001; Stephenson, 1975). They do this on the basis that if democracy caused peace, a monadic effect would be expected (Matsushita et al., 2015; McCorkell and Gillard, 2010; Meyer and Thein, 2014; Mikhaylova, Babich, and Smirnova, 2017). In effect, this is a rejection of the simplistic models of international politics that seek to describe the actions of sovereign nations in an overly deterministic way that does not capture some of the nuances of foreign policy (Mlambo, 2005; Mobley, 2002; Porter, 1978; Rowe, 1999, 2001; Stephenson, 1975; Strack and Strack, 1978). Besides, we know that many countries (particularly those that are under sanctions regimes) can be unpredictable in terms of the way that they respond to aggression from foreign actors (Mobley, 2002; Porter, 1978; Rowe, 1999, 2001; Stephenson, 1975; Strack and Strack, 1978).

Perhaps the simplest explanation to such perceived anomaly is that democracies are not peaceful to each other because they are democratic, but rather because they are similar (Fridell, 2014; Fu et al., 2020; Genzberger et al., 1994; Gharehgozli, 2017; Goodhart, 2016). That means that they respond to challenges and conflict in very similar ways (Porter, 1978; Rowe, 1999, 2001; Stephenson, 1975; Strack and Strack, 1978). Besides, the strength of these democracies has allowed them to lead the world into a set of values and norms that are considered to be ideal (Rowe, 1999, 2001; Stephenson, 1975; Strack and Strack, 1978). The nations that then face sanctions are the ones that are unable to meet these standards (Austin, 1966; Boczek, 1968; Cohen, 2011; Curtin, 1969; Fenwick, 1967; Galtung, 1967; Harris, 1968; Hintz, 1972). As the case of Iran shows (see), economic sanctions create a cyclic series of crises that do not allow for democratization (Wallensteen and Staibano, 2005).

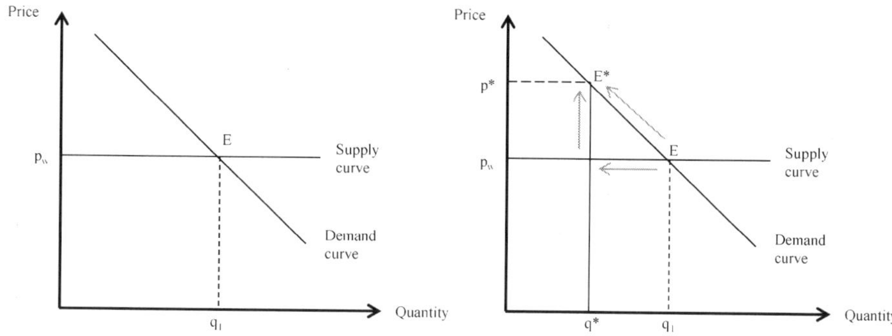

Figure 4.1. Impact of sanctions on Iranian economy.

Source: MDPI.

Hence, it could be argued that it is the sanctions, rather than the "undemocratic" nature of the regime that is ultimately responsible for the downturn in that nation (Escribà-Folch, 2010, 2012; Escribà-Folch and Wright, 2010; Farzanegan, 2013; Farzanegan and Hayo, 2019). Indeed, some nations have argued that sanctions have been used in a neo-Mercantilist way to stifle the development of rival nations or ones that threaten the dominance of one nation (Figure 4.1) (Kreczko, 1980; Kuyper, 1975; McDougal and Reisman, 1968; McKinnell, 1968; Minter and Schmidt, 1988).

This line of thought started with several independent observations of an "Autocratic Peace" effect (Mlambo, 2005; Mobley, 2002; Porter, 1978; Rowe, 1999, 2001; Stephenson, 1975; Strack and Strack, 1978). Under this paradigm, there was a reduced probability of war between states which are both non-democratic and highly autocratic (Hultman and Peksen, 2017; Hurd, 2017; Igami, 2015; Ivanov, Sypchenko, and Webster, 2017; James, 2013). This has led to the hypothesis that democratic peace emerges as a particular case when analyzing a subset of states which are similar (Levy, 1999; Leyton-Brown, 2017; Li and Saghaian, 2013; Lutz and Lux, 1995; Mahmud, 2001). The problem with such an analysis and conclusion is that it does not account for autocratic nations that are simultaneously peaceful (Abunimah, 2002; Al-Ali, 2005; Bolton, 1997; Byman, Pollack, and Waxman, 1998; Clawson, 1993; Cordesman, 1999). In fact, there is empirical evidence of autocratic states that have a specific policy of non-interference in the internal and external affairs of other sovereign nations (Al-Ali, 2005; Bolton, 1997; Byman, Pollack, and Waxman, 1998; Clawson, 1993; Cordesman, 1999, 2018; Delmonte, 2001). By way of contrast, developed nations that are considered democratic often consider it their responsibility to enforce democracy in other nations, regardless of whether an invitation has come from those nations (Bolton, 1997; Byman, Pollack, and Waxman, 1998; Clawson, 1993; Cordesman, 1999, 2018; Delmonte, 2001).

Alternatively, it can be argued that similarity in general does not solely affect the probability of war (Nossal, 1989; Ogden, 2008; Ozawa and Castello, 2001). For example, the similarities or differences between nations may be so subtle that they cannot even be detected in the overall assessment of the security risks of those nations (Byman, Pollack, and Waxman, 1998; Clawson, 1993; Cordesman, 1999, 2018; Delmonte, 2001; Falk, 2002). At other times, populations have links between and among nations which can cause or reduce the possibility of wars (Clawson, 1993; Cordesman, 1999, 2018; Delmonte, 2001; Falk, 2002; Gause III, 1999). A case in point is where foreigners become so many in each locality that they begin to ask for autonomy or even greater dependence on their home countries (Cordesman, 1999, 2018; Delmonte, 2001; Falk, 2002; Gause III 1999; Ismael and Ismael, 2005). Nevertheless, only coherence of strong political regimes such as full democracies and stark autocracies can be legitimately linked to peace (Carter, 1987; Caruso, 2003; Chachavalpongpun, 2014; Chan,

2000; Chan and Drury, 2000; Chen et al., 2019). Autocratic peace and the explanation based on political similarity is a relatively recent development (Cordesman, 2018; Delmonte, 2001; Falk, 2002; Gause III 1999; Ismael and Ismael, 2005; Joyner, 2003; Karsh and Rautsi, 1991). That perhaps explains why opinions about its value are varied (Escribà-Folch and Wright, 2010; Farzanegan, 2013; Farzanegan and Hayo, 2019; Franzway and Fonow, 2011). For example, some researchers have proposed a model considering political similarity, geographic distance, and economic interdependence as its main variables (Denzin, 2008; Devarajan and Mottaghi, 2015; Dobler, 2008; Doxey, 1972). Whereas such models can be reductivist, there is some evidence to prove their associations, if not causality (Karsh and Rautsi, 1991; Lopez, 1998; Lopez and Cortright, 2004; Mackey, 2003; Nagy, 2001). Researchers who follow this line of thinking subsequently concluded that democratic peace is a statistical artifact which disappears when the above variables are considered (Bolander, 2011; Borszik, 2014, 2016; Bosco, 2012; Bradley and Galbraith, 2016; Brzoska, 2015; Buck, Gallant, and Nossal, 1998). Others identify a conflict reducing effect from political similarity in general (Hultman and Peksen, 2017; Hurd, 2017; Igami, 2015; Ivanov, Sypchenko, and Webster, 2017; James, 2013). Whereas these debates are often carried out in abstract, war, and peace happens in real-life situations where the dynamics are complex and therefore difficult to control, let alone predict accurately (Joyner, 2003; Karsh and Rautsi, 1991; Lopez, 1998; Lopez and Cortright, 2004; Mackey, 2003; Nagy, 2001).

This is particularly true for democratic dyads and those nations that have a similar political system (Jiang, Chen, and Liu, 2010; Jing, Kaempfer, and Lowenberg, 2003). However, there are some differences in behavior between democratic and autocratic dyads with respect to the ways in which they forge alliances (Ismael and Ismael, 2005; Joyner, 2003; Karsh and Rautsi, 1991; Lopez, 1998; Lopez and Cortright, 2004; Mackey, 2003). Those differences also extend to the way in which these states exercise power and how that power is evaluated (Ryngaert, 2015; Saeidnia and Abdollahi, 2013). Researchers use neural networks to show two distinct low probability zones which have slightly different patterns of behavior (Gause III 1999; Ismael and Ismael, 2005; Joyner, 2003; Karsh and Rautsi, 1991; Lopez, 1998; Lopez and Cortright, 2004). In turn, these zones correspond to high democracy and high autocracy contexts depending on the subjective definitions of these two terms (Jiang, Chen, and Liu, 2010; Jing, Kaempfer, and Lowenberg, 2003; Kaempfer and Lowenberg, 1999). Some analysts use a different statistical model. Based on this model, they have produced data indicating that autocratic peace is not statistically significant (Ross, 1989; Rothwell and Stephens, 2016; Ryngaert, 2015; Saeidnia and Abdollahi, 2013). However, there are others who have questioned the veracity and consistency of these models when dealing with emerging nations that may have to react to circumstances outside their control (Falk, 2002; Gause III 1999; Ismael and Ismael, 2005; Joyner, 2003; Karsh and Rautsi, 1991; Lopez, 1998; Lopez and Cortright, 2004).

Moreover, results suggest that the effect attributed to similarity is mostly driven by the pacifying effect of joint democracy (Kaempfer and Lowenberg, 2000; Kaempfer, Lowenberg, and Mertens, 2004; Kendall, 2000). In this case, the fact that two democracies are the closest neighbors means that there is a low likelihood of these countries engaging in war (Delmonte, 2001; Falk, 2002; Gause III 1999; Ismael and Ismael, 2005; Joyner, 2003; Karsh and Rautsi, 1991; Lopez, 1998). The opposite relationship is then considered to be true when autocratic regimes are naturally aggressive and may end up attacking other neighboring autocratic regimes (Cordesman, 1999, 2018; Delmonte, 2001; Falk, 2002; Gause III, 1999; Ismael and Ismael, 2005). The problematic aspect of this are situations when autocracies band together against the world, particularly if they are both subjected to international sanctions (Cordesman, 2018; Delmonte, 2001; Falk, 2002; Gause III, 1999; Ismael and Ismael, 2005; Joyner, 2003; Karsh and Rautsi, 1991). There can be a form of brotherhood among pariah states as they attempt to respond to international isolation (Clawson, 1993; Cordesman, 1999, 2018; Delmonte, 2001; Falk, 2002; Gause III, 1999). Indeed, there have been examples which regimes that would otherwise fall, have successfully endured because of the collaboration of other pariah regimes (Byman, Pollack, and Waxman, 1998; Clawson, 1993; Cordesman, 1999, 2018; Delmonte, 2001; Falk, 2002).

Others similarly dispute the weight of the argument on logical grounds. They argue for example that claiming that statistical analysis on "political similarity" uses a main variable which is an extension of "joint democracy" (Bolton, 1997; Byman, Pollack, and Waxman, 1998; Clawson, 1993; Cordesman, 1999, 2018; Delmonte, 2001). This is in effect, nothing more than a linguistic redefinition of political systems (Biersteker, Eckert, and Tourinho, 2016; Blyton, 2004; Bolander, 2011). Hence, it is expected that the war reducing effects are carried on in the new analysis (Cranmer, Heinrich, and Desmarais, 2014; Crawford and Klotz, 1999; Crook, 2013; David and Holliday, 2012; Daviron and Ponte, 2007). At the crux of the problem is the challenge of trying to delineate the positive effects of democracy so that one can understand what causes war, what reduces war, and what has no effect whatsoever (Al-Ali, 2005; Bolton, 1997; Byman, Pollack, and Waxman, 1998; Clawson, 1993; Cordesman, 1999, 2018; Delmonte, 2001). Moreover, the fact that democracies are generally stable means that they do not often have violent regime change (Abunimah, 2002; Al-Ali, 2005; Bolton, 1997; Byman, Pollack, and Waxman, 1998; Clawson, 1993; Cordesman, 1999). It means that there is a generalized consensus on policy (Delmonte, 2001; Falk, 2002; Gause III 1999; Ismael and Ismael, 2005; Joyner, 2003; Karsh and Rautsi, 1991; Lopez, 1998). As such, it can be difficult to distinguish between the positive aspects of the policies that are adopted by the government and the actual system of government that is being used (Falk, 2002; Gause III 1999; Ismael and Ismael, 2005; Joyner, 2003; Karsh and Rautsi, 1991; Lopez, 1998; Lopez and Cortright, 2004).

There is a direct statistical model based on a triadic classification of states into "democratic," "autocratic" and "mixed" (Cheraghali, 2013; Drury and Peksen, 2014; Hafner-Burton and Montgomery, 2008). The problem with these classifications is that they do not always account for the complexity of nations that do not fit into a straight jack of typologies (Gause III 1999; Ismael and Ismael, 2005; Joyner, 2003; Karsh and Rautsi, 1991; Lopez, 1998; Lopez and Cortright, 2004). There are regimes that have different aspects of democratic and autocratic government (Ismael and Ismael, 2005; Joyner, 2003; Karsh and Rautsi, 1991; Lopez, 1998; Lopez and Cortright, 2004; Mackey, 2003). Indeed, few governments are completely democratic or completely autocratic (Joyner, 2003; Karsh and Rautsi, 1991; Lopez, 1998; Lopez and Cortright, 2004; Mackey, 2003; Nagy, 2001). Nevertheless, researchers posit that autocratic dyads have about 35% reduced chance of going into any type of armed conflict with respect to a reference mixed dyad (Rothwell and Stephens, 2016; Solingen, 2012; Stephanides et al., 2002). Such a statistic is based on a selected sample and may not always apply in a real-world situation where there are many considerations that might prevent a country from going to war despite its predilection for war (Karsh and Rautsi, 1991; Lopez, 1998; Lopez and Cortright, 2004; Mackey, 2003; Nagy, 2001). Another statistic that has been discussed is the possibility that democratic dyads have a 55% reduced chance of going to war (Abunimah, 2002; Al-Ali, 2005; Bolton, 1997; Byman, Pollack, and Waxman, 1998; Clawson, 1993). However, such a statistic is developed in quasi-experimental situations that may not be reflected in real life situations (Cordesman, 1999, 2018; Delmonte, 2001; Falk, 2002; Gause III, 1999).

In any case, this effect gets stronger when looking at more severe or highly impactful conflicts (Ponte, 2004; Reilly, 2012; Reisman and Stevick,

1998; Richard and Raimo, 1999). In other words, even those regimes that tend to go to war, will be less likely to do so if the conflict has serious costs and consequences (Ismael and Ismael, 2005; Joyner, 2003; Karsh and Rautsi, 1991; Lopez, 1998; Lopez and Cortright, 2004; Mackey, 2003; Nagy, 2001). This is particularly true if those consequences cannot be easily mitigated, a case in point being punitive international sanctions (Barry, 2000; Boas, 2000; Cain, 1994; Copeland, Jolly, and Thompson, 2011; Drain and Barry, 2010; Falk, 1996). That is why some have concluded that autocratic peace exists (Boas, 2000; Cain, 1994; Copeland, Jolly, and Thompson, 2011; Drain and Barry, 2010; Falk, 1996; Fandl, 2017). Indeed, we have seen autocratic nations surviving in a sanctions regime and actually not really going to war with the aggressors, partly because the consequences for them are greater than any benefits that might accrue from war (Cain, 1994; Copeland, Jolly, and Thompson, 2011; Drain and Barry, 2010; Falk, 1996; Fandl, 2017; Fisk, 2000).

It is also true that democratic peace exists as well and this has been the mainstay argument for democratizing the world (Copeland, Jolly, and Thompson, 2011; Drain and Barry, 2010; Falk, 1996; Fandl, 2017; Fisk, 2000; Garfield and Santana, 1997). However, the critical point is that the predilection for peace is clearly stronger among democracies than it is among autocracies (Kaempfer and Lowenberg, 2000; Kaempfer, Lowenberg, and Mertens, 2004; Kendall, 2000). Others have questioned whether this is merely a reflection of Western imperialist thinking in which only systems that arise from the Anglo-Saxon model of democracy or constitutional monarchy are democratic (Drain and Barry, 2010; Falk, 1996; Fandl, 2017; Fisk, 2000; Garfield and Santana, 1997; Gordon, 2012; Kirkpatrick, 1996). It is possible for an apparently repressive regime to engage in democratic processes such as elections (Falk, 1996; Fandl, 2017; Fisk, 2000; Garfield and Santana, 1997; Gordon, 2012; Kirkpatrick, 1996). Nevertheless, there is no significant and relevant pacifying effect of political similarity (Fandl, 2017; Fisk, 2000; Garfield and Santana, 1997; Gordon, 2012; Kirkpatrick, 1996; Kuntz and Jackson, 1994). The only exceptions that have been seen in existing literature tend to lie at the extremes of the scale (Wallensteen and Staibano, 2005). Besides, all these assumptions have caveats relating to the context which may cause nations to behave differently from their predilections (Fisk, 2000; Garfield and Santana, 1997; Gordon, 2012; Kirkpatrick, 1996; Kuntz and Jackson, 1994; LeoGrande, 1997).

The capitalist peace theory (or capitalist peace theory in some literature) posits that according to given criteria for economic development (capitalism), developed economies have not engaged in war with each other (Garfield and Santana, 1997; Gordon, 2012; Kirkpatrick, 1996; Kuntz and Jackson, 1994; LeoGrande, 1997; Osieja, 2006). It also argues that capitalist regimes rarely enter low-level disputes (Farzanegan and Hayo, 2019; Franzway and Fonow, 2011; Frick, Humphreys, and Scheel, 2015; Fridell, 2014). Some may argue that capitalist peace theory is nothing more than an attempt to justify attacks against socialist or non-capitalist regimes (Gordon, 2012; Kirkpatrick, 1996; Kuntz and Jackson, 1994; LeoGrande, 1997; Osieja, 2006; Purcell and Rothkopf, 2000). Indeed, in the case of Cuba, there has been a specific interested from the USA to portray socialism as inherently evil while capitalism is portrayed as being ideal (Kirkpatrick, 1996; Kuntz and Jackson, 1994; LeoGrande, 1997; Osieja, 2006; Purcell and Rothkopf, 2000; Reinisch, 1996). There are positive things about socialism and negative things about capitalism (Kuntz and Jackson, 1994; LeoGrande, 1997; Osieja, 2006; Purcell and Rothkopf, 2000; Reinisch, 1996). However, these subtleties are often ignored for political expediency (LeoGrande, 1997; Osieja, 2006; Purcell and Rothkopf, 2000; Reinisch, 1996; Roman, 1995; Smugula, 1995; Spadoni, 2010).

These capitalist peace theories have been proposed as an explanation for the democratic peace by accounting for both democracy and the peace among democratic nations (Eliat and Einav, 2004; Eriksson, 2016; Escribà-Folch, 2010, 2012; Escribà-Folch and Wright, 2010; Farzanegan, 2013; Farzanegan and Hayo, 2019). The exact nature of the causality depends upon both the proposed variable and the measure of the indicator for the concept used (Frick, Humphreys, and Scheel, 2015; Fridell, 2014; Fu et al., 2020; Genzberger et al., 1994; Gharehgozli, 2017). As we know, both the variables and the relationships among them can be subject to cultural norms and values (Osieja, 2006; Purcell and Rothkopf, 2000; Reinisch, 1996; Roman, 1995; Smugula, 1995; Spadoni, 2010; Zimbalist, 1993). For example, a socialist regime will have a different view of social good from a capitalist one (Barry, 2000; Boas, 2000; Cain, 1994; Copeland, Jolly, and Thompson, 2011; Drain and Barry, 2010). Similarly, the attitudes to conflict and war may vary between capitalist and non-capitalist regimes (Purcell and Rothkopf, 2000; Reinisch, 1996; Roman, 1995; Smugula, 1995; Spadoni, 2010; Zimbalist, 1993).

Nevertheless, most researchers on the determinants of democracy agree that economic development is a primary factor which allows the formation of a stable and healthy democracy (Lee, 2018; Levy, 1999; Leyton-Brown, 2017; Li and Saghaian, 2013). Others argue that the interest in protecting capital, means that entrepreneurs are less likely to support a war (Falk, 1996; Fandl, 2017; Fisk, 2000; Garfield and Santana, 1997; Gordon, 2012). Of course, there are situations in which entrepreneurs that are operating within a defense industry would encourage war as a means of ensuring a steady supply of demand for their products (Kirkpatrick, 1996; Kuntz and Jackson, 1994; LeoGrande, 1997; Osieja, 2006). At other times, capitalists will encourage war if another state has encroached on their right to property and profits (Purcell and Rothkopf, 2000; Reinisch, 1996; Roman, 1995; Smugula, 1995; Spadoni, 2010; Zimbalist, 1993). For example, we know that the conflict between the USA and Cuba is partly driven by the grievances of businesspeople that lost out when Cuba decided to nationalize some of its key industries (Barry, 2000; Boas, 2000; Cain, 1994; Fandl, 2017; Fisk, 2000; Garfield and Santana, 1997; Osieja, 2006; Purcell and Rothkopf, 2000). If anything, the motivations and conduct of war are so complex that they cannot be easily reduced to a binary of capitalist versus socialist regime (Copeland, Jolly, and Thompson, 2011; Gordon, 2012; Kirkpatrick, 1996; Reinisch, 1996; Roman, 1995). Thus, some researchers have argued that economic development also plays a factor in the establishment of peace (Caruso, 2003; Chachavalpongpun, 2014; Chan, 2000; Chan and Drury, 2000; Chen et al., 2019; Cheraghali, 2013). The realist perspective, which we are going to cover in the next section, has a more nuanced understanding of war and peace beyond economics and democratic similarities.

4.2. REALIST EXPLANATIONS OF INTERNATIONAL SANCTIONS

Many studies supporting the democratic similarity and economic factor theories have controlled for many possible alternative causes of the peace (Jing, Kaempfer, and Lowenberg, 2003; Kaempfer and Lowenberg, 1999, 2000). Examples of factors controlled for are geographic distance, geographic contiguity, power status, alliance ties, militarization, economic wealth and economic growth, power ratio, and political stability (Bolander, 2011; Cranmer, Heinrich, and Desmarais, 2014; Escribà-Folch, 2012; Hovdenak, 2009; Kiriya, 2017). These studies have often found very different results depending on methodology and included variables, which has caused criticism (Igami, 2015; Ivanov, Sypchenko, and Webster, 2017; James, 2013). It is important to acknowledge that few (if any) researchers argue democracy is the only thing affecting the risk of military conflict (Ozawa and Castello, 2001; Pape, 1997, 1998).

As we have seen democracies causing and sustaining conflict, the assumptions of democratic peace have been continuously critiqued (Drain and Barry, 2010; Falk, 1996; Kuntz and Jackson, 1994; LeoGrande, 1997; Smugula, 1995; Spadoni, 2010; Zimbalist, 1993). Indeed, there have been cases where democracies have ended up behaving like modern imperial powers once they have acquired sufficient political, economic, and social clout on the international stage (Purcell and Rothkopf, 2000; Reinisch, 1996; Roman, 1995; Smugula, 1995; Spadoni, 2010; Zimbalist, 1993). They continuously stifle the development of rival nations in ways that would not be alien to a mercantilist monarchy in the 15th and 16th century (Osieja, 2006; Purcell and Rothkopf, 2000; Reinisch, 1996; Roman, 1995; Smugula, 1995; Spadoni, 2010; Zimbalist, 1993). In light of those criticisms, other factors have emerged as being important in moderating the warlike tendencies of nations (LeoGrande, 1997; Osieja, 2006; Purcell and Rothkopf, 2000; Reinisch, 1996; Roman, 1995; Smugula, 1995; Spadoni, 2010). Many of these additional factors favoring peace are rooted in the realist perspective (Caron, 1989; Genzberger et al., 1994). Figure 4.2 summarizes some of the reasons for the actions of states in respect to war, peace, and foreign policy.

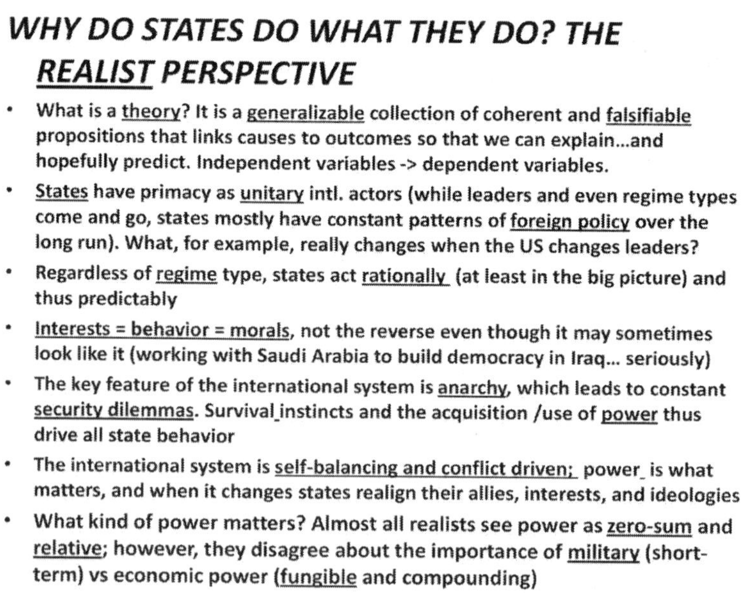

Figure 4.2. Realist explanations of a nation's behavior.

Source: Slide Player.

Several studies have also controlled for the possibility of reverse causality from peace to democracy (Koskenniemi, 2014; Kunz, 1960; Laub, 2015; Lee, 2018; Levy, 1999; Leyton-Brown, 2017). Some literature supports the theory of simultaneous causation in which dyads involved in wars are likely to experience a decrease in joint democracy (Kuntz and Jackson, 1994; LeoGrande, 1997; Osieja, 2006; Purcell and Rothkopf, 2000; Reinisch, 1996). This in turn increases the probability of further war (Ogden, 2008; Ozawa and Castello, 2001; Pape, 1997). So, they argue that disputes between democratizing or democratic states should be resolved externally at a very early stage, in order to stabilize the system (Franzway and Fonow, 2011; Frick, Humphreys, and Scheel, 2015; Fridell, 2014; Fu et al., 2020). Indeed, the international systems or international law relies on this assumption (Kirkpatrick, 1996; Kuntz and Jackson, 1994; LeoGrande, 1997; Osieja, 2006; Purcell and Rothkopf, 2000; Reinisch, 1996). Rather than fighting over the smallest of squabbles, nations can come to the negotiating table (Gordon, 2012; Kirkpatrick, 1996; Kuntz and Jackson, 1994; LeoGrande, 1997; Osieja, 2006; Purcell and Rothkopf, 2000). Where the conflict has escalated, the nations may impose diplomatic and economic sanctions as a means of dealing with the infringement before considering the last resort of outright military conflict (Garfield and Santana, 1997; Gordon, 2012; Kirkpatrick, 1996; Kuntz and Jackson, 1994; LeoGrande, 1997; Osieja, 2006). Indeed, some researchers have pointed out the reduction in international wars as being an example of how and why the international system works (Fisk, 2000; Garfield and Santana, 1997; Gordon, 2012; Kirkpatrick, 1996; Kuntz and Jackson, 1994; LeoGrande, 1997).

Others find that peace does not spread democracy in a linear or direct way (Fandl, 2017; Fisk, 2000; Garfield and Santana, 1997; Gordon, 2012; Kirkpatrick, 1996; Kuntz and Jackson, 1994). Instead, they argue that spreading democracy is likely to spread peace (Richard and Raimo, 1999; Ross, 1989; Rothwell and Stephens, 2016; Ryngaert, 2015). This is a very subtle difference that is often lost when classifying nations as being peaceful and democratic (Falk, 1996; Fandl, 2017; Fisk, 2000; Garfield and Santana, 1997; Gordon, 2012; Kirkpatrick, 1996). A different kind of reverse causation lies in the suggestion that impending war could destroy or decrease democracy (Gui, 1991; Hafner-Burton and Montgomery, 2008; Hanushek and Woessmann, 2010; Haugh and Kitson, 2007). This is because the preparation for war might include political restrictions, which may be the cause for the findings of democratic peace (Genzberger et al., 1994; Gharehgozli, 2017; Goodhart, 2016; Grauvogel and Von Soest, 2014).

This explanation would predict a monadic effect, although weaker than the dyadic one (James, 2013; Jiang, Chen, and Liu, 2010; Jing, Kaempfer, and Lowenberg, 2003).

There are researchers who argue that the peacefulness appears and disappears rapidly when democracy appears and disappears (Takian, Raoofi, and Kazempour-Ardebili, 2020; Taylor, 2012; Thaver and Ekanayake, 2010). Hence, it is unlikely that variables that change more slowly are the explanation (Meyer and Thein, 2014; Mikhaylova, Babich, and Smirnova, 2017). Such propositions have been criticized for not offering any quantitative analysis to support them (Huebner, 2009; Hultman and Peksen, 2017; Hurd, 2017; Igami, 2015; Ivanov, Sypchenko, and Webster, 2017). Wars tend very strongly to be between neighboring states (Von Glahn and Taulbee, 2015). Research has shown that the average distance between democracies is about 8000 miles, the same as the average distance between all states (Devarajan and Mottaghi, 2015; Dobler, 2008; Doxey, 1972, 1983). Some researchers believe that the effect of distance in preventing war, modified by the democratic peace, explains the incidence of war as fully as it can be explained (Mahmud, 2001; Mikhaylova, Babich, and Smirnova, 2017; Ponte, 2004).

Supporters of realism in international relations (IRs) in general argue that not democracy or its absence, but considerations and evaluations of power, cause peace or war (Chiquiar, 2008; Dunn and Shaw, 2001; Hanushek and Woessmann, 2010; Kaempfer and Lowenberg, 1999). Specifically, many realist critics claim that the effect ascribed to democratic, or liberal, peace, is in fact due to alliance ties between democratic states, which in turn are caused, one way or another, by realist factors (Caron, 1989; Genzberger et al., 1994). Such researchers find evidence for peace between democracies to be statistically significant only in the period from 1945 onwards (Dunoff, Ratner, and Wippman, 2015; Eliat and Einav, 2004; Eriksson, 2016; Escribà-Folch, 2010, 2012; Escribà-Folch and Wright, 2010; Farzanegan, 2013). They consider such peace an artifact of the Cold War, when the threat from the communist states forced democracies to ally with one another (Crawford and Klotz, 1999; Crook, 2013; David and Holliday, 2012; Daviron and Ponte, 2007; De Visscher, 2015). There have been studies that have identified several instances of wars between democracies (Ross, 1989; Rothwell and Stephens, 2016; Ryngaert, 2015; Saeidnia and Abdollahi, 2013). These studies are in effect arguing that evidence in favor of the theory might be not so vast as other authors report (Afesorgbor, 2019; Brzoska, 2015; Denzin, 2008; Frick, Humphreys, and Scheel, 2015; Huebner, 2009; Kunz, 1960).

Moreover, there is skepticism about evidence which consists of peace between allied states with shared objectives (Tridimas and Guiterrex-Fons, 2008).

Generally, researchers acknowledge that democratic states might have a somewhat greater tendency to ally with one another (Ogden, 2008; Ozawa and Castello, 2001; Pape, 1997). Hence, they argue that this is the only real effect of democratic peace. Most of the significant evidence for democratic peace has been observed after World War II where it has happened within a broad alliance including NATO and its satellite nations (Morgan and Schwebach, 1997; Mueller and Mueller, 1999). Such alliances are imposed and maintained by American dominance (Pape, 1997, 1998; Ponte, 2004; Reilly, 2012; Reisman and Stevick, 1998). Whereas the USA has never engaged in open war with another liberal democracy during the Cold War, it intervened openly or covertly in the political affairs of democratic states several times (Denzin, 2008; Devarajan and Mottaghi, 2015; Dobler, 2008; Doxey, 1972). Examples of this include the Chilean coup of 1973, the 1953 coup in Iran and the 1954 coup in Guatemala (Levy, 1999; Leyton-Brown, 2017; Li and Saghaian, 2013). This is what some researchers have referred to as an "imperial peace" rather than a democratic one (Doxey, 1980, 1983, 1987; Drezner, 2000, 2011, 2015; Drezner and Drezner, 1999; Drury and Peksen, 2014). The USA in particular has been fond of using sanctions as a form of deterrent, a practice that we will explore further in the next section.

4.3. SANCTIONS AS A FORM OF DETERRENT

Sanctions have been deployed as a deterrent, particularly with regards to the accumulation and deployment of weapons of mass destruction (Lutz and Lux, 1995; Mahmud, 2001; Matsushita et al., 2015; McCorkell and Gillard, 2010; Meyer and Thein, 2014). The "nuclear deterrent" is one of the arguments that are continuously referenced by the USA and its allies when imposing pernicious sanctions on Iran and North Korea (Kirshner, 1997; Klotz, 1995; Koskenniemi, 2014; Kunz, 1960; Laub, 2015; Lee, 2018). However, it is also notable that Iran has never used a nuclear weapon, unlike the USA (Taylor, 2012; Thaver and Ekanayake, 2010; Tridimas and Guiterrex-Fons, 2008). Indeed, many allies of the USA have nuclear capabilities and have a history of oppressing and attacking other nations in the past (Crawford and Klotz, 1999; Crook, 2013; David and Holliday, 2012; Daviron and Ponte, 2007; De Visscher, 2015; De Vos, 2010). This calls into question the logical conclusions of the "nuclear deterrent" (Rothwell and Stephens, 2016;

Ryngaert, 2015; Saeidnia and Abdollahi, 2013). Figure 4.3 summarizes the deterrent justification for international sanctions.

	Possible Objectives	Possible Mechanisms
1	To *change or prevent* objectionable/unlawful policy/behaviour	*Indirect Mechanisms:* Economic Pressure Non-Economic Pressure *Direct Mechanism:* Direct Denial of Resources
2	To *send a message*	Imposition alone should send message
3	To *punish* objectionable/unlawful behaviour	Infliction of economic harm as a penalty and/or sanctions express international condemnation

Figure 4.3. Sanctions as a form of deterrent.

Source: Internet Encyclopedia of Philosophy.

A different kind of realist criticism stresses the role of nuclear weapons in maintaining peace. In realist terms, this means that, in the case of disputes between nuclear powers, respective evaluation of power might be irrelevant (Solingen, 2012; Stephanides et al., 2002; Strack and Strack, 1978). This is because of mutual assured destruction preventing both sides from foreseeing what could be reasonably called a "victory" (Mahmud, 2001; Mikhaylova, Babich, and Smirnova, 2017; Ponte, 2004). The 1999 Kargil War between India and Pakistan has been cited as a counterexample to this argument (Matsushita et al., 2015; Nossal, 1989; Reilly, 2012; Strack and Strack, 1978). However, it is also notable that this was a small, regional conflict and the threat of WMDs (Weapons of Mass Destruction) being used contributed to its de-escalation (Igami, 2015; Ivanov, Sypchenko, and Webster, 2017; James, 2013).

Some supporters of the democratic peace do not deny that realist factors are also important (Biersteker, Eckert, and Tourinho, 2016; Cleveland, 2001; Eriksson, 2016; Hiraide and Chakraborty, 2012). Research supporting the theory has also shown that factors such as alliance ties and major power status influence interstate conflict behavior (Takian, Raoofi, and Kazempour-Ardebili, 2020; Taylor, 2012; Thaver and Ekanayake, 2010). The democratic peace theory has been extremely divisive among political scientists (Gui,

1991; Hafner-Burton and Montgomery, 2008; Hanushek and Woessmann, 2010). It is rooted in the idealist and classical liberalist traditions and is opposed to the dominant theory of realism (Igami, 2015; Ivanov, Sypchenko, and Webster, 2017; James, 2013).

In the United States, presidents from both major parties have expressed support for the theory (Kaempfer and Lowenberg, 1999; Kaempfer and Lowenberg, 2000; Kaempfer, Lowenberg, and Mertens, 2004). Some fear that the democratic peace theory may be used to justify wars against non-democracies to bring lasting peace, in a democratic crusade (Nossal, 1989; Ogden, 2008). Woodrow Wilson in 1917 asked Congress to declare war against Imperial Germany, citing Germany's sinking of American ships due to unrestricted submarine warfare and the Zimmermann telegram, but also stating that "A steadfast concert for peace can never be maintained except by a partnership of democratic nations" and "The world must be made safe for democracy" (Levy, 1999; Leyton-Brown, 2017; Li and Saghaian, 2013; Lutz and Lux, 1995; Mahmud, 2001). Rummel is a notable proponent of war for the purpose of spreading democracy, based on this theory (Daviron and Ponte, 2007; Franzway and Fonow, 2011; Koskenniemi, 2014; Thaver and Ekanayake, 2010).

Some point out that the democratic peace theory has been used to justify the 2003 Iraq War (Drezner and Drezner, 1999; Drury and Peksen, 2014; Dunn and Shaw, 2001; Dunoff, Ratner, and Wippman, 2015; Eliat and Einav, 2004; Eriksson, 2016). Yet, others argue that this justification was used only after the war had already started (Kirshner, 1997; Klotz, 1995; Koskenniemi, 2014; Kunz, 1960; Laub, 2015; Lee, 2018). Furthermore, there are experts who have argued that the justification is extremely weak, because forcibly democratizing a country surrounded by non-democracies (Doxey, 1987; Drezner, 2000, 2011, 2015; Drezner and Drezner, 1999; Drury and Peksen, 2014; Dunn and Shaw, 2001). Indeed, most of Iraq's neighbors are full autocracies (Kendall, 2000; Kiriya, 2017; Kirshner, 1997; Klotz, 1995; Koskenniemi, 2014; Kunz, 1960; Laub, 2015; Lee, 2018). Hence, Iraq was at least as likely to increase the risk of war as it is to decrease it (Ryngaert, 2015; Saeidnia and Abdollahi, 2013). Some studies show that dyads formed by one democracy and one autocracy are the most warlike (Jiang, Chen, and Liu, 2010; Jing, Kaempfer, and Lowenberg, 2003). Indeed, several papers find that the risk of war is greatly increased in democratizing countries surrounded by non-democracies (Bosco, 2012; David and Holliday, 2012; Farzanegan and Hayo, 2019; Klotz, 1995; Pape, 1998; Taylor, 2012).

According to some researchers, if the United States and its allies wanted to adopt a rationale strategy of forced democratization based on democratic peace; it would be best to start intervening in countries which border with at least one or two stable democracies (Bosco, 2012; David and Holliday, 2012; Farzanegan and Hayo, 2019; Klotz, 1995; Pape, 1998; Taylor, 2012). This would then set the rationale to expand gradually. Moreover, research shows that attempts to create democracies by using external force has often failed (Bacchiega and Borzaga, 2003; Baldwin and Pape, 1998; Barber, 1979). Commentators argue that forced democratization by interventionism may initially have partial success. However, such interventions often create an unstable democratizing country, which can have dangerous consequences in the long run (Ozawa and Castello, 2001; Pape, 1997, 1998; Ponte, 2004; Reilly, 2012). Those attempts which had a permanent and stable success (e.g., democratization in Austria, West Germany, and Japan after World War II) mostly involved countries which had an advanced economic and social structure already (Bacchiega and Borzaga, 2003; Chan, 2000; Drezner, 2000; Grauvogel, Licht, and von Soest, 2017). Hence, the democratization process implied a drastic change of the whole political culture (Seyfi and Hall, 2019; Solingen, 2012; Stephanides et al., 2002). Supporting internal democratic movements and using diplomacy may be far more successful and less costly (Blyton, 2004; Bolander, 2011; Borszik, 2014, 2016; Bosco, 2012; Bradley and Galbraith, 2016; Brzoska, 2015; Buck, Gallant, and Nossal, 1998). Thus, the theory and related research, if they were correctly understood, may be an argument against a democratic crusade (De Visscher, 2015; Ross, 1989; Von Glahn and Taulbee, 2015). All this falls within the realms of IRs theory which will be explored in the next section.

4.4. INTERNATIONAL RELATIONS (IRS) THEORY

International relations (IRs) theory is the study of IRs from a theoretical perspective (Richard and Raimo, 1999; Ross, 1989; Rothwell and Stephens, 2016; Ryngaert, 2015). It attempts to provide a conceptual framework upon which IRs can be analyzed (Tridimas and Guiterrex-Fons, 2008). Ole Holsti describes IRs theories as acting like pairs of colored sunglasses that allow the wearer to see only salient events relevant to the theory (Doxey, 1972, 1980, 1983, 1987; Drezner, 2000, 2011, 2015; Drezner and Drezner, 1999; Drury and Peksen, 2014). For example, an adherent of realism may completely disregard an event that a constructivist might pounce upon as crucial, and vice versa (Drezner, 2011, 2015; Drezner and Drezner, 1999;

Drury and Peksen, 2014; Dunn and Shaw, 2001; Dunoff, Ratner, and Wippman, 2015). The three most prominent theories are realism, liberalism, and constructivism (Attia, Grauvogel, and von Soest, 2020; Bacchiega and Borzaga, 2003; Baldwin and Pape, 1998). Sometimes, institutionalism proposed and developed by Keohane and Nye is discussed as a paradigm that differed from liberalism (Defourny, 2013; Denzin, 2008; Devarajan and Mottaghi, 2015; Dobler, 2008). Figure 4.4 is a demonstration of one typology of states that are subject to theories of IRs.

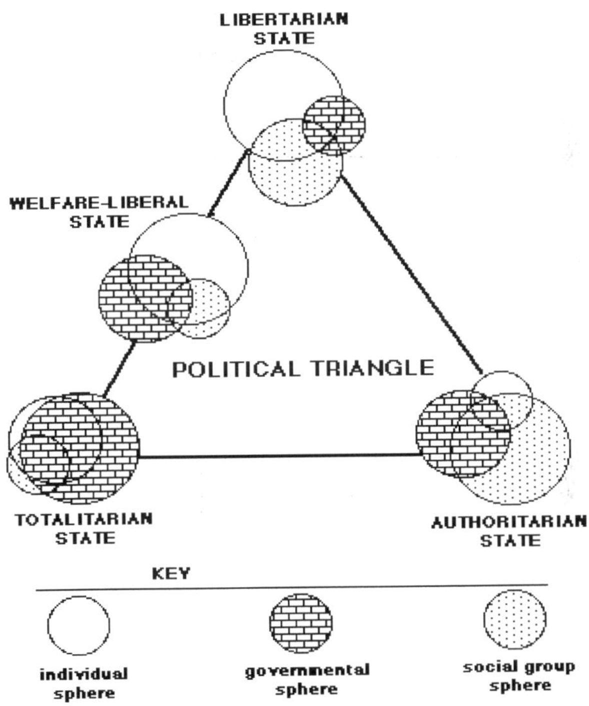

Figure 4.4. Typologies of states and spheres of autonomy.

Source: University of Hawaii System.

IRs theories can be divided into two broad categories. The first are the "positivist or rationalist" theories which focus on a principally state-level analysis (Solingen, 2012; Stephanides et al., 2002; Strack and Strack, 1978). Second, are the "post-positivist or reflectivist" ones which incorporate expanded meanings of security, ranging from class, to gender, to postcolonial security (McCorkell and Gillard, 2010; Meyer and Thein, 2014;

Mikhaylova, Babich, and Smirnova, 2017). Many often-conflicting ways of thinking exist in IR theory, including constructivism, institutionalism, Marxism, neo-Gramscianism, and others (Morgan and Schwebach, 1997; Mueller and Mueller, 1999). However, two positivist schools of thought are most prevalent: realism and liberalism (Jiang, Chen, and Liu, 2010; Jing, Kaempfer, and Lowenberg, 2003; Kaempfer and Lowenberg, 1999). Early IRs scholarship in the interwar years focused on the need for the balance of power system to be replaced with a system of collective security (Strack and Strack, 1978; Takian, Raoofi, and Kazempour-Ardebili, 2020; Taylor, 2012). These thinkers were later described as "Idealists" (Bradley and Galbraith, 2016; Defourny, 2013; Huang, Xu, and Lu, 2011). The leading critique of this school of thinking was the "realist" analysis offered by Carr (Nossal, 1989; Ogden, 2008).

Nevertheless, a more recent study by David Long and Brian Schmidt in 2005, offers a revisionist account of the origins of the field of IRs (Nossal, 1989; Ogden, 2008). They claim that the history of the field can be traced back to late 19th Century imperialism and internationalism (Bradley and Galbraith, 2016; Defourny, 2013; Huang, Xu, and Lu, 2011). The fact that the history of the field is presented by "great debates," such as the realist-idealist debate, does not correspond with the historical evidence found in earlier works (Strack and Strack, 1978; Takian, Raoofi, and Kazempour-Ardebili, 2020; Taylor, 2012). Their revisionist account claims that, up until 1918, IRs already existed in the form of colonial administration, race science, and race development (Jiang, Chen, and Liu, 2010; Jing, Kaempfer, and Lowenberg, 2003; Kaempfer and Lowenberg, 1999). A clear distinction is made between explanatory and constitutive approaches when classifying IRs theories (Morgan and Schwebach, 1997; Mueller and Mueller, 1999).

Realism or political realism has been the dominant theory of IRs since the conception of the discipline (McCorkell and Gillard, 2010; Meyer and Thein, 2014; Mikhaylova, Babich, and Smirnova, 2017). The theory claims to rely upon an ancient tradition of thought which includes writers such as Thucydides, Machiavelli, and Hobbes (Solingen, 2012; Stephanides et al., 2002; Strack and Strack, 1978). Early realism can be characterized as a reaction against interwar idealist thinking (Afesorgbor, 2019; Alam, 2008; Al-Jawaheri, 2008). The outbreak of World War II was seen by realists as evidence of the deficiencies of idealist thinking (Defourny, 2013; Denzin, 2008; Devarajan and Mottaghi, 2015; Dobler, 2008). There are various strands of modern-day realist thinking (Attia, Grauvogel, and von Soest, 2020; Bacchiega and Borzaga, 2003; Baldwin and Pape, 1998). However, the main tenets of the theory have been identified as statism, survival, and self-help (Drezner, 2011, 2015; Drezner and Drezner, 1999; Drury and Peksen, 2014; Dunn and Shaw, 2001; Dunoff, Ratner, and Wippman, 2015).

Realists believe that nation states are the main actors in international politics (Doxey, 1972, 1980, 1983, 1987; Drezner, 2000, 2011, 2015; Drezner and Drezner, 1999; Drury and Peksen, 2014). As such it is a state-centric theory of IRs (Tridimas and Guiterrex-Fons, 2008). This contrasts with liberal IRs theories which accommodate roles for non-state actors and international institutions (Richard and Raimo, 1999; Ross, 1989; Rothwell and Stephens, 2016; Ryngaert, 2015). This difference is sometimes expressed by describing a realist world view as one which sees nation-states as billiard balls; liberals would consider relationships between states to be more of a cobweb (De Visscher, 2015; Ross, 1989; Von Glahn and Taulbee, 2015). Realists believe that the international system is governed by anarchy, meaning that there is no central authority (Blyton, 2004; Bolander, 2011; Borszik, 2014, 2016; Bosco, 2012; Bradley and Galbraith, 2016; Brzoska, 2015; Buck, Gallant, and Nossal, 1998). Therefore, international politics is a struggle for power between self-interested states (Seyfi and Hall, 2019; Solingen, 2012; Stephanides et al., 2002). Realists believe that no other states can be relied upon to help guarantee the state's survival (Bacchiega and Borzaga, 2003; Chan, 2000; Drezner, 2000; Grauvogel, Licht, and von Soest, 2017).

Realism makes several key assumptions. It assumes that nation-states are unitary, geographically based actors in an anarchic international system with no authority above capable of regulating interactions between states as no true authoritative world government exists (Ozawa and Castello, 2001; Pape, 1997, 1998; Ponte, 2004; Reilly, 2012). Secondly, it assumes that sovereign states, rather than intergovernmental organizations, non-governmental organizations (NGOs), or multinational corporations, are the primary actors in international affairs (Bacchiega and Borzaga, 2003; Baldwin and Pape, 1998; Barber, 1979). Thus, states, as the highest order, are in competition with one another (Escribà-Folch, 2010, 2012; Escribà-Folch and Wright, 2010; Farzanegan, 2013; Farzanegan and Hayo, 2019; Franzway and Fonow, 2011). As such, a state acts as a rational autonomous actor in pursuit of its own self-interest with a primary goal to maintain and ensure its own security; and thus, its sovereignty and survival (Bosco, 2012; David and Holliday, 2012; Farzanegan and Hayo, 2019; Klotz, 1995; Pape, 1998; Taylor, 2012). Realism holds that in pursuit of their interests, states will attempt to amass resources and that relations between states are determined by their relative levels of power (Jiang, Chen, and Liu, 2010; Jing, Kaempfer, and Lowenberg, 2003). That level of power is in turn determined by the state's military, economic, and political capabilities (Ryngaert, 2015; Saeidnia and Abdollahi, 2013).

Some realists, known as human nature realists or classical realists, believe that states are inherently aggressive (Kendall, 2000; Kiriya, 2017; Kirshner, 1997; Klotz, 1995; Koskenniemi, 2014; Kunz, 1960; Laub, 2015; Lee, 2018). Furthermore, that territorial expansion is constrained only by opposing powers (Doxey, 1987; Drezner, 2000, 2011, 2015; Drezner and Drezner, 1999; Drury and Peksen, 2014; Dunn and Shaw, 2001). Others (known as offensive or defensive realists) believe that states are obsessed with the security and continuation of the state's existence (Kirshner, 1997; Klotz, 1995; Koskenniemi, 2014; Kunz, 1960; Laub, 2015; Lee, 2018). The defensive view can lead to a security dilemma, where increasing one's own security can bring along greater instability as the opponents builds up their own arms (Drezner and Drezner, 1999; Drury and Peksen, 2014; Dunn and Shaw, 2001; Dunoff, Ratner, and Wippman, 2015; Eliat and Einav, 2004; Eriksson, 2016). This has the effect of making security a zero-sum game where only relative gains can be made (Daviron and Ponte, 2007; Franzway and Fonow, 2011; Koskenniemi, 2014; Thaver and Ekanayake, 2010).

Neorealism or structural realism is a development of realism advanced by Kenneth Waltz in "*Theory of International Politics*" (Levy, 1999; Leyton-Brown, 2017; Li and Saghaian, 2013; Lutz and Lux, 1995; Mahmud, 2001). It is, however, only one strand of neorealism (Nossal, 1989; Ogden, 2008). Joseph Grieco has combined neo-realist thinking with more traditional realists (Kaempfer and Lowenberg, 1999; Kaempfer and Lowenberg, 2000; Kaempfer, Lowenberg, and Mertens, 2004). This strand of theory is sometimes called "modern realism" (Igami, 2015; Ivanov, Sypchenko, and Webster, 2017; James, 2013). Waltz's neorealism contends that the effect of structure must be considered in explaining state behavior (Gui, 1991; Hafner-Burton and Montgomery, 2008; Hanushek and Woessmann, 2010). It shapes all foreign policy choices of states in the international arena (Takian, Raoofi, and Kazempour-Ardebili, 2020; Taylor, 2012; Thaver and Ekanayake, 2010). For instance, any disagreement between states derives from lack of a common power (central authority) to enforce rules and maintain them constantly (Biersteker, Eckert, and Tourinho, 2016; Cleveland, 2001; Eriksson, 2016; Hiraide and Chakraborty, 2012).

Thus, there is constant anarchy in the international system that makes it necessary for states the obtainment of strong weapons to guarantee their survival (Igami, 2015; Ivanov, Sypchenko, and Webster, 2017; James, 2013). Additionally, in an anarchic system, states with greater power tend to increase its influence further (Matsushita et al., 2015; Nossal, 1989; Reilly, 2012; Strack and Strack, 1978). According to neo-realists, structure is considered an extremely important element in IR and defined twofold (Mahmud, 2001; Mikhaylova, Babich, and Smirnova, 2017; Ponte, 2004). First, it is conceptualized as the ordering principle of the international system which is anarchy (Solingen, 2012; Stephanides et al., 2002; Strack and Strack, 1978). Secondly, it can be conceptualized as the distribution of capabilities across units (Rothwell and Stephens, 2016; Ryngaert, 2015; Saeidnia and Abdollahi, 2013). Waltz also challenges traditional realism's emphasis on traditional military power, instead characterizing power in terms of the combined capabilities of the state (Crawford and Klotz, 1999; Crook, 2013; David and Holliday, 2012; Daviron and Ponte, 2007; De Visscher, 2015; De Vos, 2010). This chapter will close with a review of the relationship between liberalism and international sanctions.

4.5. LIBERALISM AND INTERNATIONAL SANCTIONS

Research has shown that seemingly Western "liberal" countries are the ones most likely to instigate and sustain international sanctions (Taylor, 2012; Thaver and Ekanayake, 2010; Tridimas and Guiterrex-Fons, 2008). Many of them justify their actions based on democratization, even if that means overthrowing legitimate regimes within their target areas of influence (Kirshner, 1997; Klotz, 1995; Koskenniemi, 2014; Kunz, 1960; Laub, 2015; Lee, 2018). The application of the democratization principle can also be uneven since these powers tend to ignore human rights abuses by their allies while highlighting any failings in their enemies (Lutz and Lux, 1995; Mahmud, 2001; Matsushita et al., 2015; McCorkell and Gillard, 2010; Meyer and Thein, 2014). That is why for example, Saudi Arabia and Iran are treated very differently in the international sanctions business yet they both have seemingly appalling human rights abuse records (Doxey, 1980, 1983, 1987; Drezner, 2000, 2011, 2015; Drezner and Drezner, 1999; Drury and Peksen, 2014). These contradictions between liberal rhetoric and aggressive or oppressive action have led many to reconsider the ethics of international sanctions (Levy, 1999; Leyton-Brown, 2017; Li and Saghaian, 2013). Sometimes international crises present dilemmas for liberal democracies, a case in point being the response to the Russian annexation of Crimea (see Figure 4.5 for examples of policy responses).

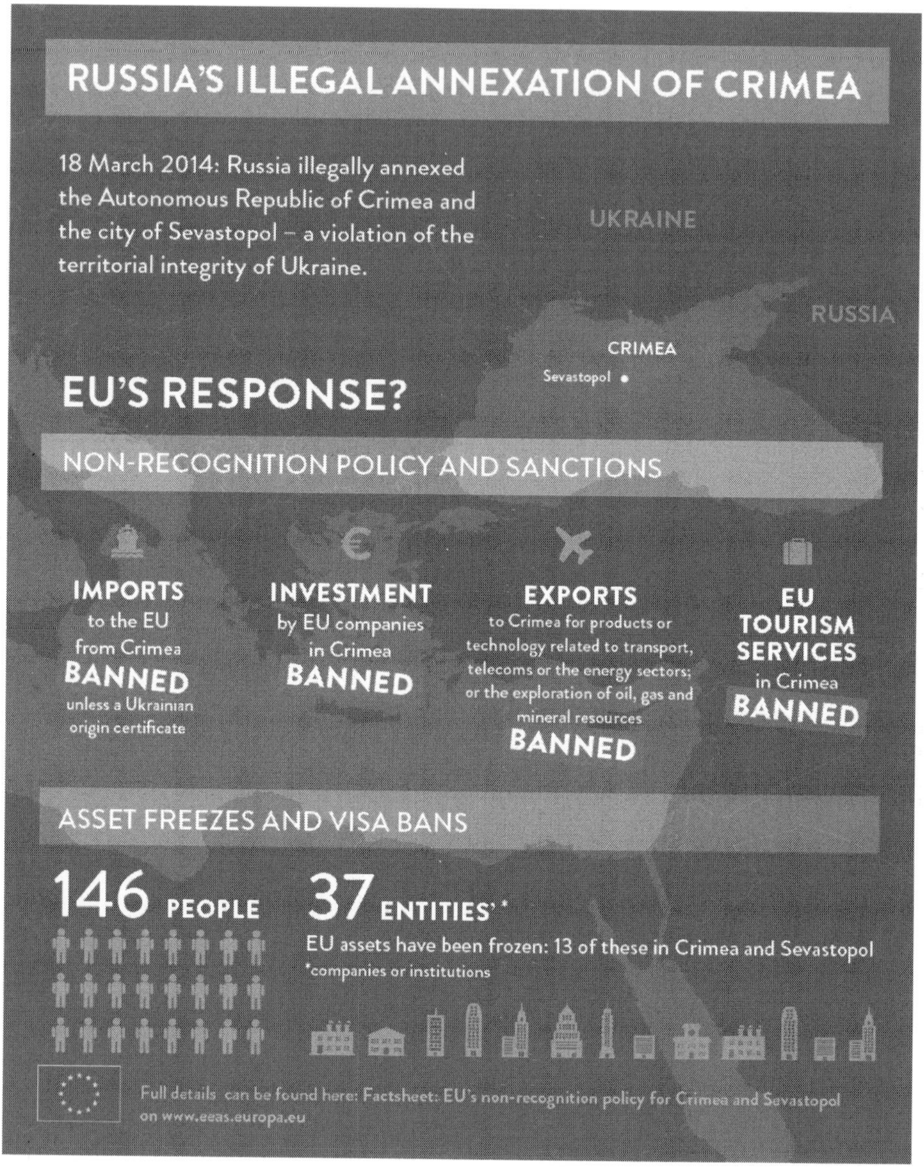

Figure 4.5. Use of international sanctions after the Russian annexation of Ukraine.

Source: European Union.

There are several liberal theories of internationalism or foreign policy. These are invariably used to describe and predict the behavior of liberal democracies. Such theories tend to focus on the determinants and preventative factors in terms of justifying the systematic international sanctions against less liberal states (Denzin, 2008; Devarajan and Mottaghi, 2015; Dobler, 2008; Doxey, 1972). In other words, these theories provide an organized rationale for the international conduct of foreign policy in the context of a sanctions regime. Prior to these liberal IRs theory, there existed the notion of "idealism" which imbued sanctions with a sense of noble purpose for the greater good of the international community. In some sense, idealism (or utopianism) was critiqued by the "realists," for failing to fully account for the selfish and sometimes destructive interests of nations that impose sanctions on others. One of the notable examples of these critics is Carr who advanced the notion that international sanctions mainly serve the interests of powerful nations that use their power to impose stifling conditions on their adversaries (Pape, 1997, 1998; Ponte, 2004; Reilly, 2012; Reisman and Stevick, 1998). Those taking an IRs slant, take to reconstruct idealism (or "Wilsonianism" from Woodrow Wilson). This is a school of thought which advocates that states should make their internal political philosophy the goal of foreign policy. In other words, there is no homogenous international interest, but rather the expression of state interests through their actions on the global stage (Morgan and Schwebach, 1997; Mueller and Mueller, 1999). For example, an idealist might believe that ending poverty at home should be coupled with tackling poverty abroad. Such an approach is too expensive because it involves dealing with the root of the problem rather than merely protecting one's borders and citizens (Ogden, 2008; Ozawa and Castello, 2001; Pape, 1997). Wilson's idealism predated and gave birth to liberal IRs theory. More precisely, this arose among the "institution-builders" who emerged following World War I (Tridimas and Guiterrex-Fons, 2008;).

According to liberalism, the preferences of the state take precedence over its capabilities when determining the behavior of that state (Afesorgbor, 2019; Brzoska, 2015; Denzin, 2008; Frick, Humphreys, and Scheel, 2015; Huebner, 2009; Kunz, 1960). In that sense, a state might spend more than it can afford to achieve its strategic objectives on the global stage. This is in stark contrast to realism in as far as the state becomes a unitary actor and tends to restrict its resources to the furtherment of internalized ambitions. The implication is that liberalism allows for plurality in state actions, a key foundational principle of international bodies such as the UN (Ross, 1989; Rothwell and Stephens, 2016; Ryngaert, 2015; Saeidnia and Abdollahi, 2013). It follows on from the assertions above that the preferences of the actors will vary from state to state. This is the diversity of interests and actions that makes international law so complex. The action that is taken by states will depend on a range of complex factors including the prevailing culture, the economic system, and the type of government which dominates that state (Crawford and Klotz, 1999; Crook, 2013; David and Holliday, 2012; Daviron and Ponte, 2007; De Visscher, 2015). For example, dictatorships may have an entirely different approach to international law when compared to liberal democracies (Pape, 1997, 1998; Ponte, 2004; Reilly, 2012; Reisman and Stevick, 1998).

According to liberalism, the interaction between states is not limited to the political or security, which is also known as "high politics." Instead, it incorporates element of economic or cultural interests, which are known as "low politics." States practice high and low politics depending on the context within which they are furthering their interests. This holds true regardless of whether or not, the influence is exercised through commercial firms, organizations or individuals (Dunoff, Ratner, and Wippman, 2015; Eliat and Einav, 2004; Eriksson, 2016; Escribà-Folch, 2010, 2012; Escribà-Folch and Wright, 2010; Farzanegan, 2013). It is on that basis, that soft power is used to make changes in circumstances where military force might be too expensive or even counterproductive (Crawford and Klotz, 1999; Crook, 2013; David and Holliday, 2012; Daviron and Ponte, 2007; De Visscher, 2015). Many critics of Multinational Corporations have argued that they are conduit for the performance of foreign policy through their unique commercial resources (Levy, 1999; Leyton-Brown, 2017; Li and Saghaian, 2013).

Such an assertion is an alternative to an anarchic international system under which nations are called upon to engage in aggressive and often counterproductive skirmishes against each other. To that extent, there are many opportunities for cooperation rather than creating instability on the global stage for the purpose of furthering parochial interests. In one sense, this means that there are broader notions of power and its deployment, beyond the mercantilist interest of individual sovereign states (Caron, 1989; Genzberger et al., 1994). An example of this cooperation is the notion of cultural capital which is a real commodity and source of power for some of the most industrialized nations on earth (Chiquiar, 2008; Dunn and Shaw, 2001; Hanushek and Woessmann, 2010; Kaempfer and Lowenberg, 1999). For instance, the influence of films may lead to the popularity of the country's culture and creating a market for its exports worldwide. The USA in particular has used its entertainment industry in order to drive forward the narrative of the country as being a beacon of freedom, prosperity, power, and inclusion. Another assumption is that absolute gains can be made through co-operation and interdependence (Mahmud, 2001; Mikhaylova, Babich, and Smirnova, 2017; Ponte, 2004). Nations no longer must win or lose an argument, but instead can gain insight and mutual advantages through a negotiated settlement. This then becomes a precursor for peace and is often used to bring together factions that initially appear to be diametrically opposed to each other.

According to the democratic peace theory, it is rare that liberal democracies engage in conflict against each other (Dunoff, Ratner, and Wippman, 2015; Eliat and Einav, 2004; Eriksson, 2016; Escribà-Folch, 2010, 2012; Escribà-Folch and Wright, 2010; Farzanegan, 2013). This has been used as justification for imposing the philosophy on less liberal states. Apparently liberal states are less likely to upset the global peace. Even where there is conflict, it never rises to the extent of an outright war. One of the reasons for this are the multiple channels for dialog and cooperation that can resolve the problems. Indeed, there have been cases where some minor sanctions have been used to avoid war or more serious conflict among liberal democracies (Devarajan and Mottaghi, 2015; Dobler, 2008; Doxey, 1972, 1983). This is seen as contradicting realist theories. In fact, such an empirical claim has been contested extensively in political science (Von Glahn and Taulbee, 2015).

Numerous explanations have been proposed for the democratic peace (Huebner, 2009; Hultman and Peksen, 2017; Hurd, 2017; Igami, 2015; Ivanov, Sypchenko, and Webster, 2017). It has also been argued that democracies conduct diplomacy in general very differently from non-democracies (Meyer and Thein, 2014; Mikhaylova, Babich, and Smirnova, 2017). Realists and neo-realists disagree with liberals over the theory, often citing structural reasons for the peace, as opposed to the state's government (Takian, Raoofi, and Kazempour-Ardebili, 2020; Taylor, 2012; Thaver and Ekanayake, 2010). Sebastian Rosato, a critic of democratic peace theory, points to America's behavior towards left-leaning democracies in Latin America during the Cold War to challenge democratic peace (James, 2013; Jiang, Chen, and Liu, 2010; Jing, Kaempfer, and Lowenberg, 2003). One argument is that economic interdependence makes war between trading partners less likely. In contrast realists claim that economic interdependence increases rather than decreases the likelihood of conflict (Genzberger et al., 1994; Gharehgozli, 2017; Goodhart, 2016; Grauvogel and Von Soest, 2014).

Neoliberalism, liberal institutionalism, or neo-liberal institutionalism is an advancement of liberal thinking (Gui, 1991; Hafner-Burton and

Montgomery, 2008; Hanushek and Woessmann, 2010; Haugh and Kitson, 2007). It argues that international institutions can allow nations to successfully cooperate in the international system (Richard and Raimo, 1999; Ross, 1989; Rothwell and Stephens, 2016; Ryngaert, 2015). This is based on an acknowledgment of the complex interdependence that exists between and among nations (Franzway and Fonow, 2011; Frick, Humphreys, and Scheel, 2015; Fridell, 2014; Fu et al., 2020). This presupposes that international politics creates multiple channels that connect societies exceeding the conventional Westphalian system of states (Ogden, 2008; Ozawa and Castello, 2001; Pape, 1997). This manifests itself in many forms ranging from informal governmental ties to multinational corporations and organizations (Koskenniemi, 2014; Kunz, 1960; Laub, 2015; Lee, 2018; Levy, 1999; Leyton-Brown, 2017). It is through these channels that political exchange occurs, not through the limited interstate channel as championed by realists (Caron, 1989; Genzberger et al., 1994).

This way of thinking rejects the notion of a hierarchy among issues, meaning that not only is the martial arm of foreign policy not the supreme tool by which to carry out a state's agenda (Ozawa and Castello, 2001; Pape, 1997, 1998). However, there are a multitude of different agendas that come to the forefront (Igami, 2015; Ivanov, Sypchenko, and Webster, 2017; James, 2013). The line between domestic and foreign policy becomes blurred in this case, as realistically there is no clear agenda in interstate relations (Bolander, 2011; Cranmer, Heinrich, and Desmarais, 2014; Escribà-Folch, 2012; Hovdenak, 2009; Kiriya, 2017). Moreover, the use of military force is not exercised when complex interdependence prevails (Jing, Kaempfer, and Lowenberg, 2003; Kaempfer and Lowenberg, 1999, 2000). The idea is developed that between countries in which a complex interdependence exists, the role of the military in resolving disputes is negated (Caruso, 2003; Chachavalpongpun, 2014; Chan, 2000; Chan and Drury, 2000; Chen et al., 2019; Cheraghali, 2013).

One version of post-liberal theory argues that within the modern, globalized world, states in fact are driven to cooperate in order to ensure security and sovereign interests (Lee, 2018; Levy, 1999; Leyton-Brown, 2017; Li and Saghaian, 2013). The departure from classical liberal theory is most notably felt in the re-interpretation of the concepts of sovereignty and autonomy (Frick, Humphreys, and Scheel, 2015; Fridell, 2014; Fu et al., 2020; Genzberger et al., 1994; Gharehgozli, 2017). Autonomy becomes a problematic concept in shifting away from a notion of freedom, self-determination, and agency to a heavily responsible and duty laden concept

(Eliat and Einav, 2004; Eriksson, 2016; Escribà-Folch, 2010, 2012; Escribà-Folch and Wright, 2010; Farzanegan, 2013; Farzanegan and Hayo, 2019). Importantly, autonomy is linked to a capacity for good governance. Similarly, sovereignty also experiences a shift from a right to a duty (Farzanegan and Hayo, 2019; Franzway and Fonow, 2011; Frick, Humphreys, and Scheel, 2015; Fridell, 2014). In the global economy, International organizations hold sovereign states to account, leading to a situation where sovereignty is co-produced among "sovereign" states (Wallensteen and Staibano, 2005).

The concept of sovereignty becomes a variable capacity of good governance and can no longer be accepted as an absolute right (Kaempfer and Lowenberg, 2000; Kaempfer, Lowenberg, and Mertens, 2004; Kendall, 2000). One possible way to interpret this theory, is the idea that to maintain global stability and security and solve the problem of the anarchic world system in IRs, no overarching, global, sovereign authority is created (Ponte, 2004; Reilly, 2012; Reisman and Stevick, 1998; Richard and Raimo, 1999). Instead, states collectively abandon some rights for full autonomy and sovereignty (Rothwell and Stephens, 2016; Solingen, 2012; Stephanides et al., 2002). Another version of post-liberalism, drawing on work in political philosophy after the end of the Cold War, as well as on democratic transitions in Latin America, argues that social forces from below are essential in understanding the nature of the state and the international system (Cheraghali, 2013; Drury and Peksen, 2014; Hafner-Burton and Montgomery, 2008). Whereas these theories partially explain the actions of liberal democracies in terms of international sanctions, they are not entirely satisfactory justifications for the actual imposition of some of these pernicious measures (Cranmer, Heinrich, and Desmarais, 2014; Crawford and Klotz, 1999; Crook, 2013; David and Holliday, 2012; Daviron and Ponte, 2007). Instead, they tend to expose the self-interest and latent hypocrisy that is at the heart of modern IRs (Biersteker, Eckert, and Tourinho, 2016; Blyton, 2004; Bolander, 2011).

CHAPTER 4 SUMMARY

This chapter has attempted to rationale international relations (IRs) from a number of perspectives. Some of them include political similarity, economic self-interest, realist views of international politics, deterrence, and liberalism. All these explanations are broadly rooted in the theory of IRs. However, this chapter has also exposed some of the inconsistencies that are at the heart of sanctions regimes. The next chapter will summarize the constructivist view of IRs generally, and sanctions.

Chapter 5

Constructivist Perspective on International Sanctions

CONTENTS

The constructivist perspective has been generally critical of reductivist international politics. Instead, it argues that hegemony is a socially constructed modality that is sustained through culture and human relations. This chapter will reference other critiques such as Marxism and Humanism. In doing so, this chapter will hope to add to the reader's knowledge of the philosophy of war and its relevance to international sanctions.

5.1. THE CONSTRUCTIVIST CRITIQUE OF HEGEMONY

The standing of constructivism as an international relations (IRs) theory increased after the fall of the Berlin wall and Communism in Eastern Europe, since these events had not been predicted by the existing mainstream theories (Kaempfer and Lowenberg, 2000; Kaempfer, Lowenberg, and Mertens, 2004; Kendall, 2000). Constructivism or social constructivism has been described as a challenge to the dominance of neo-liberal and neo-realist IRs theories (Ross, 1989; Rothwell and Stephens, 2016; Ryngaert, 2015; Saeidnia and Abdollahi, 2013).

Figure 5.1. Use of military bases for USA global hegemony.

Source: Peak Oil News.

Hence constructivist IRs theories are concerned with how ideas define international structure, how this structure defines the interests and identities of states and how states and non-state actors reproduce this structure (Jiang, Chen, and Liu, 2010; Jing, Kaempfer, and Lowenberg, 2003; Kaempfer and

Lowenberg, 1999). For example, the construction of USA bases near Russia (see Figure 5.1) would be seen as a constructed solution to a constructed problematizing of Russian imperial ambitions (Ryngaert, 2015; Saeidnia and Abdollahi, 2013). The key element of constructivism is the belief that international politics is shaped by persuasive ideas, collective values, culture, and social identities (Hultman and Peksen, 2017; Hurd, 2017; Igami, 2015; Ivanov, Sypchenko, and Webster, 2017; James, 2013). Constructivism argues that international reality is socially constructed by cognitive structures which give meaning to the material world (Bolander, 2011; Borszik, 2014, 2016; Bosco, 2012; Bradley and Galbraith, 2016; Brzoska, 2015; Buck, Gallant, and Nossal, 1998). The theory emerged from debates concerning the scientific method of IRs theories and theory's role in the production of international power (Denzin, 2008; Devarajan and Mottaghi, 2015; Dobler, 2008; Doxey, 1972). Emanuel Adler states that constructivism occupies a middle ground between rationalist and interpretative theories of IRs (Escribà-Folch and Wright, 2010; Farzanegan, 2013; Farzanegan and Hayo, 2019; Franzway and Fonow, 2011).

Constructivist theory criticizes the static assumptions of traditional IRs theory and emphasizes that IRs is a social construction (Carter, 1987; Caruso, 2003; Chachavalpongpun, 2014; Chan, 2000; Chan and Drury, 2000; Chen et al., 2019). Constructivism is a theory critical of the ontological basis of rationalist theories of IRs (Nossal, 1989; Ogden, 2008; Ozawa and Castello, 2001). Whereas realism deals mainly with security and material power, and liberalism looks primarily at economic interdependence and domestic-level factors; constructivism most concerns itself with the role of ideas in shaping the international system (Levy, 1999; Leyton-Brown, 2017; Li and Saghaian, 2013; Lutz and Lux, 1995; Mahmud, 2001). In any case, it is possible there is some overlap between constructivism and realism or liberalism. However, they remain separate schools of thought (Hultman and Peksen, 2017; Hurd, 2017; Igami, 2015; Ivanov, Sypchenko, and Webster, 2017; James, 2013).

By "ideas" constructivists refer to the goals, threats, fears, identities, and other elements of perceived reality that influence states and non-state actors within the international system (Escribà-Folch, 2010, 2012; Escribà-Folch and Wright, 2010; Farzanegan, 2013; Farzanegan and Hayo, 2019). Constructivists believe that these ideational factors can often have far-reaching effects, and that they can trump materialistic power concerns (Wallensteen and Staibano, 2005). In that sense, the constructivists perceive sanctions as a socially defined punishment whose effectiveness depends on mutually accepted perceptions of its consequences (Fridell, 2014; Fu et al.,

2020; Genzberger et al., 1994; Gharehgozli, 2017; Goodhart, 2016). For example, Iran has effectively used its "pariah state" status on the global stage to harness nationalistic fervor at home (Matsushita et al., 2015; McCorkell and Gillard, 2010; Meyer and Thein, 2014; Mikhaylova, Babich, and Smirnova, 2017). That means that in some ways, the sanctions actually help to entrench the very regime that they were meant to overturn (Barber, 1979; Bederman and Keitner, 2016). The next section focuses on the Marxist critique.

5.2. MARXIST CRITIQUE OF INTERNATIONAL RELATIONS (IRS)

Marxist and Neo-Marxist IRs theories are structuralist paradigms which reject the realist or liberal view of state conflict or cooperation (Chan, 2000; Chan and Drury, 2000; Chen et al., 2019; Cheraghali, 2013; Chiquiar, 2008; Choi and Luo, 2013; Clegg and Palmer, 1996). They instead focus on the economic and material aspects (Blyton, 2004; Cortright et al., 2000; Escribà-Folch, 2010; Ho-Chuan, Yi-Chen, and Chih-Chuan, 2012; Kendall, 2000). Marxist approaches argue the position of historical materialism and assume that the economic concerns transcend others (Laub, 2015; Lee, 2018; Levy, 1999; Leyton-Brown, 2017; Li and Saghaian, 2013). This has the effect of allowing for the elevation of class as the focus of study (Carter, 1987; Doxey, 1972; Gharehgozli, 2017; Lee, 2018; Ozawa and Castello, 2001).

Marxists view the international system as an integrated capitalist system in pursuit of capital accumulation (Franzway and Fonow, 2011; Frick, Humphreys, and Scheel, 2015; Fridell, 2014). A sub-discipline of Marxist IR is Critical Security Studies (Kendall, 2000; Kiriya, 2017; Kirshner, 1997; Klotz, 1995; Koskenniemi, 2014; Kunz, 1960). Gramscian approaches rely on the ideas of Italian Antonio Gramsci whose writings concerned the hegemony that capitalism holds as an ideology (Drury and Peksen, 2014; Dunn and Shaw, 2001; Dunoff, Ratner, and Wippman, 2015; Eliat and Einav, 2004; Eriksson, 2016). Marxist approaches have also inspired Critical Theorists such as Robert W. Cox, who argues that theory is always for someone and for some purpose (Doxey, 1972, 1980, 1983, 1987; Drezner, 2000, 2011, 2015; Drezner and Drezner, 1999). As Figure 5.2, the world remains an undemocratic place despite all the agencies that are deployed towards democratization (Buck, Gallant, and Nossal, 1998; Caron, 1989; Carter, 1987; Caruso, 2003; Chachavalpongpun, 2014).

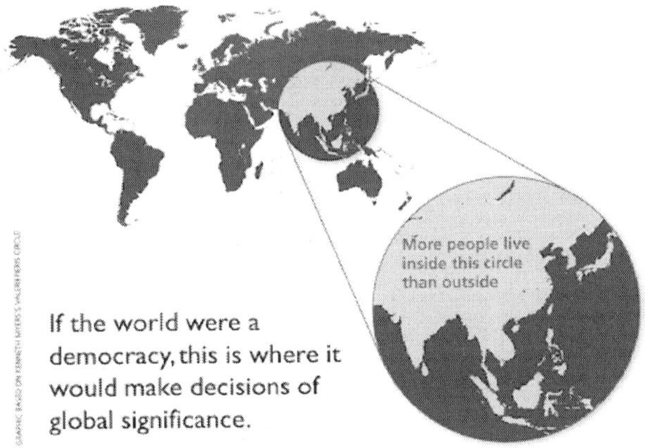

Figure 5.2. The world as an undemocratic place.

Source: Danny Quah.

One notable Marxist approach to IRs theory is Immanuel Wallerstein's World-system theory which can be traced back to the ideas expressed by Lenin in "*Imperialism: The Highest Stage of Capitalism*" (Attia, Grauvogel, and von Soest, 2020; Chachavalpongpun, 2014; Doxey, 1980; Goodhart, 2016; Ivanov, Sypchenko, and Webster, 2017). World-system theory argues that globalized capitalism has created a core of modern industrialized countries which exploit a periphery of exploited "Third World" countries (Solingen, 2012; Stephanides et al., 2002; Strack and Strack, 1978; Takian, Raoofi, and Kazempour-Ardebili, 2020). These ideas were developed by the Latin American Dependency School (Huebner, 2009; Hultman and Peksen, 2017; Hurd, 2017; Igami, 2015; Ivanov, Sypchenko, and Webster, 2017).

"Neo-Marxist" or "New Marxist" approaches have returned to the writings of Karl Marx for their inspiration (Drezner and Drezner, 1999; Drury and Peksen, 2014; Dunn and Shaw, 2001; Dunoff, Ratner, and Wippman, 2015; Eliat and Einav, 2004; Eriksson, 2016). Key "New Marxists" include Justin Rosenberg and Benno Teschke (Bederman and Keitner, 2016; Chen et al., 2019; Drezner and Drezner, 1999; Gui, 1991; Jing, Kaempfer, and Lowenberg, 2003). Marxist approaches have enjoyed a renaissance since the collapse of communism in Eastern Europe (McCorkell and Gillard, 2010; Ogden, 2008; Richard and Raimo, 1999).

In that sense, international sanctions are a tool and expression of hegemony that is exercised by largely Western liberal democracies that routinely target developing countries with a view to further exploit them in the postcolonial settlement (Borszik, 2014; Crawford and Klotz, 1999; Escribà-Folch and Wright, 2010; Li and Saghaian, 2013). That means that sanctions are not about the law or even justice, but rather the exploitation of those who are on the peripheral of the developed nations (Farzanegan, 2013; Farzanegan and Hayo, 2019; Franzway and Fonow, 2011; Frick, Humphreys, and Scheel, 2015). Hence, one explanation for the sanctions against Iran and Iraq is the search for oil resources which the existing regimes are not willing to allow to be siphoned off by the Western powers (Hanushek and Woessmann, 2010; Haugh and Kitson, 2007; Hinds, 1997; Hiraide and Chakraborty, 2012; Ho-Chuan, Yi-Chen, and Chih-Chuan, 2012). Criticisms of Marxists' approaches to IRs theory include the narrow focus on material and economic aspects of life (Jiang, Chen, and Liu, 2010; Jing, Kaempfer, and Lowenberg, 2003; Kaempfer and Lowenberg, 1999). The next section highlights some examples of alternative criticisms.

5.3. ALTERNATIVE CRITIQUES OF INTERNATIONAL SANCTIONS

There have been other critical perspectives the complement Marxism or even challenge it (Afesorgbor, 2019; Brzoska, 2015; Denzin, 2008; Frick, Humphreys, and Scheel, 2015; Huebner, 2009; Kunz, 1960). For example, Feminist approaches to IRs became popular in the early 1990s. Such approaches emphasize that women's experiences continue to be excluded from the study of IRs (McCorkell and Gillard, 2010; Ogden, 2008; Richard and Raimo, 1999). IRs Feminists who argue that gender relations are integral to IRs focus on the role of diplomatic wives and marital relationships that facilitate sex trafficking (Nossal, 1989; Ogden, 2008; Ozawa and Castello, 2001).

Early feminist IR approaches were part of the "Third Great Debate" between positivists and post-positivists (Mueller and Mueller, 1999; Nossal, 1989; Ogden, 2008). They argued against what they saw as the positivism and state-centrism of mainstream IRs (Ozawa and Castello, 2001; Pape, 1997, 1998; Ponte, 2004). Others argue that these approaches did not describe what a feminist perspective on world politics would look like (Crawford and Klotz, 1999; Crook, 2013; David and Holliday, 2012; Daviron and Ponte, 2007; De Visscher, 2015). It is nevertheless not clear how the feminist perspective might explain the postcolonial imperialist ambitions of nations like China (see Figure 5.3).

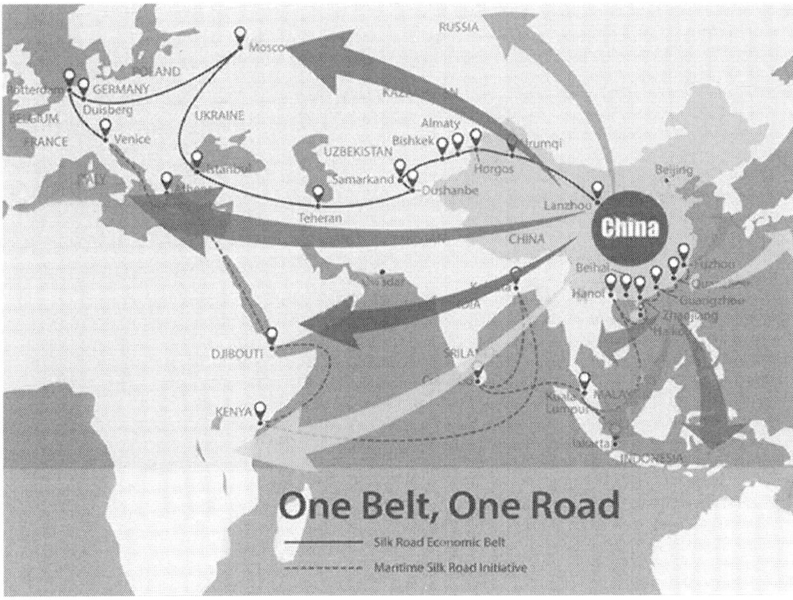

Figure 5.3. Chinese postcolonial imperial ambitions.

Source: China GNews.

The feminist IRs scholar Jacqui True differentiates between empirical feminism, analytical feminism, and normative feminism (Doxey, 1972, 1980, 1983, 1987; Drezner, 2000, 2011, 2015; Drezner and Drezner, 1999; Drury and Peksen, 2014). Empirical feminism sees women and gender relations as empirical aspects of IRs (Takian, Raoofi, and Kazempour-Ardebili, 2020; Taylor, 2012; Thaver and Ekanayake, 2010). It is argued that mainstream IRs emphasis on anarchy and statecraft mean that areas of study that make the reproduction of the state system possible are marginalized (Caruso, 2003; Chachavalpongpun, 2014; Chan, 2000; Chan and Drury, 2000; Chen et al., 2019; Cheraghali, 2013). Analytical feminism claims that the theoretical framework of IRs has a gender bias (Reilly, 2012; Reisman and Stevick, 1998; Richard and Raimo, 1999; Ross, 1989; Rothwell and Stephens, 2016). Here gender refers not to the "biological" differences between men and women but the social constructs of masculine and feminine identity (Kunz, 1960; Laub, 2015; Lee, 2018; Levy, 1999; Leyton-Brown, 2017; Li and Saghaian, 2013).

It is claimed that in mainstream IRs masculinity is associated with objectivity (Attia, Grauvogel, and von Soest, 2020; Chachavalpongpun,

2014; Doxey, 1980; Goodhart, 2016; Ivanov, Sypchenko, and Webster, 2017). Analytical feminists would see neo-realism's dislike of domestic explanations for explaining interstate behavior as an example of this bias (Hurd, 2017; Igami, 2015; Ivanov, Sypchenko, and Webster, 2017; James, 2013). Normative feminist sees theorizing as part of an agenda for change. Criticisms of feminist IRs theory include its portrayal of women in developing countries (Barber, 1979; Drezner, 2015; Jiang, Chen, and Liu, 2010; Leyton-Brown, 2017).

Feminist IRs is sometimes oversimplified into a women's issue or simply a need to 'add women and stir' (Saeidnia and Abdollahi, 2013; Seyfi and Hall, 2019). Hence, the hyper-masculinity used in IRs has a negative impact on all genders. It privileges only a certain kind of man, forcing all others to fit into the constraints of one vision of masculinity (Lutz and Lux, 1995; Meyer and Thein, 2014; Mueller and Mueller, 1999; Ryngaert, 2015). Some researchers also argue that this gendered lens requires a complete overhaul of traditional methods, rather than just adding women to the study (Reilly, 2012; Reisman and Stevick, 1998; Richard and Raimo, 1999; Ross, 1989; Rothwell and Stephens, 2016). Traditional methods do not meet the needs of men or women (Solingen, 2012; Stephanides et al., 2002; Strack and Strack, 1978; Takian, Raoofi, and Kazempour-Ardebili, 2020). They attempt to reduce our needs to security, failing to consider class, education level, gender, or experience (Lutz and Lux, 1995; Mahmud, 2001; Matsushita et al., 2015; McCorkell and Gillard, 2010). Hence, traditional studies of IRs are causing us to miss many factors for more than just women and children (Hafner-Burton and Montgomery, 2008; Hanushek and Woessmann, 2010; Haugh and Kitson, 2007; Hinds, 1997).

Other pockets of critique have subsequently emerged. For example, green theory in IRs is a sub-field of IRs theory which concerns international environmental cooperation (Solingen, 2012; Stephanides et al., 2002; Strack and Strack, 1978; Takian, Raoofi, and Kazempour-Ardebili, 2020). Several alternative approaches have been developed based on foundationalism, anti-foundationalism, positivism, behavioralism, structuralism, and post-structuralism (Chan, 2000; Chan and Drury, 2000; Chen et al., 2019; Cheraghali, 2013; Chiquiar, 2008; Choi and Luo, 2013; Clegg and Palmer, 1996). These theories, however, are not widely known and tend to be restricted to ontological and epistemological discussions in academia (Goodhart, 2016; Grauvogel and Von Soest, 2014; Grauvogel, Licht, and von Soest, 2017). Behavioralism in IRs theory is an approach to IRs theory which believes in the unity of science, the idea that the social sciences are not fundamentally different from the natural sciences (Matsushita et al., 2015; Nossal, 1989; Reilly, 2012; Strack and Strack, 1978). The "English School" of IRs theory, also known as International Society, Liberal Realism, Rationalism, or the British institutionalists, maintains that there is a 'society of states' at the international level, despite the condition of "anarchy," i.e., the lack of a ruler or world state (Li and Saghaian, 2013; Lutz and Lux, 1995; Mahmud, 2001; Matsushita et al., 2015). In the next section, we discuss the neuroscientific and queer view of IRs and its relevance to sanctions.

5.4. NEUROSCIENCE AND QUEER INTERNATIONAL RELATIONS (IRS)

In recent years, with significant advances in neuroscience and neuroimaging tools, IRs Theory has benefited from further multidisciplinary contributions (Bolander, 2011; Borszik, 2014, 2016; Bosco, 2012; Bradley and Galbraith, 2016; Brzoska, 2015; Buck, Gallant, and Nossal, 1998). Some have argued that neuroscience can significantly advance the IR debate as it brings forward new insights about human nature, which is at the center of political theory (Dunoff, Ratner, and Wippman, 2015; Eliat and Einav, 2004; Eriksson, 2016; Escribà-Folch, 2010, 2012; Escribà-Folch and Wright, 2010; Farzanegan, 2013). New tools to scan the human brain, and studies in neurochemistry allow us to grasp what drives divisiveness, conflict, and human nature in general (De Vos, 2010; Defourny, 2013; Denzin, 2008; Devarajan and Mottaghi, 2015; Dobler, 2008). The theory of human nature in Classical Realism, developed long before the advent of neuroscience, stressed that egoism and competition were central to human behavior, to politics and social relations (Seyfi and Hall, 2019; Solingen, 2012; Stephanides et al., 2002). Neuroscience has more sympathy with the humanistic view of nature than the economistic view (see Figure 5.4).

Human nature	Economistic view	Humanistic view
Foundation	Wants	Drives
Goal	Maximization	Balance
Operating modes	Fixed utility curves/ Opportunity sets	Routines, Learning, Practical wisdom
Focal point	Individual	Relational
Role of dignity	Absent	Critical
Role of morality	Amoral	Moral/Immoral
Aspiration	Wealth/Status/Power/Reputation	Well -being

Figure 5.4. Contrasting the economistic and humanistic view of human nature.

Source: Cambridge University Press.

Evidence from neuroscience, however, provides a more nuanced understanding of human nature which can be emotional, amoral, and egoistic (Levy, 1999; Leyton-Brown, 2017; Li and Saghaian, 2013). These three features can be summarized as follows: First, emotionality is more pervasive than rationality and central to decision-making (De Vos, 2010; Reisman and Stevick, 1998; Seyfi and Hall, 2019;). Second, we are born neither moral, nor immoral but amoral, and circumstances decide how our moral compass will develop (Solingen, 2012; Stephanides et al., 2002; Strack and Strack, 1978). Third, we are egoistic insofar as we seek to ensure our survival, a basic form of egoism (Drezner, 2015; Drezner and Drezner, 1999; Drury and Peksen, 2014; Dunn and Shaw, 2001; Dunoff, Ratner, and Wippman, 2015; Eliat and Einav, 2004). This neuro-philosophy of human nature can also be applied to states in ways that are like the Realist analogy between the character (and flaws) of man and the state in international politics (Biersteker, Eckert, and Tourinho, 2016; Cleveland, 2001; Eriksson, 2016; Hiraide and Chakraborty, 2012). Leading researchers in neuro-philosophy argue there are significant examples in history and contemporary politics that demonstrate states behave less rationality than IR dogma would have us believe (Doxey, 1972, 1980, 1983, 1987; Drezner, 2000, 2011). These aspects may include different strategic cultures, habits, identity politics influence state conduct, geopolitics, and diplomacy in profound ways (Haugh and Kitson, 2007; Hinds, 1997; Hiraide and Chakraborty, 2012; Ho-Chuan, Yi-Chen, and Chih-Chuan, 2012; Hovdenak, 2009).

Another humanist approach is that of Queer IRs scholarship which aims to broaden the scope and method of traditional IRs theory to include sexed and gendered approaches that are often excluded in the discipline at large (Genzberger et al., 1994; Gharehgozli, 2017; Goodhart, 2016; Grauvogel and Von Soest, 2014). While affiliated with feminist theory and gender studies, as well as post-structuralism, queer IR theory is not reducible to any other field of IR's scholarship (Nossal, 1989; Ogden, 2008; Ozawa and Castello, 2001). Queer IRs theory works to expose the many ways in which sexualities and gender affect international politics (Drezner, 2015; Drezner and Drezner, 1999; Drury and Peksen, 2014; Dunn and Shaw, 2001; Dunoff, Ratner, and Wippman, 2015; Eliat and Einav, 2004). This includes the ways in which queer subjects and practices are disciplined, normalized, or capitalized on by traditional sites of power (Chan, 2000; Chan and Drury, 2000; Chen et al., 2019; Cheraghali, 2013; Chiquiar, 2008; Choi and Luo, 2013). Queer theory is concerned with how queer identities have often been the focus of domestic and foreign policy in heteronormative states (Lutz and Lux, 1995; Mahmud, 2001; Matsushita et al., 2015). It also examines how the order-versus-anarchy dichotomy in traditional IRs theory socially manifests itself in normal-versus-perverse and hetero/homo-normative versus queer dichotomies (Saeidnia and Abdollahi, 2013; Seyfi and Hall, 2019). Queer IR theory takes sites of traditional IRs scholarship (war and peace, international political economy, and state and nation-building) as its subjects of study (Clegg and Palmer, 1996; Eliat and Einav, 2004; Hinds, 1997; Kaempfer, Lowenberg, and Mertens, 2004). It also expands its scope and methods beyond those traditionally utilized in Realist IR scholarship (Tridimas and Guiterrex-Fons, 2008). Ontologically, queer IR utilizes a different scope from traditional IR, as it aims to non-monolithically address the needs of various queer groups, including trans-, inter-, cross-, and pan-gendered, sexed, and sexualized bodies (Afesorgbor, 2019; Alam, 2008; Al-Jawaheri, 2008).

Epistemologically, queer IR explores alternative methodologies to those traditionally used in IR, as it emphasizes the sexual dimension of knowledge within IRs (Koskenniemi, 2014; Kunz, 1960; Laub, 2015; Lee, 2018; Levy, 1999; Leyton-Brown, 2017). Criticism for queer theory in general, and queer IRs, addresses the worry of the minimization or exclusion of certain groups (Farzanegan and Hayo, 2019; Franzway and Fonow, 2011; Frick, Humphreys, and Scheel, 2015; Fridell, 2014). While queer IR incorporates transgender individuals in its expanded scope; some argue its emphasis on sexuality fails to adequately capture transgender experiences (Gui, 1991; Hafner-Burton and Montgomery, 2008). That is why some researchers advocate for allying trans-theorizing and feminist theorizing in IR (Bacchiega and Borzaga, 2003; Baldwin and Pape, 1998; Barber, 1979; Bederman and Keitner, 2016). They suggest some possible improvements that trans-theorizing may offer for feminist IR theory, which include a more nuanced understanding of gender hierarchy through a pluralist approach to sex (Daviron and Ponte, 2007; De Visscher, 2015; De Vos, 2010; Defourny, 2013; Denzin, 2008; Devarajan and Mottaghi, 2015; Dobler). This would lead to a holistic view of gender that resists viewing gender entirely either as a social construction or as biologically essential (McCorkell and Gillard, 2010; Meyer and Thein, 2014; Mikhaylova, Babich, and Smirnova, 2017). Another potential benefit is an increased awareness of gender as involving power relations among different sexes and genders (Fridell, 2014; Fu et al., 2020; Genzberger et al., 1994; Gharehgozli, 2017; Goodhart, 2016). This chapter will close with a general view of the philosophy of war.

5.5. PHILOSOPHY OF WAR

The philosophy of war is the area of philosophy devoted to examining issues such as the causes of war, the relationship between war and human nature, and the ethics of war (Hovdenak, 2009; Huang, Xu, and Lu, 2011; Huebner, 2009; Hultman and Peksen, 2017; Hurd, 2017). Certain aspects of the philosophy of war overlap with the philosophy of history, political philosophy, IRs and the philosophy of law (Bederman and Keitner, 2016; Biersteker, Eckert, and Tourinho, 2016).

Perhaps the greatest and most influential work in the philosophy of war is On War by Carl von Clausewitz (Askari et al., 2003; Attia, Grauvogel, and von Soest, 2020; Bacchiega and Borzaga, 2003). It combines observations on strategy with questions about human nature and the purpose of war. Clausewitz especially examines the teleology of war in terms of whether war is a means to an end outside itself or whether it can be an end in itself (Leyton-Brown, 2017; Li and Saghaian, 2013; Lutz and Lux, 1995; Mahmud, 2001). He concludes that the latter cannot be so, and that war is "politics by different means"; that is to say that war must not exist only for its own sake (Tridimas and Guiterrex-Fons, 2008). It must serve some purpose for the state. Figure 5.5 highlights some key points in war history that have served to question or solidify the philosophy of war (Farzanegan, 2013; Farzanegan and Hayo, 2019; Franzway and Fonow, 2011; Frick, Humphreys, and Scheel, 2015).

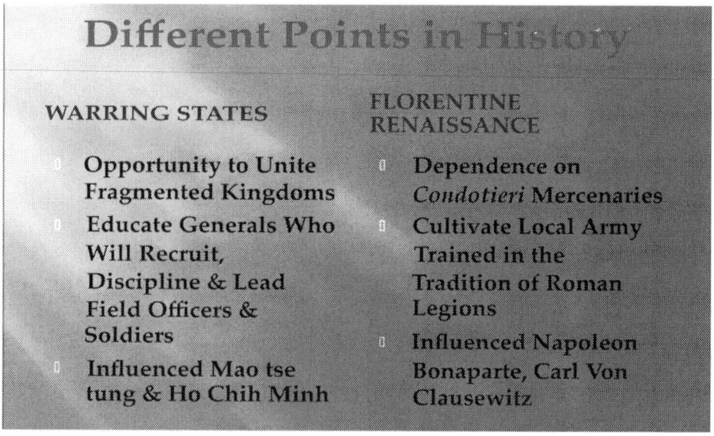

Figure 5.5. Historical key points in war.

Source: Slide Share.

Leo Tolstoy's novel "*War and Peace*" contains frequent philosophical digressions on the philosophy of war (Hafner-Burton and Montgomery, 2008; Hanushek and Woessmann, 2010; Haugh and Kitson, 2007; Hinds, 1997). For example, it references broader metaphysical speculations derived from Christianity and from Tolstoy's observations of the Napoleonic Wars (Blyton, 2004; Cortright et al., 2000; Escribà-Folch, 2010; Ho-Chuan, Yi-Chen, and Chih-Chuan, 2012; Kendall, 2000). This work was influential on later thought about war. Tolstoy's Christian-centered philosophy of war (especially his essays "*A Letter to a Hindu*" and "*The Kingdom of God is Within You*") was a direct influence on Gandhi's Hinduism-centered non-violent resistance philosophy (Biersteker, Eckert, and Tourinho, 2016; Blyton, 2004; Bolander, 2011). While Sun Tzu's The Art of War, focuses mostly on weaponry and strategy instead of philosophy, his observations are often broadened into a philosophy applied in situations extending well beyond war itself (Ozawa and Castello, 2001; Pape, 1997, 1998; Ponte, 2004; Reilly, 2012). Parts of Niccolò Machiavelli's masterpiece "*The Prince*" (as well as "*Discourses*") and parts of his own work titled "*The Art of War*" discuss some philosophical points relating to war, though neither book could be said to be a work in the philosophy of war (Von Glahn and Taulbee, 2015).

The philosophy of war is often treated as a subset of another branch of philosophy, such as political philosophy or the philosophy of law (Ponte, 2004; Reilly, 2012; Reisman and Stevick, 1998; Richard and Raimo, 1999; Ross, 1989). Hence, it would be difficult to define any clear-cut schools of thought in the same sense that (e.g., Existentialism or Objectivism) can be described as distinct movements (Doxey, 1987; Grauvogel and Von Soest, 2014; James, 2013). The Stanford Encyclopedia of Philosophy refers to Carl von Clausewitz as "the only (so-called) philosopher of war," implying that he is the only (major) philosophical writer who develops a philosophical system focusing exclusively on war (Borszik, 2016; Crook, 2013; Farzanegan, 2013; Kirshner, 1997; Pape, 1997; Takian, Raoofi, and Kazempour-Ardebili, 2020). However, discernible traditions of thought on war have developed over time, so that some writers have been able to distinguish broad categories (Doxey, 1980, 1987; Drezner, 2000, 2011, 2015; Drezner and Drezner, 1999; Drury and Peksen, 2014; Dunn and Shaw, 2001).

Just war theory, along with pacifism, holds that morals do apply to war (Thaver and Ekanayake, 2010; Tridimas and Guiterrex-Fons, 2008). However, unlike pacifism, according to just war theory, it is possible for a war to be morally justified (Askari et al., 2003; Attia, Grauvogel, and von Soest, 2020; Bacchiega and Borzaga, 2003). The concept of a morally justified war underlies much of the concept of International Law, such as the Geneva Conventions (Bosco, 2012; Bradley and Galbraith, 2016; Brzoska, 2015; Buck, Gallant, and Nossal, 1998; Caron, 1989). Aristotle, Cicero, Augustine, Aquinas, and Hugo Grotius are among the philosophers who have espoused some form of a just war philosophy (Cortright et al., 2000; Cranmer, Heinrich, and Desmarais, 2014; Crawford and Klotz, 1999; Crook, 2013; David and Holliday, 2012). One common just war theory evaluation of war is that war is only justified if it meets two conditions (Kiriya, 2017; Kirshner, 1997; Klotz, 1995; Koskenniemi, 2014; Kunz, 1960; Laub, 2015; Lee, 2018). First, it is waged in a state or nation's self-defense (Huang, Xu, and Lu, 2011; Huebner, 2009; Hultman and Peksen, 2017; Hurd, 2017; Igami, 2015). Second, the war is waged to end gross violations of human rights (Biersteker, Eckert, and Tourinho, 2016). Political philosopher John Rawls advocated these criteria as justification for war. Interestingly, the philosophy of war has been directly and indirectly referenced when justifying certain international sanctions (Morgan and Schwebach, 1997; Mueller and Mueller, 1999).

CHAPTER 5 SUMMARY

This chapter has explored various critical perspectives on war. These include constructivist, Marxist, green, feminist, queer, and humanist critiques. Whereas many of these criticisms are often suppressed at the international level when war is being waged or when sanctions are being triggered; they nevertheless play an important role in helping us understand the behavior of nations. Moreover, they contribute to the development of a coherent philosophy of war, even if that philosophy becomes disparate and diverse as a consequence of adding many perspectives. The next chapter examines how conflicts are triggered, organized, and resolved across the globe.

Chapter 6

Organization of Conflict in the World

CONTENTS

One of the consequences of an international community is that there are ground rules for organizing, sustaining, and concluding conflict. Certainly, there are “red lines” such as the use of chemical weapons on civilian populations, the crossing of which might lead to sanctions and even an invasion. This chapter examines some of the key principles that underpin the process of conflict including antimilitarism, just war theories, criteria for escalation, the military-industrial complex, and the notion of peace through strength. By the end of this chapter, the reader should have a good idea of the ground rules for military or non-military.

6.1. ANTIMILITARISM AND INTERNATIONAL SANCTIONS

Antimilitarism is a doctrine that opposes war, relying heavily on a critical theory of imperialism (Kiriya, 2017; Kirshner, 1997; Klotz, 1995; Koskenniemi, 2014; Kunz, 1960; Laub, 2015; Lee, 2018). Whereas pacifism is the doctrine that disputes (especially between countries) should be settled without recourse to violence, antimilitarism comprises ideology and activities aimed at reducing the civil power of the military and ultimately, preventing international war (Grauvogel and Von Soest, 2014; Grauvogel, Licht, and van Soest, 2017). An anti-militarist movement is one opposed to military rule, high military expenditure, or the imposition of foreign bases in their country (Doxey, 1987; Grauvogel and Von Soest, 2014; James, 2013).

Antimilitarism is sometimes equated with pacificism, a general opposition to war or violence, except in cases where force is deemed necessary to advance the cause of peace (David and Holliday, 2012; Daviron and Ponte, 2007; De Visscher, 2015; De Vos, 2010; Defourny, 2013; Denzin, 2008; Devarajan and Mottaghi, 2015). It is important to draw distinctions between antimilitarism and pacifism because they impact on international relations (IRs) in relatively different ways (Hinds, 1997; Hiraide and Chakraborty, 2012; Ho-Chuan, Yi-Chen, and Chih-Chuan, 2012; Hovdenak, 2009; Huang, Xu, and Lu, 2011). Figure 6.1 is an example of an antiwar poster that might be utilized as a propaganda tool or even as an information sheet when fostering the goals and objectives of antimilitarism.

Figure 6.1. Example of an anti-war poster.

Source: WNPJ.

Pacifism is the belief that disputes between nations can and should be settled peacefully (Bederman and Keitner, 2016; Biersteker, Eckert, and Tourinho, 2016). It is the opposition to war and the use of violence as a means of settling disputes (Stephanides et al., 2002; Strack and Strack, 1978; Takian, Raoofi, and Kazempour-Ardebili, 2020). It can include the refusal to participate in military action (Igami, 2015; Ivanov, Sypchenko, and Webster, 2017; James, 2013). Antimilitarism does not reject war in all circumstances but rejects the belief or desire to maintain a large and strong military organization in aggressive preparedness for war (Hovdenak, 2009; Huang, Xu, and Lu, 2011; Huebner, 2009; Hultman and Peksen, 2017; Hurd, 2017). Anarcho-syndicalist Georges Sorel advocated the use of violence as a form of direct action, calling it "revolutionary violence," which he opposed in "*Reflections on Violence*" (1908) to the violence inherent in class struggle (Mahmud, 2001; Matsushita et al., 2015; McCorkell and Gillard, 2010; Meyer and Thein, 2014). This is an argument that was already advanced in critical Marxism (Ho-Chuan, Yi-Chen, and Chih-Chuan, 2012; Hovdenak, 2009; Huang, Xu, and Lu, 2011; Huebner, 2009; Hultman and Peksen, 2017).

The effect of antimilitarism might be the reduction in the military capabilities of nations who then look to other ways of controlling enemies and friends (Mueller and Mueller, 1999; Nossal, 1989; Ogden, 2008). Sanctions are one of these tools, a case in point being Germany which continues to hold significant sway over international affairs despite having been forced to degrade its military capabilities following World War II (Gui, 1991; Hafner-Burton and Montgomery, 2008; Hanushek and Woessmann, 2010). Some who are on the antimilitarism spectrum require justification for war (Von Glahn and Taulbee, 2015; Wallensteen and Staibano, 2005). That brings in the just war theories that we will explore in the next section.

6.2. THE JUST WAR THEORY

Just war theory is a doctrine, also referred to as a tradition, of military ethics studied by military leaders, theologians, ethicists, and policymakers (Taylor, 2012; Thaver and Ekanayake, 2010; Tridimas and Guiterrex-Fons, 2008). The purpose of the doctrine is to ensure war is morally justifiable through a series of criteria, all of which must be met for a war to be considered just (Choi and Luo, 2013; Clegg and Palmer, 1996; Cleveland, 2001; Cortright et al., 2000; Cranmer, Heinrich, and Desmarais, 2014). The criteria are split into two groups: "right to go to war" and "right conduct in war" (Baldwin and Pape, 1998; Barber, 1979; Bederman and Keitner, 2016). The first concerns the morality of going to war, and the second the moral conduct within war (Kaempfer, Lowenberg, and Mertens, 2004; Kendall, 2000; Kiriya, 2017; Kirshner, 1997).

Recently there have been calls for the inclusion of a third category of just war theory dealing with the morality of post-war settlement and reconstruction (Ozawa and Castello, 2001; Pape, 1997, 1998; Ponte, 2004). According to the theory, whereas war is not an ideal solution, it can be less terrible with the right conduct (Genzberger et al., 1994; Gharehgozli, 2017; Goodhart, 2016; Grauvogel and Von Soest, 2014). Secondly, that war is not always the worst option. Important responsibilities, undesirable outcomes, or preventable atrocities may justify war (Kendall, 2000; Kiriya, 2017; Kirshner, 1997; Klotz, 1995; Koskenniemi, 2014; Kunz, 1960). Figure 6.2 summarizes the constituent elements of a just war.

Opponents of just war theory may be either inclined to a stricter pacifist standard (Bolander, 2011; Cranmer, Heinrich, and Desmarais, 2014; Escribà-Folch, 2012; Hovdenak, 2009; Kiriya, 2017). They do this by proposing that there has never been and can never be a justifiable basis for war (Pape, 1997, 1998; Ponte, 2004; Reilly, 2012; Reisman and Stevick, 1998). Alternatively, they may toward a more permissive nationalist standard by proposing that a war need only serve a nation's interests to be justifiable (Alam, 2008; Buck,

Gallant, and Nossal, 1998; Devarajan and Mottaghi, 2015; Fridell, 2014; Hultman and Peksen, 2017).

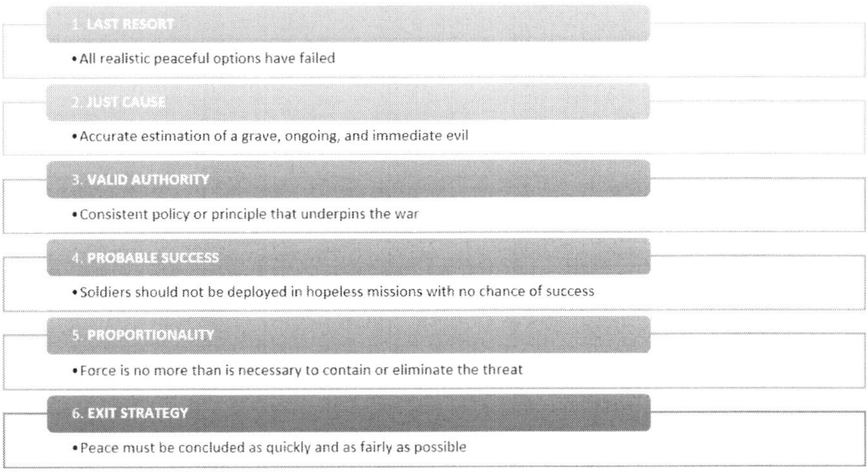

Figure 6.2. Elements of a just war.

Source: Duke University.

In many cases, philosophers state that individuals need not be of guilty conscience if required to fight (Askari et al., 2003; Attia, Grauvogel, and von Soest, 2020; Bacchiega and Borzaga, 2003; Baldwin and Pape, 1998). A few ennoble the virtues of the soldier while declaring their apprehensions for war itself (Stephanides et al., 2002; Strack and Strack, 1978; Takian, Raoofi, and Kazempour-Ardebili, 2020). A few, such as Rousseau, argue for insurrection against oppressive rule (Bacchiega and Borzaga, 2003; Baldwin and Pape, 1998; Barber, 1979).

The historical aspect, or the "just war tradition," deals with the historical body of rules or agreements that have applied in various wars across the ages (Afesorgbor, 2019; Alam, 2008; Al-Jawaheri, 2008). The just war tradition also considers the writings of various philosophers and lawyers through history and examines both their philosophical visions of war's ethical limits (Grauvogel, Licht, and von Soest, 2017; Gui, 1991). It also examines whether their thoughts have contributed to the body of conventions that have evolved to guide war and warfare (Tridimas and Guiterrex-Fons, 2008).

The just war tradition can be traced as far back as to Ancient Egypt (Kaempfer and Lowenberg, 1999; Kaempfer and Lowenberg, 2000; Kaempfer, Lowenberg, and Mertens, 2004). This helps in demonstrating that just war thought developed beyond the boundaries of Europe (Hiraide and Chakraborty, 2012; Ho-Chuan, Yi-Chen, and Chih-Chuan, 2012; Hovdenak, 2009; Huang, Xu, and Lu, 2011). It existed many centuries earlier than the advent of Christianity or even the emergence of Greco-Roman doctrine (Morgan and Schwebach, 1997; Mueller and Mueller, 1999; Nossal, 1989).

Chinese philosophy produced a massive body of work on warfare, much of it during the Zhou dynasty, especially the Warring States era (Meyer and Thein, 2014; Mikhaylova, Babich, and Smirnova, 2017). War was justified only as a last resort and only by the rightful sovereign (Doxey, 1972, 1980, 1983, 1987; Drezner, 2000, 2011). However, questioning the decision of the emperor concerning the necessity of a military action was not permissible (Afesorgbor, 2019; Alam, 2008; Al-Jawaheri, 2008; Askari et al., 2003). The success of a military campaign was sufficient proof that the campaign had been righteous (Franzway and Fonow, 2011; Frick, Humphreys, and Scheel, 2015; Fridell, 2014; Fu et al., 2020). Though Japan did not develop its own doctrine of just war, between the 5th and 7th centuries, they drew heavily from Chinese philosophy, and especially Confucian views (Mahmud, 2001; Matsushita et al., 2015; McCorkell and Gillard, 2010; Meyer and Thein, 2014). As part of the Japanese campaign to take the northeastern island Honshu, Japanese military action was portrayed as an effort to "pacify" the Emishi people who were likened to "bandits" and "wild-hearted wolf cubs" and accused of invading Japan's frontier lands (Saeidnia and Abdollahi, 2013; Seyfi and Hall, 2019).

The Indian Hindu epic, the Mahabharata, offers the first written discussions of a "just war" or "righteous war" (Blyton, 2004; Bolander, 2011; Borszik, 2014, 2016; Bosco, 2012; Bradley and Galbraith, 2016; Brzoska, 2015). In it, one of five ruling brothers ask if the suffering caused by war can ever be justified. A long discussion then ensues between the siblings, establishing criteria like proportionality (Askari et al., 2003; Attia, Grauvogel, and von Soest, 2020). These criteria include the reassurance that chariots cannot attack cavalry, only other chariots; no attacking people in distress, use of just means (no poisoned or barbed arrows), just cause (no attacking out of rage), and fair treatment of captives and the wounded. The war in the Mahabharata is preceded by context that develops the "just cause" for the war, including last minute efforts to reconcile differences to avoid war. At the beginning of the war, there is the discussion of "just conduct" appropriate to the context of war. In Sikhism, the term dharamyudh describes a war that is fought for just, righteous, or religious reasons, especially in defense of one's own beliefs (Frick, Humphreys, and Scheel, 2015; Fridell,

2014; Fu et al., 2020; Genzberger et al., 1994). Though some core tenets in the Sikh religion are understood to emphasize peace and nonviolence, especially before the 1606 execution of Guru Arjan by Mughal emperor Jahangir (Bradley and Galbraith, 2016; Brzoska, 2015; Buck, Gallant, and Nossal, 1998; Caron, 1989; Carter, 1987). In that case, military force may be justified if all peaceful means to settle a conflict have been exhausted, thus resulting in a dharamyudh (Dunn and Shaw, 2001; Dunoff, Ratner, and Wippman, 2015; Eliat and Einav, 2004; Eriksson, 2016; Escribà-Folch, 2010, 2012).

It was Aristotle who first introduced the concept and terminology to the Hellenic world where war was a last resort and required a conduct that would not make impossible the restoration of peace (Li and Saghaian, 2013; Lutz and Lux, 1995; Mahmud, 2001; Matsushita et al., 2015). Aristotle generally has a favorable opinion of war and warfare to "avoid becoming enslaved to others" is justified as self-defense (Clegg and Palmer, 1996; Eliat and Einav, 2004; Hinds, 1997; Kaempfer, Lowenberg, and Mertens, 2004). As an exception to this, Aristotelian just war theory permitted warfare to enslave what Aristotle called "natural slaves" (Biersteker, Eckert, and Tourinho, 2016; Blyton, 2004). For this reason, Aristotelian just war theory is not well regarded in present-day (Askari et al., 2003; Attia, Grauvogel, and von Soest, 2020). In Aristotelian philosophy, the abolition of what he considers "natural slavery" would undermine civic freedom (Strack and Strack, 1978; Takian, Raoofi, and Kazempour-Ardebili, 2020; Taylor, 2012; Thaver and Ekanayake, 2010). The pursuit of freedom is inseparable from pursuing mastery over "those who deserve to be slaves" (Jiang, Chen, and Liu, 2010; Jing, Kaempfer, and Lowenberg, 2003; Kaempfer and Lowenberg, 1999). According to The Cambridge Companion to Aristotle's Politics, the targets of this aggressive warfare were non-Greeks, noting Aristotle's view that "our poets say, 'it is proper for Greeks to rule non-Greeks'" (Buck, Gallant, and Nossal, 1998; Caron, 1989; Carter, 1987; Caruso, 2003; Chachavalpongpun, 2014). It is interesting to note that all this theory tends to set out specific criteria that demonstrate justification for war, a topic that we will explore further in the next section.

6.3. CRITERIA FOR ENGAGING IN ARMED CONFLICT

As a starting point for war, there must be a just cause for that war (Pape, 1998; Ponte, 2004; Reilly, 2012; Reisman and Stevick, 1998; Richard and Raimo,

1999). The reason for going to war needs to be just and cannot therefore be solely for recapturing things taken or punishing people who have done wrong (Reilly, 2012; Reisman and Stevick, 1998; Richard and Raimo, 1999; Ross, 1989; Rothwell and Stephens, 2016). For example, 'innocent' or civilian life must be in imminent danger and intervention must be to protect life (Jiang, Chen, and Liu, 2010; Jing, Kaempfer, and Lowenberg, 2003; Kaempfer and Lowenberg, 1999). A contemporary view of just cause was expressed in 1993 when the US Catholic Conference suggested that force may be used only to correct a grave, public evil (Caron, 1989; Carter, 1987; Caruso, 2003; Chachavalpongpun, 2014; Chan, 2000; Chan and Drury, 2000). Examples may include aggression or massive violation of the basic human rights of entire populations (Frick, Humphreys, and Scheel, 2015; Fridell, 2014; Fu et al., 2020; Genzberger et al., 1994). As Figure 6.3 satirically demonstrates, the failure to justify a war or to alternatively justify it on shaky grounds can underpin public confidence in the government as well as its foreign policy (Askari et al., 2003; Caruso, 2003; Doxey, 1983; Igami, 2015).

Figure 6.3. Satirical view of the Bush war on Iraq.

Source: Amazon.

The notion of comparative justice can be instructive in these cases (Hiraide and Chakraborty, 2012; Ho-Chuan, Yi-Chen, and Chih-Chuan, 2012; Hovdenak, 2009; Huang, Xu, and Lu, 2011). There may be rights and wrongs on all sides of a conflict (Matsushita et al., 2015; McCorkell and Gillard, 2010; Meyer and Thein, 2014; Mikhaylova, Babich, and Smirnova, 2017). However, to overcome the presumption against the use of force; the injustice suffered by one party must significantly outweigh that suffered by the other (Reilly, 2012; Reisman and Stevick, 1998; Richard and Raimo, 1999; Ross, 1989; Rothwell and Stephens, 2016). Some theorists such as Brian Orend omit this term, seeing it as fertile ground for exploitation by bellicose regimes (Al-Jawaheri, 2008; Dobler, 2008; Fu et al., 2020; Hurd, 2017; Laub, 2015).

There should be a competent authority to conduct the war (Bosco, 2012; Bradley and Galbraith, 2016; Brzoska, 2015; Buck, Gallant, and Nossal, 1998; Caron, 1989). Only duly constituted public authorities may wage war (Alam, 2008; Buck, Gallant, and Nossal, 1998; Devarajan and Mottaghi, 2015; Fridell, 2014; Hultman and Peksen, 2017). A just war must be initiated by a political authority within a political system that allows distinctions of justice (Chiquiar, 2008; Dunn and Shaw, 2001; Hanushek and Woessmann, 2010; Kaempfer and Lowenberg, 1999). Dictatorships (e.g., Hitler's Regime) or deceptive military actions (e.g., the 1968 US bombing of Cambodia) are typically considered as violations of this criterion (Drury and Peksen, 2014; Dunn and Shaw, 2001; Dunoff, Ratner, and Wippman, 2015; Eliat and Einav, 2004; Eriksson, 2016; Escribà-Folch, 2010). It is not possible to have a genuine process of judging a just war within a system that represses the process of genuine justice (Seyfi and Hall, 2019; Solingen, 2012; Stephanides et al., 2002). A just war must be initiated by a political authority within a political system that allows distinctions of justice (Ivanov, Sypchenko, and Webster, 2017; James, 2013).

There must be a right intention behind the war. Force may be used only in a truly just cause and solely for that purpose (Biersteker, Eckert, and Tourinho, 2016; Blyton, 2004; Bolander, 2011; Borszik, 2014, 2016). This may involve correcting a suffered wrong is considered a right intention (Solingen, 2012; Stephanides et al., 2002; Strack and Strack, 1978; Takian, Raoofi, and Kazempour-Ardebili, 2020). However, material gain or maintaining economies is not an appropriate justification for war, although many may believe otherwise (Ponte, 2004; Reilly, 2012; Reisman and Stevick, 1998; Richard and Raimo, 1999; Ross, 1989). That is why the Western powers have always bristled at the suggestion that their engagement in the Middle East is nothing but a smokescreen for accessing the oil reserves in that region (Drezner, 2000, 2011, 2015; Drezner and Drezner, 1999; Drury and Peksen, 2014; Dunn and Shaw, 2001; Dunoff, Ratner, and Wippman, 2015).

A just war should have a good probability of success (Ozawa and Castello, 2001; Pape, 1997, 1998). This criterion helps to reduce the unnecessary loss of lives and resources (Mikhaylova, Babich, and Smirnova, 2017; Morgan and Schwebach, 1997). Arms may not be used in a futile cause and that has always been a rallying cry for some antiwar protesters (Eliat and Einav, 2004; Eriksson, 2016; Escribà-Folch, 2010, 2012; Escribà-Folch and Wright, 2010; Farzanegan, 2013; Farzanegan and Hayo, 2019). The decision must be taken in a case where disproportionate measures are required to achieve success (Pape, 1998; Ponte, 2004; Reilly, 2012; Reisman and Stevick, 1998; Richard and Raimo, 1999). It is for this reason that nuclear weapons are disproportionate, although Western powers seem to claim exclusive rights to access and use them (Devarajan and Mottaghi, 2015; Dobler, 2008; Doxey, 1972, 1983).

A just war is a last resort measure, and not the immediate option (Grauvogel, Licht, and von Soest, 2017; Gui, 1991; Hafner-Burton and Montgomery, 2008). It is for this reason that the public is always suspicious of post-event justifications for war when the government always intended to go to war anyway (Chachavalpongpun, 2014; Chan, 2000; Chan and Drury, 2000; Chen et al., 2019; Cheraghali, 2013; Chiquiar, 2008). Force may be used only after all peaceful and viable alternatives have been seriously tried and exhausted or are clearly not practical (Lutz and Lux, 1995; Mahmud, 2001; Matsushita et al., 2015; McCorkell and Gillard, 2010). It may be clear that the other side is using negotiations as a delaying tactic and will not make meaningful concessions (Barber, 1979; Drezner, 2015; Jiang, Chen, and Liu, 2010; Leyton-Brown, 2017).

The principle of proportionality reduces the risk of revenge wars that are meant to destroy people and communities (David and Holliday, 2012; Daviron and Ponte, 2007; De Visscher, 2015; De Vos, 2010; Defourny, 2013; Denzin, 2008; Devarajan and Mottaghi, 2015). The anticipated benefits of waging a war must be proportionate to its expected evils or harms (De Visscher, 2015; De Vos, 2010; Defourny, 2013; Denzin, 2008; Devarajan and Mottaghi, 2015; Dobler, 2008). Sanctions and other diplomatic measures may be used as an interim measure to avoid war (Borszik, 2016; Crook, 2013; Farzanegan, 2013; Kirshner, 1997; Pape, 1997; Takian, Raoofi, and

Kazempour-Ardebili, 2020). This principle is also known as the principle of macro-proportionality, to distinguish it from the jus in bello principle of proportionality (Crawford and Klotz, 1999; Crook, 2013; David and Holliday, 2012; Daviron and Ponte, 2007; De Visscher, 2015; De Vos, 2010). In modern terms, just war is waged in terms of self-defense, or in defense of another; with sufficient evidence of that fact (Von Glahn and Taulbee, 2015). In the next section, we explore the notion of a military-industrial complex in which there is a permanent and ready apparatus that is just "itching for war."

6.4. THE MILITARY-INDUSTRIAL COMPLEX

The military-industrial complex (MIC) is an informal alliance between a nation's military and the defense industry that supplies it, seen together as a vested interest which influences public policy (Hovdenak, 2009; Huang, Xu, and Lu, 2011; Huebner, 2009; Hultman and Peksen, 2017; Hurd, 2017). A driving factor behind this relationship between the government and defense-minded corporations is that both sides benefit (Biersteker, Eckert, and Tourinho, 2016; Blyton, 2004; Bolander, 2011; Borszik, 2014, 2016; Bosco, 2012). For example, the defense ministry benefits from obtaining war weapons, and weapons industry benefits from being paid to supply them (Levy, 1999; Leyton-Brown, 2017; Li and Saghaian, 2013; Lutz and Lux, 1995; Mahmud, 2001). The term is most often used in reference to the system behind the military of the United States, where it is most prevalent due to close links between defense contractors, the Pentagon and politicians (Gui, 1991; Hafner-Burton and Montgomery, 2008; Hanushek and Woessmann, 2010; Haugh and Kitson, 2007). The term gained popularity after a warning on its detrimental effects in the farewell address of President Dwight D. Eisenhower on January 17, 1961. Figure 6.4 is a demonstration of the intricate relationships between the supply and demand of tax funding for weapons (Reisman and Stevick, 1998; Richard and Raimo, 1999; Ross, 1989; Rothwell and Stephens, 2016; Ryngaert, 2015).

In the context of the United States, the appellation is sometimes extended to military-industrial-congressional complex (MICC), adding the US Congress to form a three-sided relationship termed an iron triangle (Bradley and Galbraith, 2016; Brzoska, 2015; Buck, Gallant, and Nossal, 1998; Caron, 1989; Carter, 1987). These relationships include political contributions, political approval for military spending, lobbying to support bureaucracies, and oversight of the industry (Ponte, 2004; Reilly, 2012; Reisman and Stevick, 1998; Richard and Raimo, 1999). They more broadly include the entire network of contracts and flows of money and resources among individuals as well as corporations and institutions of the defense contractors, private military contractors, The Pentagon, Congress, and the executive branch (Pape, 1997, 1998; Ponte, 2004; Reilly, 2012; Reisman and Stevick, 1998).

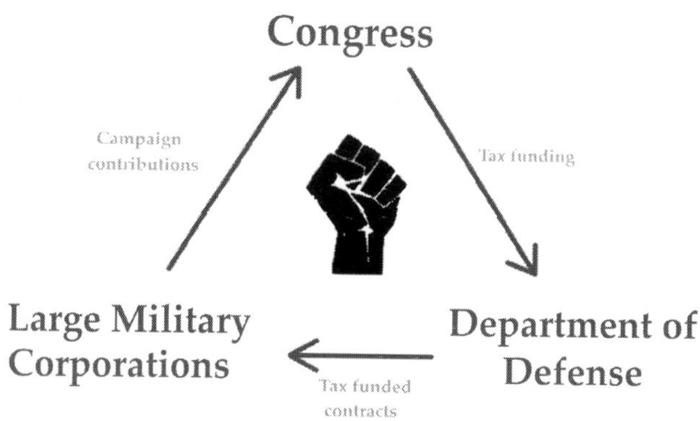

Figure 6.4. The military-industrial complex.

Source: Medium.

Attempts to conceptualize something like a modern "MIC" existed before Eisenhower's address (Caron, 1989; Carter, 1987; Caruso, 2003; Chachavalpongpun, 2014; Chan, 2000; Chan and Drury, 2000). Ledbetter finds the precise term used in 1947 in close to its later meaning in an article in Foreign Affairs by Winfield W. Riefler (Lutz and Lux, 1995; Mahmud, 2001; Matsushita et al., 2015). In 1956, sociologist C. Wright Mills had claimed in his book "*The Power Elite*" that a class of military, business, and political leaders, driven by mutual interests, were the real leaders of the state, and were effectively beyond democratic control (Carter, 1987; Caruso, 2003; Chachavalpongpun, 2014; Chan, 2000; Chan and Drury, 2000; Chen et al., 2019). Friedrich Hayek mentions in his 1944 book "*The Road to Serfdom*" the danger of a support of monopolistic organization of industry from World War II political remnants (Matsushita et al., 2015; McCorkell and Gillard, 2010; Meyer and Thein, 2014; Mikhaylova, Babich, and Smirnova, 2017).

At the end of the Cold War, American defense contractors were concerned about what they called declining government weapons spending (Thaver and Ekanayake, 2010; Tridimas and Guiterrex-Fons, 2008). They saw escalation of tensions, such as with Russia over Ukraine, as new opportunities for increased weapons sales (James, 2013; Jiang, Chen, and

Liu, 2010; Jing, Kaempfer, and Lowenberg, 2003). Hence, they have pushed the political system, both directly and through industry groups such as the National Defense Industrial Association, to spend more on military hardware (Escribà-Folch and Wright, 2010; Farzanegan, 2013; Farzanegan and Hayo, 2019; Franzway and Fonow, 2011). Pentagon contractor-funded American think tanks such as the Lexington Institute and the Atlantic Council have also demanded increased spending in view of the perceived Russian threat (Levy, 1999; Leyton-Brown, 2017; Li and Saghaian, 2013; Lutz and Lux, 1995; Mahmud, 2001). Independent Western observers such as William Hartung argue that Russian saber-rattling has additional benefits for weapons makers because it has become a standard part of the argument for higher Pentagon spending (Takian, Raoofi, and Kazempour-Ardebili, 2020; Taylor, 2012; Thaver and Ekanayake, 2010). This spending rise continues even though the Pentagon already has more than enough money to address any actual threat to the United States (Grauvogel, Licht, and von Soest, 2017; Gui, 1991; Hafner-Burton and Montgomery, 2008). The accumulation of military strength due to perceived and actual threats is closely aligned with the doctrine of "peace through strength," which will be covered in the next section.

6.5. PEACE THROUGH STRENGTH

Peace through strength" is a phrase which suggests that military power can help preserve peace (Drezner, 2011, 2015; Drezner and Drezner, 1999; Drury and Peksen, 2014; Dunn and Shaw, 2001; Dunoff, Ratner, and Wippman, 2015). It is quite old and has famously been used by many leaders from Roman Emperor Hadrian in the first century AD to former US President Ronald Reagan in the 1980s (Nossal, 1989; Ogden, 2008; Ozawa and Castello, 2001). The concept has long been associated with realpolitik. The idea has critics who argue that in reality 'peace through strength' has become 'peace through war' (Bacchiega and Borzaga, 2003; Baldwin and Pape, 1998; Barber, 1979; Bederman and Keitner, 2016). Roman Emperor Hadrian (AD 76–138) is said to have sought "peace through strength or, failing that, peace through threat" (Baldwin and Pape, 1998; Chan and Drury, 2000; Drezner, 2011; Levy, 1999). Hadrian's Wall was a symbol of this policy. The first American President, George Washington, enunciated a policy of peace through strength in his 5th annual message to Congress, the 1793 State of the Union Address (Baldwin and Pape, 1998; Barber, 1979; Bederman and Keitner, 2016). President Ronald Reagan embraced the same mantra (see Figure 6.5).

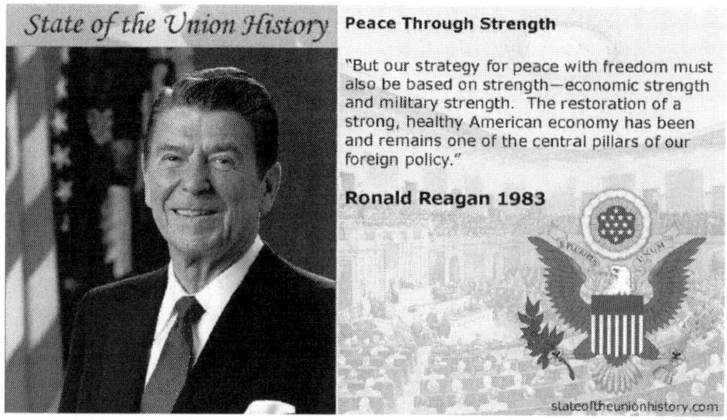

Figure 6.5. Peace through strength.

Source: State of the Union History.

In Federalist No. 24, Alexander Hamilton argued for peace through strength, stating that strong garrisons in the west and a navy in the east would protect the Union from the threat of Britain and Spain (Kunz, 1960; Laub, 2015; Lee, 2018; Levy, 1999; Leyton-Brown, 2017; Li and Saghaian, 2013). "*Peace Through Strength*" (1952) is the title of a book about a defense plan by Bernard Baruch, a World War II adviser to US President Franklin D. Roosevelt. During the 1964 presidential campaign in the United States, the Republican party spent about $5 million on "Peace through Strength" TV spots (Bederman and Keitner, 2016; Chen et al., 2019; Drezner and Drezner, 1999; Gui, 1991; Jing, Kaempfer, and Lowenberg, 2003). For supporters of the MX missile in the 1970s, the missile symbolized "peace through strength" (Pape, 1997, 1998; Ponte, 2004; Reilly, 2012; Reisman and Stevick, 1998). In 1980, Ronald Reagan used the phrase during his election challenge against Jimmy Carter, accusing the incumbent of weak, vacillating leadership that invited enemies to attack the United States and its allies (Morgan and Schwebach, 1997; Wallensteen and Staibano, 2005). Reagan later considered it one of the mainstays of his foreign policy as President. In reality,the mantra has become a rallying cry or an excuse for those that wish to support the Military-Industrial Complex (Blyton, 2004; Bolander, 2011; Borszik, 2014, 2016; Bosco, 2012; Bradley and Galbraith, 2016; Brzoska, 2015; Buck, Gallant, and Nossal, 1998).

CHAPTER 6 SUMMARY

This chapter has shown that there are several rules of engagement that determine the ways in which conflict is handled. Some of the contributors to these rules include perspectives such as antimilitarism and pacificism. The just war theory provides a coherent set of principles that might be used to justify armed conflict. However, this is subject to individual interpretations such as the "peace through strength" mantra and the emergence of the military-industrial complex that perpetuates conflicts for commercial reasons. The next chapter in this book will consider how these rules are then reinterpreted and adopted to justify international sanctions.

Chapter 7

Rationalizing International Sanctions

CONTENTS

In many ways, the justification for international sanctions often mirrors the justification for wars, the former acting as an interim measure or one that is used to placate a skeptical populace. This chapter examines some of the rationalizations for international sanctions, including deterrence, safety, democratization, and responsiveness to aggression. The chapter also shows the difficulties of launching an effective response to crises such as the one that happened in Crimea when Russian annexed parts of Ukraine.

7.1. ROLE OF THE DETERRENCE THEORY

Deterrence theory is the idea that an inferior force, by virtue of the destructive power of the force's weapons, could deter a more powerful adversary, provided that this force could be protected against destruction by a surprise attack (Laub, 2015; Lee, 2018; Levy, 1999; Leyton-Brown, 2017; Li and Saghaian, 2013). This doctrine gained increased prominence as a military strategy during the Cold War about the use of nuclear weapons and is related to, but distinct from, the concept of Mutual assured destruction, which models the preventative nature of the full-scale nuclear attack that would devastate both parties in a nuclear war (Von Glahn and Taulbee, 2015).

Deterrence is a strategy intended to dissuade an adversary from taking an action not yet started by means of threat of reprisal (Escribà-Folch, 2010, 2012; Escribà-Folch and Wright, 2010; Farzanegan, 2013; Farzanegan and Hayo, 2019). Alternatively, it can be used to prevent them from doing something that another state desires. The strategy is based on the psychological concept of the same name (Askari et al., 2003; Caruso, 2003; Doxey, 1983; Igami, 2015). A credible nuclear deterrent, Bernard Brodie wrote in 1959, must be always at the ready, yet never used (Nossal, 1989; Ogden, 2008; Ozawa and Castello, 2001). Figure 7.1 summarizes the kind of deterrent theory that might be used when making decisions about going to war.

Schelling (1966) presents the concept that military strategy can no longer be defined as the science of military victory (Hovdenak, 2009; Huang, Xu, and Lu, 2011; Huebner, 2009; Hultman and Peksen, 2017; Hurd, 2017). Instead, it is argued that military strategy was now equally, if not more, the art of coercion, intimidation, and deterrence (Chan, 2000; Chan and Drury, 2000; Chen et al., 2019; Cheraghali, 2013; Chiquiar, 2008). Schelling says the capacity to harm another state is now used as a motivating factor for other states to avoid it and influence another state's behavior (Al-Jawaheri, 2008; Dobler, 2008; Fu et al., 2020; Hurd, 2017; Laub, 2015).

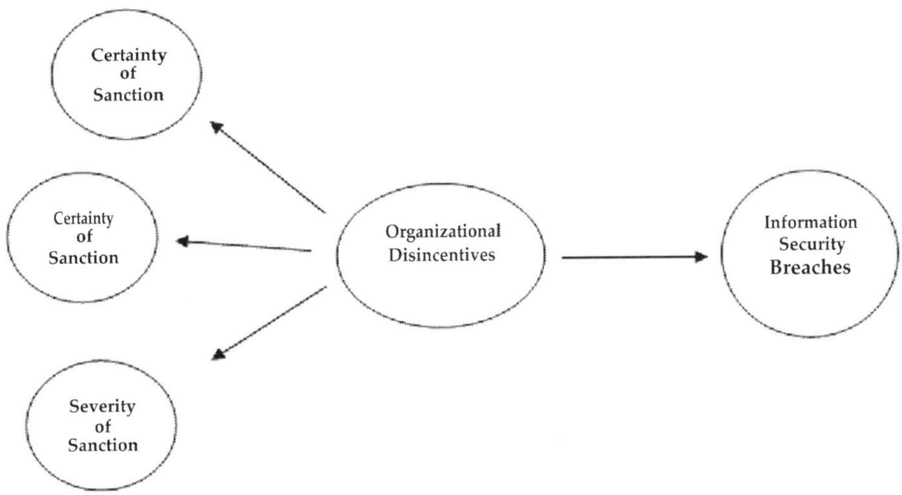

Figure 7.1. Role of the deterrence theory.

Source: Research Gate.

To be coercive or deter another state, violence must be anticipated and avoidable by accommodation (Crook, 2013; David and Holliday, 2012; Daviron and Ponte, 2007; De Visscher, 2015; De Vos, 2010; Defourny, 2013; Denzin, 2008). It can therefore be summarized that the use of the power to hurt as bargaining power is the foundation of deterrence theory and is most successful when it is held in reserve (Cranmer, Heinrich, and Desmarais, 2014; Crawford and Klotz, 1999; Crook, 2013; David and Holliday, 2012; Daviron and Ponte, 2007). In 2004 Zagare made the case that deterrence theory is logically inconsistent, not empirically accurate, and that it is deficient as a theory (Rothwell and Stephens, 2016; Solingen, 2012; Stephanides et al., 2002). In place of classical deterrence, rational choice scholars have argued for perfect deterrence, which assumes that states may vary in their internal characteristics and especially in the credibility of their threats of retaliation (Eriksson, 2016; Escribà-Folch, 2010, 2012; Escribà-Folch and Wright, 2010; Farzanegan, 2013; Farzanegan and Hayo, 2019; Franzway and Fonow, 2011).

Deterrence theory holds that nuclear weapons are intended to deter other states from attacking with their nuclear weapons, through the promise of retaliation and possibly mutually assured destruction or MAD (Kiriya, 2017; Kirshner, 1997; Klotz, 1995; Koskenniemi, 2014; Kunz, 1960; Laub, 2015; Lee, 2018). Nuclear deterrence can also be applied to an attack by conventional forces; for example, the doctrine of massive retaliation threatened to launch US nuclear weapons in response to Soviet attacks (Drezner, 2000, 2011, 2015; Drezner and Drezner, 1999; Drury and Peksen, 2014; Dunn and Shaw, 2001; Dunoff, Ratner, and Wippman, 2015). A successful nuclear deterrent requires that a country preserve its ability to retaliate, either by responding before its own weapons are destroyed or by ensuring a second-strike capability (Caron, 1989; Carter, 1987; Caruso, 2003; Chachavalpongpun, 2014; Chan, 2000; Chan and Drury, 2000). A nuclear deterrent is sometimes composed of a nuclear triad, as in the case of the nuclear weapons owned by the United States, Russia, the People's Republic of China and India (Rothwell and Stephens, 2016; Ryngaert, 2015; Saeidnia and Abdollahi, 2013). Other countries, such as the United Kingdom and France, have only sea- and air-based nuclear weapons (Cleveland, 2001; Cortright et al., 2000; Cranmer, Heinrich, and Desmarais, 2014; Crawford and Klotz, 1999; Crook, 2013; David and Holliday, 2012). In the next section, we consider why the possibility of weapons of mass destruction have been used as justification for sanctions.

7.2. WEAPONS OF MASS DESTRUCTION

Researchers have been prescriptive in outlining the impact of the development of nuclear weapons in the analysis of military power and deterrence (Askari et al., 2003; Attia, Grauvogel, and von Soest, 2020). This happened before the widespread use of assured second-strike capability, or immediate reprisal, in the form of SSBN submarines (Morgan and Schwebach, 1997; Wallensteen and Staibano, 2005). It is argued that nuclear weapons give nations the potential to not only destroy their enemies but humanity itself without drawing immediate reprisal because of the lack of a conceivable defense system and the speed with which nuclear weapons can be deployed (Borszik, 2014, 2016; Bosco, 2012; Bradley and Galbraith, 2016; Brzoska, 2015; Buck, Gallant, and Nossal, 1998). A nation's credible threat of such severe damage empowers their deterrence policies and fuels political coercion and military deadlock, which in turn can produce proxy warfare (Seyfi and Hall, 2019; Solingen, 2012; Stephanides et al., 2002). As Figure 7.2 shows, mutually assured destruction can break down over the years.

Historical analysis of nuclear weapons deterrent capabilities has led modern researchers to the concept of the stability-instability paradox (Chan and Drury, 2000; Chen et al., 2019; Cheraghali, 2013; Chiquiar, 2008; Choi and Luo, 2013; Clegg and Palmer, 1996). This occurs where nuclear weapons confer large scale stability between nuclear weapon states (Buck, Gallant, and Nossal, 1998; Caron, 1989; Carter, 1987; Caruso, 2003; Chachavalpongpun, 2014). For example, in over 60 years, none have engaged in large direct warfare due primarily to nuclear weapons deterrence capabilities (Gui, 1991; Hafner-Burton and Montgomery, 2008). However, these powers instead are forced into pursuing political aims by military means in the form of comparatively smaller-scale acts of instability, such as proxy wars and minor conflicts (Franzway and Fonow, 2011; Frick, Humphreys, and Scheel, 2015; Fridell, 2014).

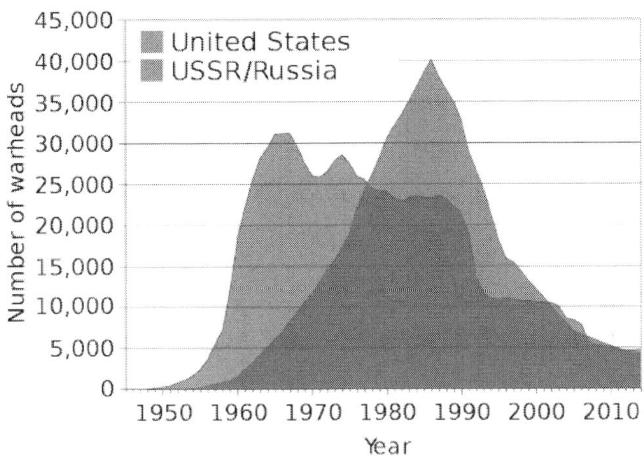

Figure 7.2. When mutually assured destruction breaks down.

Source: Stanford University.

The early stages of the Cold War were generally characterized by containment of communism, an aggressive stance on behalf of the US especially on developing nations under its sphere of influence (Doxey, 1987; Drezner, 2000, 2011, 2015; Drezner and Drezner, 1999; Drury and Peksen, 2014; Dunn and Shaw, 2001). This period was characterized by numerous proxy wars throughout most of the globe, particularly Africa, Asia, Central America, and South America (Barber, 1979; Bederman and Keitner, 2016). A notable such conflict was the Korean War. George F. Kennan, who is taken to be the founder of this ideology in his Long Telegram (Morgan and Schwebach, 1997; Mueller and Mueller, 1999). He asserted that he never advocated military intervention, merely economic support; and that his ideas were misinterpreted when espoused by the public (Grauvogel, Licht, and von Soest, 2017; Gui, 1991).

With the US drawdown from Vietnam, the normalization of US relations with China, and the Sino-Soviet Split; the policy of Containment was abandoned, and a new policy of détente was established (Askari et al., 2003; Attia, Grauvogel, and von Soest, 2020; Bacchiega and Borzaga, 2003; Baldwin and Pape, 1998). Under this policy, peaceful coexistence was sought between the United States and the Soviet Union (Ozawa and Castello, 2001; Pape, 1997, 1998). Although all factors listed above contributed to this shift, the most important factor was probably the rough parity achieved in stockpiling nuclear weapons with the clear capability of Mutual Assured Destruction (Ivanov, Sypchenko, and Webster, 2017; James, 2013). Therefore, the period of détente was characterized by a general reduction in the tension between the Soviet Union and the United States and a thawing of the Cold War, lasting from the late 1960s until the start of the 1980s (Afesorgbor, 2019; Alam, 2008; Al-Jawaheri, 2008; Askari et al., 2003). The doctrine of mutual nuclear deterrence characterized relations between the United States and the Soviet Union during this period, and relations with Russia until the onset of the New Cold War in the early 2010s (De Vos, 2010; Defourny, 2013; Denzin, 2008; Devarajan and Mottaghi, 2015; Dobler, 2008; Doxey, 1972). Since then, the relations have been less clear (Mikhaylova, Babich, and Smirnova, 2017; Morgan and Schwebach, 1997). In the next section, we examine the USA role of driving sanctions and acting as "the world's police."

7.3. THE USA AS A DRIVER OF SANCTIONS

After the failure of the Embargo Act of 1807 the federal government of the United States took little interest in imposing embargoes and economic sanctions against foreign countries until the 20th century (Daviron and Ponte, 2007; De Visscher, 2015; De Vos, 2010; Defourny, 2013; Denzin, 2008; Devarajan and Mottaghi, 2015; Dobler). United States trade policy was entirely a matter of economic policy (Drury and Peksen, 2014; Dunn and Shaw, 2001; Dunoff, Ratner, and Wippman, 2015; Eliat and Einav, 2004; Eriksson, 2016; Escribà-Folch, 2010). After World War I, interest revived and has continued to date (Ponte, 2004; Reilly, 2012; Reisman and Stevick, 1998; Richard and Raimo, 1999; Ross, 1989; Rothwell and Stephens, 2016). President Woodrow Wilson promoted such sanctions as a method for the League of Nations to enforce peace (Askari et al., 2003; Attia, Grauvogel, and von Soest, 2020). However, he failed to bring the United States into the League and the US did not join the 1935 League sanctions against Italy (Biersteker, Eckert, and Tourinho, 2016; Blyton, 2004; Bolander, 2011;

Borszik, 2014, 2016). There is a significant cost associated with some of these sanctions (see Figure 7.3).

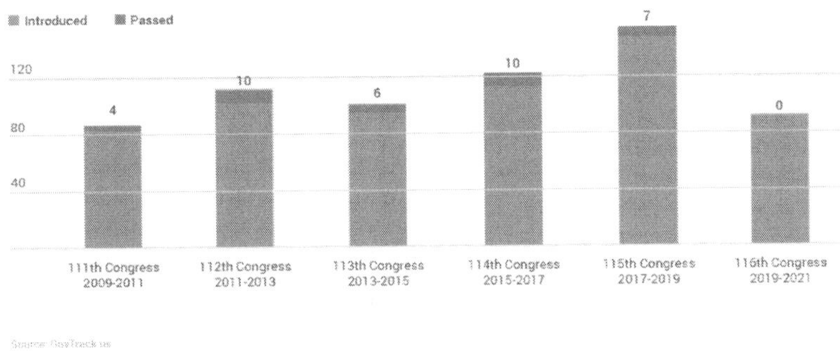

Figure 7.3. Counting the cost of financial warfare.

Source: Defense Priorities vi GovTrack.Us.

In 1940 the United States participated in the ABCD line against Japan, and the Helium Act of 1925 forbade export of that strategic commodity (Askari et al., 2003; Attia, Grauvogel, and von Soest, 2020). Interest in trade as a tool of foreign policy expanded during the Cold War era, and many economic sanctions were applied (Morgan and Schwebach, 1997; Mueller and Mueller, 1999; Nossal, 1989; Ogden, 2008). Later, sanctions were aimed against countries which the US government listed as "State Sponsors of Terrorism" (Biersteker, Eckert, and Tourinho, 2016; Blyton, 2004). Currently, the USA has one of the most extensive, detailed, far-reaching, and pernicious sanctions regime in the world (Doxey, 1980, 1983, 1987; Drezner, 2000, 2011, 2015; Drezner and Drezner, 1999; Drury and Peksen, 2014). In exercising this power, the USA relies on its economic and cultural dominance (Biersteker, Eckert, and Tourinho, 2016).

Sanctions imposed by the United States government include a ban on arms-related exports, controls over dual-use technology exports, and restrictions on economic assistance (Bosco, 2012; David and Holliday, 2012; Farzanegan and Hayo, 2019; Klotz, 1995; Pape, 1998; Taylor, 2012). There may also take the form of financial restrictions. For example, the the United States may oppose loans by the World Bank and other international financial institutions (Tridimas and Guiterrex-Fons, 2008). It can involve having diplomatic immunity waived, to allow families of terrorist victims to file for civil damages in US courts (Biersteker, Eckert, and Tourinho, 2016; Blyton, 2004; Bolander, 2011; Borszik, 2014, 2016; Bosco, 2012).

The government may offer tax credits for companies and individuals denied, for income earned in listed countries (Haugh and Kitson, 2007; Hinds, 1997; Hiraide and Chakraborty, 2012; Ho-Chuan, Yi-Chen, and Chih-Chuan, 2012; Hovdenak, 2009). Other measures include having duty-free goods exemption suspended for imports from those countries (Blyton, 2004; Bolander, 2011; Borszik, 2014, 2016; Bosco, 2012; Bradley and Galbraith, 2016; Brzoska, 2015). At other times, the government may prohibit US citizens from engaging in financial transactions with a government on the list, except by license from the US government (Cortright et al., 2000; Cranmer, Heinrich, and Desmarais, 2014; Crawford and Klotz, 1999; Crook, 2013; David and Holliday, 2012). Alternatively, there can be a prohibition of US Defense Department contracts above $100,000 with companies controlled by countries on the list (Chan and Drury, 2000; Chen et al., 2019; Cheraghali, 2013; Chiquiar, 2008; Choi and Luo, 2013; Clegg and Palmer, 1996). Countries such as Russia have responded to these sanctions in different ways, and we will explore an example in the next section.

7.4. RUSSIAN RESPONSE TO SANCTIONS

Countries like Russia have responded with sanctions of their own or even protective measures (Solingen, 2012; Stephanides et al., 2002; Strack and Strack, 1978). A case in point is the Dima Yakovlev Law. This is a law in Russia that defines sanctions against US citizens involved in "violations of the human rights and freedoms of Russian citizens" (Borszik, 2014; Crawford and Klotz, 1999; Escribà-Folch and Wright, 2010; Li and Saghaian, 2013). It creates a list of citizens who are banned from entering Russia, and allows the government to freeze their assets and investments. The law suspends the activity of politically active non-profit organizations which receive money from American citizens or organizations. It also bans citizens of the United States from adopting children from Russia. Some have argued that Russia is justified in responding to USA sanctions (Defourny, 2013; Denzin, 2008; Devarajan and Mottaghi, 2015; Dobler, 2008). This is because these sanctions severely impact on its economy (see Figure 7.4).

The law was signed by Russian President Vladimir Putin on 28th of December 2012 and took effect on 1st of January 2013. The law is informally named after a Russian orphan adopted by a family from Purcellville, Virginia, who died of heatstroke after being left in a parked car for nine hours. The law is described as a response to the Magnitsky Act in the United States, which places sanctions on Russian officials who were involved in a tax scandal exposed by Russian lawyer Sergei Magnitsky against Russian officials (Nossal, 1989; Ogden, 2008; Ozawa and Castello, 2001).

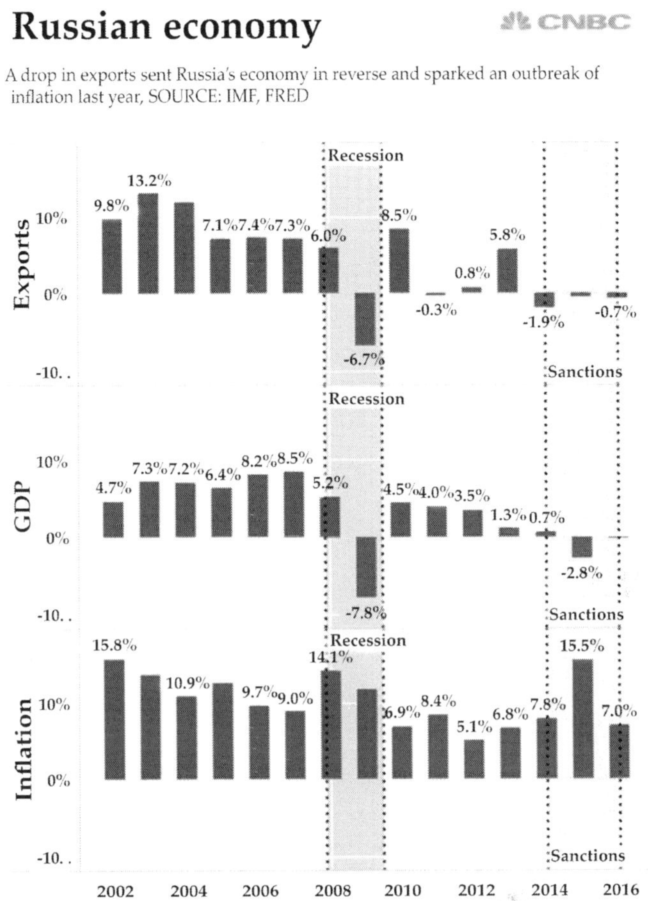

Figure 7.4. Impact of US sanctions on Russian economy.

Source: CNBC.

Magnitsky was later found to have been handcuffed and tortured while in jail. Meanwhile, Russia is also suspected of engaging in propaganda wars against the USA and in some cases interfering in US elections (Afesorgbor, 2019; Alam, 2008; Al-Jawaheri, 2008). This is not the first time that Russia has been on the receiving end of sanctions, and the last section in this chapter will consider the responses to the crisis in Ukraine where Russia was roundly condemned.

7.5. THE CASE OF THE UKRAINIAN CRISIS

International sanctions were imposed during the Russo-Ukrainian War by many countries against Russia and Crimea following the Russian invasion of Ukraine, which began in late February 2014 (Kaempfer and Lowenberg, 1999; Kaempfer and Lowenberg, 2000; Kaempfer, Lowenberg, and Mertens, 2004). The sanctions were imposed by the United States, the European Union (EU) and other countries and international organizations against individuals, businesses, and officials from Russia and Ukraine (Genzberger et al., 1994; Gharehgozli, 2017; Goodhart, 2016; Grauvogel and Von Soest, 2014). Russia responded with sanctions against several countries, including a total ban on food imports from the EU, United States, Norway, Canada, and Australia (Hinds, 1997; Hiraide and Chakraborty, 2012; Ho-Chuan, Yi-Chen, and Chih-Chuan, 2012; Hovdenak, 2009; Huang, Xu, and Lu, 2011). In December 2019, the EU announced the extension of sanctions until 31 July 2020. Figure 7.5 summarizes the geographical scope of the unrest that led to the sanctions.

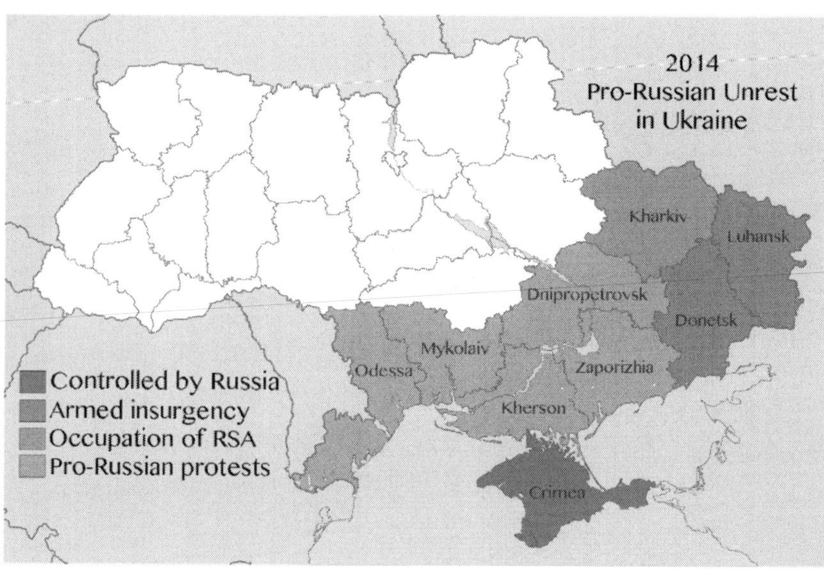

Figure 7.5. Russian incursions into Ukraine.

Source: Wikipedia.

The sanctions contributed to the collapse of the Russian ruble and the Russian financial crisis (Biersteker, Eckert, and Tourinho, 2016; Blyton, 2004; Bolander, 2011; Borszik, 2014). They also caused economic damage to several EU countries, with total losses estimated at €100 billion by 2015 (Choi and Luo, 2013; Dunoff, Ratner, and Wippman, 2015; Haugh and Kitson, 2007; Kaempfer and Lowenberg, 2000). In 2014, Russia's Finance Minister announced that the sanctions had cost Russia $40 billion, with another $100 billion loss in 2014 taken due to the decrease in the price of oil the same year driven by the 2010s oil glut. Following the latest sanctions imposed in August 2018, economic losses incurred by Russia amount to some 0.5–1.5% of foregone GDP growth (Tridimas and Guiterrex-Fons, 2008). In addition to the sanctions, Russian President Vladimir Putin has accused the United States of conspiring with Saudi Arabia to intentionally weaken the Russian economy by decreasing the price of oil (Klotz, 1995; Koskenniemi, 2014; Kunz, 1960; Laub, 2015; Lee, 2018; Levy, 1999). By mid-2016, Russia had lost an estimated $170 billion due to financial sanctions, with another $400 billion in lost revenues from oil and gas (Lutz and Lux, 1995; Mahmud, 2001; Matsushita et al., 2015; McCorkell and Gillard, 2010; Meyer and Thein, 2014).

According to Ukrainian officials, the sanctions forced Russia to change its approach towards Ukraine and undermined the Russian military advances in the region (Daviron and Ponte, 2007; Franzway and Fonow, 2011; Koskenniemi, 2014; Thaver and Ekanayake, 2010). Representatives of these countries say that they will lift sanctions against Russia only after Moscow fulfills the Minsk II agreements (Tridimas and Guiterrex-Fons, 2008). On 6 March 2014, US President Barack Obama, invoking, inter alia, the International Emergency Economic Powers Act and the National Emergencies Act, signed an executive order declaring a national emergency and ordering sanctions, including travel bans and the freezing of US assets. On 17 March 2014, the US, the EU, and Canada introduced specifically targeted sanctions, the day after the Crimean referendum and a few hours before Russian President Vladimir Putin signed a decree recognizing Crimea as an independent state, laying the groundwork for its annexation of Crimea by Russia (Morgan and Schwebach, 1997; Mueller and Mueller, 1999; Nossal, 1989; Ogden, 2008). Ultimately, Russia annexed parts of Ukraine despite the sanctions. This demonstrates the limits of international against a determined and powerful adversary.

CHAPTER 7 SUMMARY

This penultimate chapter of the book has considered some of the ways in which sanctions are rationalized on the international stage. For example, allied nations may push for sanctions to prevent and punish aggressor nations, such as the case of Russia when it annexed parts of Ukraine. However, the sanctions may not fulfill all their objectives and may have unexpected effects that are counterproductive in the long run. For example, the affected nations may build resilience and resistance. Throughout, it appears that the USA is one of the leading nations in conceiving and imposing international sanctions. Perhaps that is the reason that the sanctions are often seen as being arbitrary and unfair; with the sole purpose of serving the vested interests of powerful countries such as the USA. In that same vein, the last chapter of this book will summarize the strengths and weaknesses of international sanctions.

Chapter 8

Strengths and Weaknesses of Sanctions

CONTENTS

It is appropriate to close this book by highlighting some of the key strengths and weaknesses of international sanctions. Once again, it makes sense to go back to specific sanctions regimes to assess whether they achieved their goals. Examples include a post-Cold War settlement, quelling Iranian influence, overthrowing dictatorships such as the ones in Venezuela, and subduing the paranoid regimes of North Korea.

8.1. DEALING WITH POST-COLD WAR POLITICS

Some have argued that the Cold War between the USA and Russia has continued in a modified form which includes sanctions, aggressive rhetoric, propaganda, and electoral interference (Dunn and Shaw, 2001; Dunoff, Ratner, and Wippman, 2015; Eliat and Einav, 2004; Eriksson, 2016; Escribà-Folch, 2010, 2012). There are plenty of examples of Russia being sanctioned on a regular basis. In December 2012, the United States enacted the Magnitsky Act for example (Brzoska, 2015; Buck, Gallant, and Nossal, 1998; Caron, 1989; Carter, 1987; Caruso, 2003). This was intended to punish Russian officials responsible for the death of Russian tax accountant Sergei Magnitsky in a Moscow prison in 2009 by prohibiting their entrance to the United States and their use of its banking system (Von Glahn and Taulbee, 2015; Wallensteen and Staibano, 2005). A total of 18 individuals were originally affected by the Act.

In December 2016, Congress enacted the Global Magnitsky Act to allow the US Government to sanction foreign government officials implicated in human rights abuses anywhere in the world (Frick, Humphreys, and Scheel, 2015; Fridell, 2014; Fu et al., 2020; Genzberger et al., 1994; Gharehgozli, 2017). Other countries passed similar laws to ban foreigners deemed guilty of human rights abuses from entering their countries (Strack and Strack, 1978; Takian, Raoofi, and Kazempour-Ardebili, 2020; Taylor, 2012). These sanctions may vicariously target the Russian economy through its vulnerable points such as the oil industry (see Figure 8.1 for an illustration).

The sanctions introduced both by and against Russia slowed down the trade between Russia and the EU, causing damage to both the Russian and European economy (Attia, Grauvogel, and von Soest, 2020; Bacchiega and Borzaga, 2003; Baldwin and Pape, 1998). A 2015 data analysis suggested Russia's entry into a recession, with negative GDP growth of −2.2% for the first quarter of 2015, as compared to the first quarter of 2014 (Hanushek and Woessmann, 2010; Haugh and Kitson, 2007; Hinds, 1997; Hiraide and Chakraborty, 2012; Ho-Chuan, Yi-Chen, and Chih-Chuan, 2012).

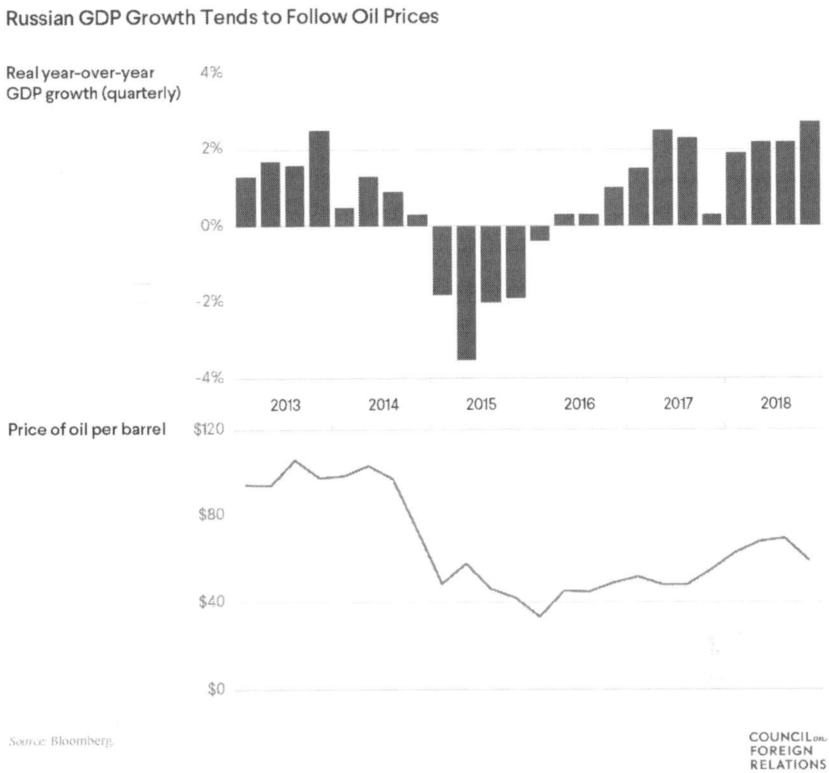

Figure 8.1. Linking oil prices to Russian GDP growth.

Source: CFA via Bloomberg.

Furthermore, the combined effect of the sanctions and the rapid decline in oil prices in 2014 has caused significant downward pressure on the value of the ruble and flight of capital out of Russia (Seyfi and Hall, 2019; Solingen, 2012; Stephanides et al., 2002). At the same time, the sanctions on access to financing have forced Russia to use part of its foreign exchange reserves to prop up the economy (Matsushita et al., 2015; McCorkell and Gillard, 2010; Meyer and Thein, 2014; Mikhaylova, Babich, and Smirnova, 2017). These events forced the Central Bank of Russia to stop supporting the value of the ruble and increase interest rates (De Visscher, 2015; De Vos, 2010; Defourny, 2013; Denzin, 2008; Devarajan and Mottaghi, 2015; Dobler, 2008).

Some believe that Russia's ban on western imports had the additional effect on these challenging events as the embargo led to higher food prices and further inflation in addition to the effects of decreased value of the ruble which had already raised the price of imported goods (Kirshner, 1997; Klotz, 1995; Koskenniemi, 2014; Kunz, 1960; Laub, 2015; Lee, 2018). In 2016 agriculture has surpassed the arms industry as Russia's second-largest export sector after oil and gas (Saeidnia and Abdollahi, 2013; Seyfi and Hall, 2019). As of 2015, the losses of EU have been estimated as at least €100 billion (Goodhart, 2016; Grauvogel and Von Soest, 2014; Grauvogel, Licht, and von Soest, 2017). The German business sector, with around 30,000 workplaces depending on trade with the Russian Federation, also reported being affected significantly by the sanctions (Escribà-Folch, 2010, 2012; Escribà-Folch and Wright, 2010; Farzanegan, 2013; Farzanegan and Hayo, 2019; Franzway and Fonow, 2011). The sanctions affected numerous European market sectors, including energy, agriculture, and aviation (Saeidnia and Abdollahi, 2013; Seyfi and Hall, 2019). In March 2016, the Finnish farmers' union MTK stated that the Russian sanctions and falling prices have put farmers under tremendous pressure (Kaempfer and Lowenberg, 1999; Kaempfer and Lowenberg, 2000; Kaempfer, Lowenberg, and Mertens, 2004). Finland's Natural Resources Institute LUKE has estimated that last year farmers saw their incomes shrink by at least 40% compared to the previous year (Strack and Strack, 1978; Takian, Raoofi, and Kazempour-Ardebili, 2020; Taylor, 2012; Thaver and Ekanayake, 2010). In February 2015, Exxon Mobil reported losing about $1 billion due to Russian sanctions (Ho-Chuan, Yi-Chen, and Chih-Chuan, 2012; Hovdenak, 2009; Huang, Xu, and Lu, 2011; Huebner, 2009; Hultman and Peksen, 2017). Nevertheless, Russia has not been broken and continues to interfere in US and European elections (Igami, 2015; Ivanov, Sypchenko, and Webster, 2017; James, 2013). The annexation of Crimea has not been reversed and some of the responses are inconsistent (Eriksson, 2016; Escribà-Folch, 2010, 2012; Escribà-Folch and Wright, 2010; Farzanegan, 2013; Farzanegan and Hayo, 2019; Franzway and Fonow, 2011). That means that the effectiveness of the sanctions is not entirely clear cut, despite their effects on all countries involved (Fu et al., 2020; Genzberger et al., 1994; Gharehgozli, 2017; Goodhart, 2016; Grauvogel and Von Soest, 2014). The next question considers the long-standing issue of Iran and how sanctions have tried to deal with it.

8.2. SANCTIONS AGAINST IRAN

There have been several sanctions against Iran imposed by a number of countries, especially the United States, and international entities (Clegg and

Palmer, 1996; Cleveland, 2001; Cortright et al., 2000; Cranmer, Heinrich, and Desmarais, 2014; Crawford and Klotz, 1999). The first sanctions were those imposed by the United States in November 1979 after a group of radical students seized the American Embassy in Tehran and took the people inside hostage (Dobler, 2008; Doxey, 1972, 1980, 1983, 1987). The sanctions by Executive Order 12170 included freezing about $12 billion in Iranian assets, including bank deposits, gold, and other properties, and a trade embargo (Daviron and Ponte, 2007; De Visscher, 2015; De Vos, 2010; Defourny, 2013; Denzin, 2008; Devarajan and Mottaghi, 2015; Dobler, 2008). These sanctions were lifted in January 1981 as part of the Algiers Accords, which was a negotiated settlement of the hostages' release (Kendall, 2000; Kiriya, 2017; Kirshner, 1997; Klotz, 1995; Koskenniemi, 2014; Kunz, 1960; Laub, 2015; Lee, 2018).

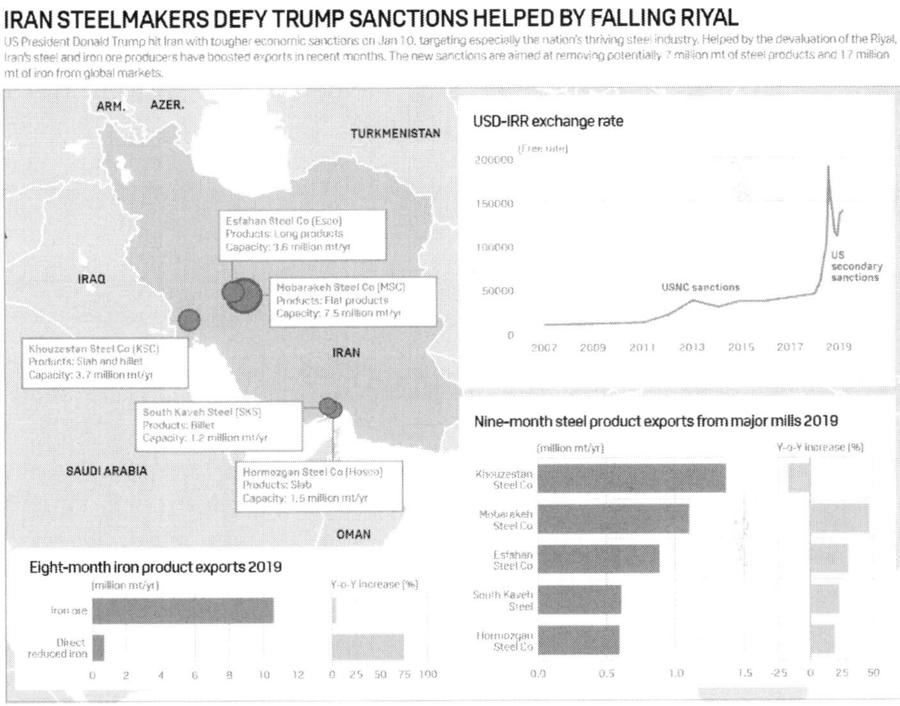

Figure 8.2. Iranian responses to US sanctions in steel.

Source: Iran Mines and Metals Holding Company.

The second sanctions by the United States were imposed under Ronald Reagan in 1987 because of Iran's actions from 1981 to 1987 against the US and other shipping vessels in the Persian Gulf and support for terrorism

(Lee, 2018; Levy, 1999; Leyton-Brown, 2017; Li and Saghaian, 2013). The sanctions were expanded in 1995 to include firms dealing with the Iranian government (Leyton-Brown, 2017; Li and Saghaian, 2013; Lutz and Lux, 1995; Mahmud, 2001). As Figure 8.2 shows, Iran can be adept at circumventing the sanctions against it through smuggling and currency manipulation (Kaempfer, Lowenberg, and Mertens, 2004; Kendall, 2000; Kiriya, 2017; Kirshner, 1997).

The third sanctions were imposed in December 2006 pursuant to UNSC Resolution 1737 after Iran refused to comply with UNSC Resolution 1696, which demanded that Iran halt its uranium enrichment program (Richard and Raimo, 1999; Ross, 1989; Rothwell and Stephens, 2016; Ryngaert, 2015). Initially, US sanctions targeted investments in oil, gas, and petrochemicals, exports of refined petroleum products, and business dealings with the Islamic Revolutionary Guard Corps (Caron, 1989; Carter, 1987; Caruso, 2003; Chachavalpongpun, 2014; Chan, 2000; Chan and Drury, 2000). It encompassed banking and insurance transactions (including with the Central Bank of Iran), shipping, web-hosting services for commercial endeavors, and domain name registration services. Subsequent UN Resolutions have expanded sanctions against Iran (Igami, 2015; Ivanov, Sypchenko, and Webster, 2017; James, 2013).

Over the years, sanctions have taken a serious toll on Iran's economy and people (Hurd, 2017; Igami, 2015; Ivanov, Sypchenko, and Webster, 2017; James, 2013). Since 1979, the United States has led international efforts to use sanctions to influence Iran's policies, including Iran's uranium enrichment program, which Western governments fear is intended for developing the capability to produce nuclear weapons (Kaempfer and Lowenberg, 2000; Kaempfer, Lowenberg, and Mertens, 2004; Kendall, 2000). Iran counters that its nuclear program is for civilian purposes, including generating electricity and medical purposes (Lutz and Lux, 1995; Meyer and Thein, 2014; Mueller and Mueller, 1999; Ryngaert, 2015). When nuclear talks between Iran and Western governments were stalled and seen as a failure, US senators cited them as a reason to enforce stronger economic sanctions on Iran (Choi and Luo, 2013; Dunoff, Ratner, and Wippman, 2015; Haugh and Kitson, 2007; Kaempfer and Lowenberg, 2000). On 2 April 2015, the P5+1 and Iran, meeting in Lausanne, Switzerland, reached a provisional agreement on a framework that, once finalized and implemented, would lift most of the sanctions in exchange for limits on Iran's nuclear programs extending for at least 10 years (Saeidnia and Abdollahi, 2013; Tridimas and Guiterrex-Fons, 2008). The final agreement, the Joint Comprehensive Plan of Action, was adopted on 18 October 2015. As a result, UN sanctions were lifted on 16 January 2016 (Kirshner, 1997; Klotz, 1995; Koskenniemi, 2014; Kunz, 1960; Laub, 2015; Lee, 2018).

On the 8th of May 2018, US President Donald Trump announced that the United States would withdraw from the Iran nuclear deal. Following the US withdrawal, the EU enacted an updated blocking statute on the 7th of August 2018 to nullify US sanctions on countries trading with Iran. The 4th sanctions by the United States came into effect in November 2018 and were intended to force Iran to dramatically alter its policies in the region, including its support for militant groups in the region and its development of ballistic missiles. In September 2019, a US official stated that the United States will sanction whoever deals with Iran or purchases its oil. Also in September 2019, in response to a suspected Iranian attack on key Saudi Arabian oil facilities, Trump said that he directed the Treasury Department to "substantially increase" sanctions on Iran. The new sanctions targeted the Iranian national bank. A senior Trump Administration official said the new sanctions targeted the financial assets of the Supreme leader's inner circle. However, according to the New York Times, Tehran has disclaimed playing any part in the attacks that affected the Saudi oil facilities.

On the 21st of February 2020, Iran was placed on the FATF blacklist. On the 14th of August 2020, the United Nations Security Council rejected a resolution proposed by the United States to extend the global arms embargo on Iran. Under the terms agreed in Iran's 2015 nuclear deal, the UN arms embargo expired on the 18th of October 2020, following which Iran was free to purchase foreign weapons as per its defense requirements (Daviron and Ponte, 2007; De Visscher, 2015; De Vos, 2010; Defourny, 2013; Denzin, 2008; Devarajan and Mottaghi, 2015; Dobler, 2008). As a response to US sanctions on persons who have visited Iran after 2011, while promoting tourism, Iran ceased affixing visas in passports and stamping passports on entry of foreigners (Hanushek and Woessmann, 2010; Haugh and Kitson, 2007; Hinds, 1997; Hiraide and Chakraborty, 2012; Ho-Chuan, Yi-Chen, and Chih-Chuan, 2012). In November 2018, Iran again ceased stamping passports or putting visa stickers in passports of foreign tourists (Saeidnia and Abdollahi, 2013; Tridimas and Guiterrex-Fons, 2008). In August 2020, the Trump Administration tried to extend the arms embargo on Iran with no success. With this event, the US moved to unilaterally trigger snapback sanctions despite having walked away from the Iran nuclear deal in 2018 (Clegg and Palmer, 1996; Cleveland, 2001; Cortright et al., 2000; Cranmer, Heinrich, and Desmarais, 2014; Crawford and Klotz, 1999). This drew skepticism and alarm from allies and experts warned it could end the agreement.

For over 40 years, the USA and its allies have tried to use sanctions to break Iran (Chan, 2000; Chan and Drury, 2000; Chen et al., 2019; Cheraghali, 2013; Chiquiar, 2008; Choi and Luo, 2013). Although, these sanctions have created hardships for both the regime and its people; the regime has not fallen (Chachavalpongpun, 2014; Chan, 2000; Chan and Drury, 2000; Chen et al., 2019; Cheraghali, 2013; Chiquiar, 2008). Indeed, Iran continues to build a hegemony in neighboring states and has been accused of sponsoring terrorism (Bacchiega and Borzaga, 2003; Baldwin and Pape, 1998; Barber, 1979; Bederman and Keitner, 2016).

For their part, the Iranians use the sanctions as an example of the unfairness and hypocrisy that is at the heart of the sanction's (Saeidnia and Abdollahi, 2013; Seyfi and Hall, 2019). If anything, the sanctions have had the effect of radicalizing Iran and also encouraging it to pursue its own arms programs regardless of international concern (Cleveland, 2001; Cortright et al., 2000; Cranmer, Heinrich, and Desmarais, 2014; Crawford and Klotz, 1999; Crook, 2013; David and Holliday, 2012). In particular, the irrational and arbitrary withdrawal by the USA from the nuclear deal has given the Iranians ammunition to suggest that the Western powers are not to be trusted (Jing, Kaempfer, and Lowenberg, 2003; Kaempfer and Lowenberg, 1999, 2000). Henceforth, they cannot be amenable to a "carrot and stick approach" (Morgan and Schwebach, 1997; Mueller and Mueller, 1999). Ultimately, the multiple sanctions against Iran have only had a limited effect in terms of achieving their primary goals (Bradley and Galbraith, 2016; Defourny, 2013; Huang, Xu, and Lu, 2011). However, they have had the effect of stifling the development of the country (Doxey, 1972, 1980, 1983, 1987; Drezner, 2000, 2011, 2015; Drezner and Drezner, 1999). The next example is that of sanctions against Venezuela, which will be covered in the next section.

8.3. SANCTIONS AGAINST VENEZUELA

During the crisis in Venezuela, governments of the United States, the European Union (EU), Canada, Mexico, Panama, and Switzerland applied individual sanctions against people associated with the administration of Nicolás Maduro (Antonopolous, Nunes, and Cottle, 2019; Bull and Rosales, 2020; Buxton, 2018; Corrales, 2020; Crabb, 2019; Dobson, 2019). The sanctions were in response to repression during the 2014 Venezuelan protests and the 2017 Venezuelan protests (Bull and Rosales, 2020; Buxton, 2018; Corrales, 2020; Crabb, 2019; Dobson, 2019; Ellner, 2015; Galbraith, 2019). Additionally, the sanctions were extensively in response to activities that occurred during the 2017 Venezuelan Constituent Assembly election (Buxton, 2018; Corrales, 2020; Crabb, 2019; Dobson, 2019; Ellner, 2015; Galbraith, 2019; Højen, 2015; Jaya, 2019). Another reason given was the conduct and outcome of the 2018 Venezuelan presidential election (Corrales, 2020; Crabb, 2019; Dobson, 2019; Ellner, 2015; Galbraith, 2019; Højen, 2015; Jaya, 2019; Malhotra, 2017).

Given the officials that were targeted, there was a strong suspicion that these sanctions were aimed at regime change (Crabb, 2019; Dobson, 2019; Ellner, 2015; Galbraith, 2019; Højen, 2015; Jaya, 2019; Malhotra, 2017; Marquina, 2018). Indeed, the then President Donald Trump indicated as such during his commentary on the sanctions (Dobson, 2019; Ellner, 2015; Galbraith, 2019; Højen, 2015; Jaya, 2019; Malhotra, 2017; Marquina, 2018; McDowell, 2020). Sanctions were placed on current and former government officials (Ellner, 2015; Galbraith, 2019; Højen, 2015; Jaya, 2019; Malhotra, 2017; Marquina, 2018; McDowell, 2020; Mills and Højen, 2014). The specific targets included members of the Supreme Tribunal of Justice (TSJ) and the 2017 Constituent National Assembly (ANC) (Galbraith, 2019; Højen, 2015; Jaya, 2019; Malhotra, 2017; Marquina, 2018; McDowell, 2020; Mills and Højen, 2014; Mirzadeh et al., 2019). The sanctions also covered members of the military and security forces (Højen, 2015; Jaya, 2019; Malhotra, 2017; Marquina, 2018; McDowell, 2020; Mills and Højen, 2014; Mirzadeh et al., 2019). Even more controversially, there were sanctions that targeted private individuals who were accused of being complicit in the repression that the Venezuelan government had been implementing throughout the years (Jaya, 2019; Malhotra, 2017; Marquina, 2018; McDowell, 2020; Mills and Højen, 2014; Mirzadeh et al., 2019; Moya Ocampos, 2018).

These entities had been accused of being involved in human rights abuses, corruption, degradation in the rule of law and repression of democracy (Malhotra, 2017; Marquina, 2018; McDowell, 2020; Mills and Højen, 2014; Mirzadeh et al., 2019; Moya Ocampos, 2018). Critics of the sanctions argued that Venezuela was doing no worse than some of America's longstanding partners such as Saudi Arabia (Marquina, 2018; McDowell, 2020; Mills and Højen, 2014; Mirzadeh et al., 2019; Moya Ocampos, 2018; Nelson, 2018). Others saw this as another example of imperial America trying to control the internal politics of a foreign sovereign nation (McDowell, 2020; Mills and Højen, 2014; Mirzadeh et al., 2019; Moya Ocampos, 2018; Nelson,

2018; Oner, 2020). As Figure 8.3 shows, the sanctions against Venezuela have divided global opinion and elicited mixed responses.

Figure 8.3. World divisions on sanctioning Venezuela.

Source: Statfor via TRANSCEND International.

As of March 2018, the Washington Office on Latin America said 78 Venezuelans associated with Maduro had been sanctioned by several countries (Mills and Højen, 2014; Mirzadeh et al., 2019; Moya Ocampos, 2018; Nelson, 2018; Oner, 2020; Romero and Mijares, 2016). Through April 2019, the US has sanctioned more than 150 companies, vessels, and individuals, in addition to revoking visas of 718 individuals associated with Maduro (Mirzadeh et al., 2019; Moya Ocampos, 2018; Nelson, 2018; Oner, 2020; Romero and Mijares, 2016; Sejersen, 2020). These sanctions included freezing of individuals' accounts and assets, prohibiting of transactions with sanctioned parties, seizing of assets, arms embargoes and travel bans (Moya Ocampos, 2018; Nelson, 2018; Oner, 2020; Romero and Mijares,

2016; Sejersen, 2020; Weisbrot and Sachs, 2019). Some argued that the sanctions targeted Maduro and Chavismo "elites" while having little impact on average Venezuelans (Nelson, 2018; Oner, 2020; Romero and Mijares, 2016; Sejersen, 2020; Weisbrot and Sachs, 2019). The Washington Post stated that the deprivation long predates recently imposed US sanctions in Venezuela (Antonopolous, Nunes, and Cottle, 2019; Bull and Rosales, 2020; Buxton, 2018; Corrales, 2020; Crabb, 2019). The implication that the sanctions had not achieved their primary objective of changing the status quo (Dobson, 2019; Ellner, 2015; Galbraith, 2019; Højen, 2015; Jaya, 2019; Malhotra, 2017; Marquina, 2018). If anything, the sanctions were strengthening Maduro who argued that this was foreign interference which required patriotic fervor to defeat the Americans (McDowell, 2020; Mills and Højen, 2014; Mirzadeh et al., 2019; Moya Ocampos, 2018; Nelson, 2018).

Beginning in January 2019, during the Venezuelan presidential crisis, the United States applied additional economic sanctions in the petroleum, gold, mining, food, and banking industries. It was anticipated that the centrality of these industries to the Venezuelan economy would eventually force the government to accept reform. A report published by the United Nations High Commissioner for Human Rights stated that although the pervasive and devastating economic and social crisis began before the imposition of the first economic sanctions. In that sense, the opponents of the actions that were proposed by the USA were of the view that the new sanctions could worsen the situation.

In April 2019, Human Rights Watch and Johns Hopkins Bloomberg School of Public Health published a joint report noting that most early sanctions did not target the Venezuelan economy in any way (Oner, 2020; Romero and Mijares, 2016; Sejersen, 2020; Weisbrot and Sachs, 2019). This exposed a serious flaw in the reasoning behind the sanctions and possibly a failure to understand the complexities and subtleties of Venezuelan society (Antonopolous, Nunes, and Cottle, 2019; Ellner, 2015; Galbraith, 2019; Mirzadeh et al., 2019; Moya Ocampos, 2018). The reported that the crisis precedes these sanctions which potentially increase repression rather than decreasing it (Bull and Rosales, 2020; Buxton, 2018; Højen, 2015; Jaya, 2019; Nelson, 2018; Oner, 2020). Through April 2019, the USA sanctioned more than 150 companies, vessels, and individuals (Corrales, 2020; Malhotra, 2017; Marquina, 2018; Romero and Mijares, 2016; Sejersen, 2020). This Was in addition to revoking visas of 718 individuals associated with Maduro that had faced earlier sanctions (Crabb, 2019; Dobson, 2019;

McDowell, 2020; Mills and Højen, 2014; Weisbrot and Sachs, 2019). It appeared at times that the US administration was relishing the prospect of acting unilaterally if other nations failed to join the sanctions (Nelson, 2018; Oner, 2020; Romero and Mijares, 2016; Sejersen, 2020; Weisbrot and Sachs, 2019).

The United States has been concerned about Venezuelan narcotics trafficking since 2005 (Moya Ocampos, 2018; Nelson, 2018; Oner, 2020; Romero and Mijares, 2016; Sejersen, 2020; Weisbrot and Sachs, 2019). Moreover, the US administrations complained about Venezuela's lack of cooperation in combatting terrorism since 2006 (Mirzadeh et al., 2019; Moya Ocampos, 2018; Nelson, 2018; Oner, 2020; Romero and Mijares, 2016; Sejersen, 2020). Of course, that raised questions about the definition of terrorism in the Venezuelan context (Mills and Højen, 2014; Mirzadeh et al., 2019; Moya Ocampos, 2018; Nelson, 2018; Oner, 2020; Romero and Mijares, 2016). This was particularly relevant given the previous record of the USA applying double standards and diplomatic umcertainly when dealing with Venezuela (McDowell, 2020; Mills and Højen, 2014; Mirzadeh et al., 2019; Moya Ocampos, 2018; Nelson, 2018; Oner, 2020). The US has used sanctions as a policy tool for at least a decade to combat terrorism-related activity (Marquina, 2018; McDowell, 2020; Mills and Højen, 2014; Mirzadeh et al., 2019; Moya Ocampos, 2018; Nelson, 2018). This instrumentality had also been used in the war against narcotics and human trafficking (Malhotra, 2017; Marquina, 2018; McDowell, 2020; Mills and Højen, 2014; Mirzadeh et al., 2019; Moya Ocampos, 2018). Additionally, the US administration felt morally empowered and compelled to sanction a regime that for long had been associated with corruption and the systematic violation of human rights violations (Jaya, 2019; Malhotra, 2017; Marquina, 2018; McDowell, 2020; Mills and Højen, 2014; Mirzadeh et al., 2019; Moya Ocampos, 2018).

In 2008, Executive Order 13224 (EO 13224) was issued, and it aimed to reduce terrorist funding in Venezuela via sanctions (Højen, 2015; Jaya, 2019; Malhotra, 2017; Marquina, 2018; McDowell, 2020; Mills and Højen, 2014; Mirzadeh et al., 2019). Additionally, the United States Department of the Treasury has used the Foreign Narcotics Kingpin Designation Act (Kingpin Act) to sanction at least 22 Venezuelans (Galbraith, 2019; Højen, 2015; Jaya, 2019; Malhotra, 2017; Marquina, 2018; McDowell, 2020; Mills and Højen, 2014; Mirzadeh et al., 2019). The institutions and individuals that have been sanctioned include current and former government officials with varying degrees of influence in the regime apparatus (Ellner, 2015; Galbraith, 2019; Højen, 2015; Jaya, 2019; Malhotra, 2017; Marquina, 2018; McDowell, 2020; Mills and Højen, 2014). Prior to the crisis in Venezuela, in 2008 the Office of Foreign Assets Control (OFAC) sanctioned three current or former Venezuelan government officials, saying there was evidence they had materially helped the Revolutionary Armed Forces of Colombia (FARC) in the illegal drug trade (Dobson, 2019; Ellner, 2015; Galbraith, 2019; Højen, 2015; Jaya, 2019; Malhotra, 2017; Marquina, 2018; McDowell, 2020). Although sometimes disputed, many believe that the Venezuelan government has given tacit approval to illegality within its sphere of influence (Crabb, 2019; Dobson, 2019; Ellner, 2015; Galbraith, 2019; Højen, 2015; Jaya, 2019; Malhotra, 2017; Marquina, 2018).

The orders issued by the USA have the effect of freezing any assets the designated entities and individuals may have under US jurisdiction (Corrales, 2020; Crabb, 2019; Dobson, 2019; Ellner, 2015; Galbraith, 2019; Højen, 2015; Jaya, 2019; Malhotra, 2017). It further prohibits US persons from conducting financial or commercial transactions involving those assets (Buxton, 2018; Corrales, 2020; Crabb, 2019; Dobson, 2019; Ellner, 2015; Galbraith, 2019; Højen, 2015; Jaya, 2019). Hugo Carvajal, former director of Venezuela's military intelligence (DGIM); Henry Rangel Silva, director National Directorate of Intelligence and Prevention Services (DISIP); and Ramón Rodríguez Chacín, former Minister of the Interior, were sanctioned (Bull and Rosales, 2020; Buxton, 2018; Corrales, 2020; Crabb, 2019; Dobson, 2019; Ellner, 2015; Galbraith, 2019). Carvajal was arrested in Spain on 12 April 2019 based on arrest warrant from the United States for the 2011 charges and the US asked Spain to extradite Carvajal (Antonopolous, Nunes, and Cottle, 2019; Bull and Rosales, 2020; Buxton, 2018; Corrales, 2020; Crabb, 2019; Dobson, 2019).

Despite the public relations storm that preceded them, the sanctions have not affected regime change or stopped the narcotics trade (Crabb, 2019; Dobson, 2019; Ellner, 2015; Galbraith, 2019; Højen, 2015; Jaya, 2019; Malhotra, 2017; Marquina, 2018). Instead, they have caused embarrassment to the USA and its allies who have been shown the limits of their sanctioning power in a foreign country (Dobson, 2019; Ellner, 2015; Galbraith, 2019; Højen, 2015; Jaya, 2019; Malhotra, 2017; Marquina, 2018; McDowell, 2020). This is the kind of mishap that has often fallen sanctions regimes that are instituted without first understanding the nature of the society that they are in effect targeting (Ellner, 2015; Galbraith, 2019; Højen, 2015; Jaya, 2019; Malhotra, 2017; Marquina, 2018; McDowell, 2020; Mills and Højen, 2014). The Venezuelan regime has shown a level of resilience that was surprising to its American enemies (Galbraith, 2019; Højen, 2015; Jaya, 2019; Malhotra, 2017; Marquina, 2018; McDowell, 2020; Mills and Højen, 2014; Mirzadeh et al., 2019). The final example is that of sanctions against North Korea.

8.4. SANCTIONS AGAINST NORTH KOREA

Several countries and international bodies have imposed sanctions against North Korea (Ogden, 2008; Ozawa and Castello, 2001; Pape, 1997). Currently, many sanctions are concerned with North Korea's nuclear weapons program and were imposed after its first nuclear test in 2006 (Tridimas and Guiterrex-Fons, 2008). The United States imposed sanctions in the 1950s and tightened them further after international bombings against South Korea by North Korean agents during the 1980s, including the Rangoon bombing and the bombing of Korean Air Flight 858 (Doxey, 1980, 1983, 1987; Drezner, 2000, 2011, 2015; Drezner and Drezner, 1999; Drury and Peksen, 2014). In 1988, the United States added North Korea to its list of state sponsors of terrorism (Fridell, 2014; Fu et al., 2020; Genzberger et al., 1994; Gharehgozli, 2017; Goodhart, 2016).

Figure 8.4. History of sanctions against North Korea.

Source: US Treasury and Reuters via Global Risk Insights.

As Figure 8.4 shows, there have been a successive list of sanctions against the North Korean state. In order to fully understand how isolated, the regime has become, it is appropriate to consider some of the specific sanctions that have been imposed over time.

Sanctions against North Korea started to ease during the 1990s when South Korea's then-liberal government pushed for engagement policies with the North (Von Glahn and Taulbee, 2015). The Clinton administration signed the Agreed Framework with North Korea in 1994 (Crawford and Klotz, 1999; Crook, 2013; David and Holliday, 2012; Daviron and Ponte, 2007; De Visscher, 2015). However, the relaxing of economic sanctions was short-lived (Solingen, 2012; Stephanides et al., 2002; Strack and Strack, 1978). North Korea continued its nuclear program and officially withdrew from the Nuclear Non-Proliferation Treaty in 2003, causing countries to reinstate various sanctions (Blyton, 2004; Bolander, 2011; Borszik, 2014, 2016; Bosco, 2012; Bradley and Galbraith, 2016; Brzoska, 2015). UN Security Council Resolutions were passed after North Korea conducted nuclear tests in 2006, 2009, 2013, 2016, and 2017 (Daviron and Ponte, 2007; Franzway and Fonow, 2011; Koskenniemi, 2014; Thaver and Ekanayake, 2010). Initially, sanctions were focused on trade bans on weapons-related materials and goods but expanded to luxury goods to target the elites (Escribà-Folch, 2010, 2012; Escribà-Folch and Wright, 2010; Farzanegan, 2013; Farzanegan and Hayo, 2019). Further sanctions expanded to cover financial assets, banking transactions, and general travel and trade (Strack and Strack, 1978; Takian, Raoofi, and Kazempour-Ardebili, 2020; Taylor, 2012; Thaver and Ekanayake, 2010).

The EU has imposed a series of sanctions against North Korea since 2006 (Von Glahn and Taulbee, 2015; Wallensteen and Staibano, 2005). These include embargoing arms and related materials (Morgan and Schwebach, 1997; Mueller and Mueller, 1999; Nossal, 1989). The EU banned the export of aviation and rocket fuel to North Korea (Chachavalpongpun, 2014; Chan, 2000; Chan and Drury, 2000; Chen et al., 2019; Cheraghali, 2013; Chiquiar, 2008). It also banned the trade of gold, precious metals, and diamonds with the North Korean government (Alam, 2008; Buck, Gallant, and Nossal, 1998; Devarajan and Mottaghi, 2015; Fridell, 2014; Hultman and Peksen, 2017). There was a prohibition on the import of minerals from North Korea, with some exemptions for coal and iron ore (Huang, Xu, and Lu, 2011; Huebner, 2009; Hultman and Peksen, 2017; Hurd, 2017; Igami, 2015). No export of luxury good was allowed and there was restricted financial support and investment for trade with North Korea (De Vos, 2010; Reisman and Stevick,

1998; Seyfi and Hall, 2019;). The EU would routinely inspect and monitor cargoes imported to and exported from North Korea. Additionally, certain individuals from the North Korean state were prohibited from entering the EU (Buck, Gallant, and Nossal, 1998; Caron, 1989; Carter, 1987; Caruso, 2003; Chachavalpongpun, 2014).

There have been several UN Security Council resolutions imposing sanctions on North Korea (Clegg and Palmer, 1996; Cleveland, 2001; Cortright et al., 2000; Cranmer, Heinrich, and Desmarais, 2014; Crawford and Klotz, 1999). Resolution 1718, passed in 2006, demanded that North Korea cease nuclear testing and prohibited the export of some military supplies and luxury goods to North Korea (Von Glahn and Taulbee, 2015; Wallensteen and Staibano, 2005). The UN Security Council Sanctions Committee on North Korea was established, supported by the Panel of Experts (Genzberger et al., 1994; Gharehgozli, 2017; Goodhart, 2016; Grauvogel and Von Soest, 2014). Resolution 1874, passed after the second nuclear test in 2009, broadened the arms embargo. Member states were encouraged to inspect ships and destroy any cargo suspected of being related to the nuclear weapons program (Borszik, 2016; Crook, 2013; Farzanegan, 2013; Kirshner, 1997; Pape, 1997; Takian, Raoofi, and Kazempour-Ardebili, 2020).

Resolution 2087, passed in January 2013 after a satellite launch, strengthened previous sanctions by clarifying a state's right to seize and destroy cargo suspected of heading to or from North Korea for purposes of military research and development (De Vos, 2010; Reisman and Stevick, 1998; Seyfi and Hall, 2019;). Resolution 2094, passed in March 2013 after the third nuclear test, imposed sanctions on money transfers and aimed to shut North Korea out of the international financial system (Drezner and Drezner, 1999; Drury and Peksen, 2014; Dunn and Shaw, 2001; Dunoff, Ratner, and Wippman, 2015; Eliat and Einav, 2004; Eriksson, 2016). Resolution 2270, passed in March 2016 after the 4th nuclear test, further strengthened existing sanctions (Ozawa and Castello, 2001; Pape, 1997, 1998; Ponte, 2004; Reilly, 2012). It banned the export of gold, vanadium, titanium, and rare earth metals (Cortright et al., 2000; Cranmer, Heinrich, and Desmarais, 2014; Crawford and Klotz, 1999; Crook, 2013; David and Holliday, 2012). The export of coal and iron were also banned, with an exemption for transactions that were purely for "livelihood purposes" (Barber, 1979; Bederman and Keitner, 2016). Resolution 2321, passed in November 2016, capped North Korea's coal exports, and banned exports of copper, nickel, zinc, and silver (Choi and Luo, 2013; Clegg and Palmer, 1996; Cleveland,

2001; Cortright et al., 2000; Cranmer, Heinrich, and Desmarais, 2014). In February 2017, a UN panel said that 116 of 193 member states had not yet submitted a report on their implementation of these sanctions, though China had (Caruso, 2003; Chachavalpongpun, 2014; Chan, 2000; Chan and Drury, 2000; Chen et al., 2019; Cheraghali, 2013). Resolution 2371, passed in August 2017, banned all exports of coal, iron, lead, and seafood (Al-Jawaheri, 2008; Dobler, 2008; Fu et al., 2020; Hurd, 2017; Laub, 2015). The resolution also imposed new restrictions on North Korea's Foreign Trade Bank and prohibited any increase in the number of North Koreans working in foreign countries (Daviron and Ponte, 2007; De Visscher, 2015; De Vos, 2010; Defourny, 2013; Denzin, 2008; Devarajan and Mottaghi, 2015; Dobler, 2008). Resolution 2375, passed on 11 September 2017, limited North Korean crude oil and refined petroleum product imports; banned joint ventures, textile exports, natural gas condensate and liquid imports; and banned North Korean nationals from working abroad in other countries (Tridimas and Guiterrex-Fons, 2008).

Resolution 2397, passed on 22 December 2017 after the launch of a Hwasong-15 intercontinental ballistic missile (Von Glahn and Taulbee, 2015). This resolution limited North Korean crude oil and refined petroleum product imports to 500,000 barrels per year, banned the export of food, machinery, and electrical equipment, called for the repatriation of all North Korean nationals earning income abroad within 24 months (Kaempfer and Lowenberg, 2000; Kaempfer, Lowenberg, and Mertens, 2004; Kendall, 2000). The resolution also authorized member states to seize and inspect any vessel in their territorial waters found to be illicitly providing oil or other prohibited products to the Democratic People's Republic of Korea (Tridimas and Guiterrex-Fons, 2008). United Nations agencies are restricted in the aid they can give to North Korea because of the sanctions, but they can help with nutrition, health, water, and sanitation (Matsushita et al., 2015; McCorkell and Gillard, 2010; Meyer and Thein, 2014; Mikhaylova, Babich, and Smirnova, 2017).

Various nations have also imposed sanctions that are separate and also in tandem with UN sanctions (Clegg and Palmer, 1996; Eliat and Einav, 2004; Hinds, 1997; Kaempfer, Lowenberg, and Mertens, 2004). For example, Australia has imposed a series of sanctions against North Korea since August 2017 (Lee, 2018; Levy, 1999; Leyton-Brown, 2017; Li and Saghaian, 2013). In February 2017, China banned all imports of coal from North Korea for the rest of the year (Ozawa and Castello, 2001; Pape, 1997, 1998; Ponte, 2004). China also banned exports of some petroleum products and imports of textiles from North Korea in line with United Nations resolutions (Drezner, 2011, 2015; Drezner and Drezner, 1999; Drury and Peksen, 2014; Dunn and Shaw, 2001; Dunoff, Ratner, and Wippman, 2015). In 2016, Japan imposed sanctions against North Korea, including banning remittances, except those made for humanitarian purposes less than ¥100,000 in value (Bradley and Galbraith, 2016; Defourny, 2013; Huang, Xu, and Lu, 2011). Japan prohibited North Korean citizens from entering Japan (Daviron and Ponte, 2007; De Visscher, 2015; De Vos, 2010; Defourny, 2013; Denzin, 2008; Devarajan and Mottaghi, 2015; Dobler, 2008). It also renewed the ban on North Korean ships entering Japanese ports and extending it to include other ships that have visited North Korea (Hanushek and Woessmann, 2010; Haugh and Kitson, 2007; Hinds, 1997; Hiraide and Chakraborty, 2012; Ho-Chuan, Yi-Chen, and Chih-Chuan, 2012). Additionally, Japan banned nuclear and missile technicians who have been to North Korea from entering Japan (Solingen, 2012; Stephanides et al., 2002; Strack and Strack, 1978).

On 30 March 2010, President Dmitry Medvedev signed a decree implementing intensified United Nations Security Council sanctions against Pyongyang's nuclear programs. The presidential decree banned the purchase of weapons and relevant materials from the DPRK by government offices, enterprises, banks, organizations, and individuals currently under Russia's jurisdiction (Barber, 1979; Drezner, 2015; Jiang, Chen, and Liu, 2010; Leyton-Brown, 2017). It also prohibited the transit of weapons and relevant materials via Russian territory or their export to the DPRK (Solingen, 2012; Stephanides et al., 2002; Strack and Strack, 1978; Takian, Raoofi, and Kazempour-Ardebili, 2020). Any financial aid and educational training that might facilitate North Korea's nuclear program and proliferation activities were also forbidden (Caron, 1989; Genzberger et al., 1994).

In December 2013, Russia joined the sanctions against North Korea, introduced in March by the UN Security Council Resolution 2087. The corresponding decree signed by President Putin specified that Russian companies were prohibited to provide North Korea any technical assistance and advice in the development and production of ballistic missiles (Caron, 1989; Carter, 1987; Caruso, 2003; Chachavalpongpun, 2014; Chan, 2000; Chan and Drury, 2000). In addition, North Korean naval vessels to call at Russian ports would be required to undergo inspection (Jiang, Chen, and Liu, 2010; Jing, Kaempfer, and Lowenberg, 2003; Kaempfer and Lowenberg, 1999). Furthermore, the authorities ordered to be vigilant when dealing with North Korean diplomats (Genzberger et al., 1994; Gharehgozli, 2017; Goodhart, 2016; Grauvogel and Von Soest, 2014).

In October 2017, Russian President Vladimir Putin signed Presidential Decree No. 484 imposing sanctions on North Korea in connection with the adoption of UN Security Council resolution 2321 of November 30, 2016. The decree supplements a number of applications, including a list of individuals and legal entities associated with the North Korean nuclear program or its ballistic missile program, which are subject to restrictions (Igami, 2015; Ivanov, Sypchenko, and Webster, 2017; James, 2013). The measures provided for by Security Council resolution 2321 introduce additional bans on trade, economic, banking, financial, scientific, and technical cooperation with North Korea (Biersteker, Eckert, and Tourinho, 2016; Blyton, 2004; Bolander, 2011; Borszik, 2014, 2016).

In the trade and economic field, the purchase of copper, nickel, silver, and zinc from North Korea is prohibited (Cheraghali, 2013; Drury and Peksen, 2014; Hafner-Burton and Montgomery, 2008). At the same time, the exception provided for by UN Security Council resolution 2270 of March 2, 2016 is retained for the project for the transit of Russian coal through Russian Railways through the North Korean port of Rajin for subsequent export to third countries (Barber, 1979; Bederman and Keitner, 2016). In addition, scientific, and technical cooperation with the participation of persons or groups representing North Korea should be suspended, except for exchanges in the field of medicine (Fridell, 2014; Fu et al., 2020; Genzberger et al., 1994; Gharehgozli, 2017; Goodhart, 2016). Furthermore, targeted restrictions are expanding on several North Korean individuals and legal entities, as well as lists of products, including "luxury goods," the import and export of which is prohibited to and from North Korea (Denzin, 2008; Devarajan and Mottaghi, 2015; Dobler, 2008; Doxey, 1972).

Russia expanded the list of dual-use goods and other items whose import into the DPRK is prohibited due to their potential use for nuclear missile program of the country and other actions that violate the North Korean sanctions regime (Doxey, 1972, 1980, 1983, 1987; Drezner, 2000, 2011). The document also provides for a complete ban on the import of textile products from North Korea. Additional restrictions on cooperation in the transport sector were introduced in the decree (Chan and Drury, 2000; Chen et al., 2019; Cheraghali, 2013; Chiquiar, 2008; Choi and Luo, 2013; Clegg and Palmer, 1996). For example, the delivery of new helicopters and ships to North Korea became prohibited (Chan, 2000; Chan and Drury, 2000; Chen et al., 2019; Cheraghali, 2013; Chiquiar, 2008; Choi and Luo, 2013). Moreover, all seagoing ships owned or controlled by North Korea were removed from state registration (Kirshner, 1997; Klotz, 1995; Koskenniemi,

2014; Kunz, 1960; Laub, 2015; Lee, 2018). North Korean aircraft and ship inspection measures were tightened on the territory of UN member states (Askari et al., 2003; Attia, Grauvogel, and von Soest, 2020).

In 2010, South Korea imposed sanctions against North Korea in response to the sinking of the South Korean naval ship, the ROKS Cheonan, known as the May 24 measures (Bradley and Galbraith, 2016; Brzoska, 2015; Buck, Gallant, and Nossal, 1998; Caron, 1989; Carter, 1987). These sanctions included banning North Korean ships from South Korean territorial waters (Askari et al., 2003; Attia, Grauvogel, and von Soest, 2020; Bacchiega and Borzaga, 2003; Baldwin and Pape, 1998). North Korea suspended inter-Korean trade except at the Kaesong Industrial Zone (Morgan and Schwebach, 1997; Wallensteen and Staibano, 2005). Additionally, most cultural exchanges were banned (Ozawa and Castello, 2001; Pape, 1997, 1998; Ponte, 2004; Reilly, 2012). In 2016, President Park Geun-Hye ordered the Kaesong Industrial Region to close in retaliation for the nuclear test in January and the rocket launch in February. In 2019, U.N. panel accused South Korea of violating sanctions by not notifying the Security Council about its deliveries of petroleum products for use at the inter-Korean joint liaison office (Carter, 1987; Doxey, 1972; Gharehgozli, 2017; Lee, 2018; Ozawa and Castello, 2001). Furthermore, in the Annex of the Updated Guidance on Addressing North Korea's Illicit Shipping Practices, issued from United States Department of the Treasury, a ship of South Korea was listed as that believed to have engaged in ship-to-ship transfers with North Korean tankers (David and Holliday, 2012; Daviron and Ponte, 2007; De Visscher, 2015; De Vos, 2010; Defourny, 2013; Denzin, 2008; Devarajan and Mottaghi, 2015).

In effect, North Korea has been significantly isolated by the various sanctions regimes that have been imposed on it (Bradley and Galbraith, 2016; Defourny, 2013; Huang, Xu, and Lu, 2011). However, some argue that these sanctions have not been effective since the secretive state has not changed course (Von Glahn and Taulbee, 2015; Wallensteen and Staibano, 2005). If anything, it has continued threatening other nations and developing nuclear capabilities (Hiraide and Chakraborty, 2012; Ho-Chuan, Yi-Chen, and Chih-Chuan, 2012; Hovdenak, 2009; Huang, Xu, and Lu, 2011). The Trump Administration made some overtures, but these were soon rebuffed since it became clear that North Korea was only interested in deluding the Western powers into a false sense of security while it continued with its nuclear programs (Farzanegan and Hayo, 2019; Franzway and Fonow, 2011; Frick, Humphreys, and Scheel, 2015; Fridell, 2014). The academic

John Delury has described the sanctions as futile and counterproductive (Cleveland, 2001; Cortright et al., 2000; Cranmer, Heinrich, and Desmarais, 2014; Crawford and Klotz, 1999; Crook, 2013; David and Holliday, 2012). He has argued that they are unenforceable and unlikely to stop North Korea's nuclear weapons program (Devarajan and Mottaghi, 2015; Dobler, 2008; Doxey, 1972, 1983). The one area in which the sanctions have been devastating is in the lives of ordinary North Koreans who are living under an increasingly paranoid and oppressive regime (Gui, 1991; Hafner-Burton and Montgomery, 2008).

Others have argued that regardless of the failures in the sanction's regime, they are the best alternative (Igami, 2015; Ivanov, Sypchenko, and Webster, 2017; James, 2013). For example, Sung-Yoon Lee, Professor in Korean Studies at the Fletcher School, and Joshua Stanton's advocate continued tightening of sanctions and targeting Pyongyang's systemic vulnerabilities. This may include blocking the regime's offshore hard currency reserves and income with financial sanctions, including secondary sanctions against its foreign enablers (Kirshner, 1997; Klotz, 1995; Koskenniemi, 2014; Kunz, 1960; Laub, 2015; Lee, 2018). The argument was that this intervention would significantly diminish (and destroy) Kim the means to pay his military, security forces and elites that repress the North Korean public (Pape, 1998; Ponte, 2004; Reilly, 2012; Reisman and Stevick, 1998; Richard and Raimo, 1999).

Nevertheless, the North Korean people continue to pay a heavy price for these diplomatic goals (Ho-Chuan, Yi-Chen, and Chih-Chuan, 2012; Hovdenak, 2009; Huang, Xu, and Lu, 2011; Huebner, 2009; Hultman and Peksen, 2017). For example, it is estimated by Kim B. Park of WHO panel that sanctions in 2018 resulted around 4000 preventable deaths due to delays in exemptions for programs by NGO's and the UN agencies that have humanitarian programs in North Korea (Reilly, 2012; Reisman and Stevick, 1998; Richard and Raimo, 1999; Ross, 1989; Rothwell and Stephens, 2016). The agricultural impact is highlighted in a report jointly made by the World Food Program and the Food and Agriculture Organization. The report outlines the negative effects on irrigation and yield in food production due to restrictions in machinery, spare parts, fuels, and fertilizers (Doxey, 1980, 1987; Drezner, 2000, 2011, 2015; Drezner and Drezner, 1999; Drury and Peksen, 2014; Dunn and Shaw, 2001).

CHAPTER 8 SUMMARY

This chapter has evaluated the success or impact of sanctions against selected countries including Russia, Iran, Venezuela, and North Korea. Several key issues emerge. First, sanctions are a form of international condemnation and serve to isolate their target. However, some countries like Russia, which have been on the receiving end of sanctions can also impose sanctions. This emphasizes the international nature of sanctions. Nevertheless, most victims of international sanctions are ordinary members of the populace who really have nothing to do with the international conflicts that are being targeted. That means that in effect, sanctions have been a very form of collective punishment. Besides, many countries have developed ingenious ways of circumventing the restrictions that are placed on them by virtue of international sanctions. Hence, the effectiveness of international sanctions must necessarily be limited.

Chapter 9

Concluding Remarks

The primary aim of this book was to explore how international sanctions are conceived, justified, implemented, and reviewed. In looking at various cases, there are countries that have emerged as international pariahs who suffer most sanctions. These have sometimes been referred to as the "axis of evil." Sanctions are a form of punishment and therefore take on the various purposes that are associated with punishment in a criminal justice system. For example, sanctions can be preventative, proactive, vindictive, and supportive. There is also an opportunity for rehabilitation if the original offending conditions are addressed. Nevertheless, there is some level of unfairness in our contemporary use of international sanctions. Not everyone that breaks international law and conventions is punished. Yet, those who are singled out as pariah states are repeatedly punished for even the smallest infringements. That is why some have argued that international sanctions have become a weapon. It is important to note that any perception of injustice means that not all countries are willing to engage in sanctions that are proposed by Western powers. Nowhere is this more visible than in the apparent opposition to the USA embargo on Cuba. Clearly, individual sovereign countries and international institutions make value judgments about the efficacy and appropriateness of any given sanctions. I hope this book has given you important insights into the sanctioning process and will stimulate further debate on this issue.

Bibliography

1. Aaslestad, K., & Joor, J., (2014). *Revisiting Napoleon's Continental System: Local, Regional and European Experiences*. Springer.
2. Abunimah, A., (2002). *Iraq Under Siege: The Deadly Impact of Sanctions and War*. South End Press.
3. Afesorgbor, S. K., (2019). The impact of economic sanctions on international trade: How do threatened sanctions compare with imposed sanctions? *European Journal of Political Economy, 56*, 11–26.
4. Al-Ali, N., (2005). Reconstructing gender: Iraqi women between dictatorship, war, sanctions and occupation. *Third World Quarterly, 26*(4, 5), 739–758.
5. Alam, S., (2008). *Sustainable Development and Free Trade, Institutional Approaches*. London: Routledge.
6. Al-Jawaheri, Y. H., (2008). *Women in Iraq: The Gender Impact of International Sanctions*. London: IB Tauris.
7. Antonopolous, P., Nunes, P. D. R., & Cottle, D., (2019). Circumventing sanctions: Venezuela's turn to cryptocurrencies. *Venezuela in Focus: Economic, Political and Social Issues*, 71–103.
8. Askari, H., Forrer, J., Teegen, H., & Yang, J., (2003). *Economic Sanctions: Examining Their Philosophy and Efficacy*. Greenwood Publishing Group.
9. Asprey, R. B., (2001). *The Reign of Napoleon Bonaparte* (p. 462). New York: Basic Books.
10. Attia, H., Grauvogel, J., & Von, S. C., (2020). The termination of international sanctions: Explaining target compliance and sender capitulation. *European Economic Review, 129*, 103565.

11. Austin, D., (1966). Sanctions and Rhodesia. *The World Today, 22*(3), 106–113.
12. Bacchiega, A., & Borzaga, C., (2003). The economics of the third sector. In: *The Study of the Nonprofit Enterprise* (pp. 27–48). Boston (MA): Springer.
13. Baldwin, D. A., & Pape, R. A., (1998). Evaluating economic sanctions. *International Security, 23*(2), 189–198.
14. Barber, J., (1979). Economic sanctions as a policy instrument. *International Affairs, 55*(3), 367–384.
15. Barry, M., (2000). Effect of the US embargo and economic decline on health in Cuba. *Annals of Internal Medicine, 132*(2), 151–154.
16. Bederman, D., & Keitner, C., (2016). *International Law Frameworks*. NY: West Academic.
17. Biersteker, T. J., Eckert, S. E., & Tourinho, M., (2016). *Targeted Sanctions*. Cambridge University Press.
18. Blyton, P., (2004). *Dynamics of Employee Relations*. London: Business & Economics.
19. Boas, T. C., (2000). The dictator's dilemma? The internet and US policy toward Cuba. *Washington Quarterly, 23*(3), 57–67.
20. Boczek, B. A., (1968). Permanent neutrality and collective security: The case of Switzerland and the United Nations sanctions against Southern Rhodesia. *Case W. Res. J. Int'l. L., 1*, 75.
21. Bolander, J., (2011). *How to Deal with Organizational Politics*. [Online] Available at: http://www.thedailymba.com/2011/02/28/how-to-deal-with-organizational-politics/ (accessed on 23 March 2021).
22. Bolton, J., (1997). *The UN Rewards Saddam* (p. 15). The Weekly Standard.
23. Borszik, O., (2014). *International Sanctions Against Iran Under President Ahmadinejad: Explaining Regime Persistence.* GIGA Working Paper, 260.
24. Borszik, O., (2016). International sanctions against Iran and Tehran's responses: Political effects on the targeted regime. *Contemporary Politics, 22*(1), 20–39.
25. Bosco, L., (2012). Competition for power and altruism. *Forum for Social Economics, 41*(2, 3), 263–296.

26. Bradley, C. A., & Galbraith, J., (2016). Presidential War powers as an interactive dynamic: International law, domestic law, and practice-based legal change. *NYUL Rev., 91*(1), 689.
27. Brzoska, M., (2015). International sanctions before and beyond UN sanctions. *International Affairs, 91*(6), 1339–1349.
28. Buck, L., Gallant, N., & Nossal, K. R., (1998). Sanctions as a gendered instrument of statecraft: The case of Iraq. *Review of International Studies*, 69–84.
29. Bull, B., & Rosales, A., (2020). Into the shadows: Sanctions, rentierism, and economic informalization in Venezuela. *European Review of Latin American and Caribbean Studies, 109*, 107–133.
30. Buxton, J., (2018). Defusing Venezuela. *Whitehead J. Dipl. and Int'l. Rel., 19*, 7.
31. Byman, D., Pollack, K., & Waxman, M., (1998). Coercing Saddam Hussein: Lessons from the past. *Survival, 40*(3), 127–151.
32. Cain, Jr. J. W., (1994). Extraterritorial Application of the united states' trade embargo against Cuba: The united nations general assembly's call for an end to the US trade embargo. *Ga. J. Int'l. and Comp. L., 24*, 379.
33. Caron, D. D., (1989). International sanctions, ocean management, and the law of the Sea: A study of denial of access to fisheries. *Ecology LQ, 16*, 311.
34. Carter, B. E., (1987). International economic sanctions: Improving the haphazard US legal regime. *Calif. L. Rev., 75*, 1159.
35. Caruso, R., (2003). The impact of international economic sanctions on trade: An empirical analysis. *Peace Economics, Peace Science, and Public Policy, 9*(2).
36. Chachavalpongpun, P., (2014). The politics of international sanctions: The 2014 coup in Thailand. *Journal of International Affairs*, 169–185.
37. Chan, A., (2000). Globalization, Chinas free (read bonded) labor market, and the Chinese trade unions. *Asia Pacific Business Review, 6*(3, 4), 260–281.
38. Chan, S., & Drury, A., (2000). *Sanctions as Economic Statecraft: Theory and Practice*. Springer.
39. Chen, Y. E., Fu, Q., Zhao, X., Yuan, X., & Chang, C. P., (2019). International sanctions' impact on energy efficiency in target states. *Economic Modeling, 82*, 21–34.

40. Cheraghali, A. M., (2013). Impacts of international sanctions on Iranian pharmaceutical market. *DARU Journal of Pharmaceutical Sciences, 21*(1), 64.
41. Chiquiar, D., (2008). Globalization, regional wage differentials and the Stolper-Samuelson theorem: Evidence from Mexico. *Journal of International Economics, 74*(1), 70–93.
42. Choi, S. W., & Luo, S., (2013). Economic sanctions, poverty, and international terrorism: An empirical analysis. *International Interactions, 39*(2), 217–245.
43. Clawson, P., (1993). *How Has Saddam Hussein Survived? Economic Sanctions, 1990–1993 (No. 22).* DIANE Publishing.
44. Clegg, S. R., & Palmer, G., (1996). *The Politics of Management Knowledge*. New York: Sage.
45. Cleveland, S. H., (2001). Norm internalization and US economic sanctions. *Yale J. Int'l. L., 26*, 1.
46. Cohen, A., (2011). Lonrho and oil sanctions against Rhodesia in the 1960s. *Journal of Southern African Studies, 37*(4), 715–730.
47. Copeland, C. C., Jolly, C. M., & Thompson, H., (2011). The history and potential of trade between Cuba and the US. *Journal of Business and Economics, 2*(3), 163–174.
48. Corbett, J. S., (2017). Napoleon and the British navy after Trafalgar. In: *Naval History 1680–1850* (pp. 1–18). Routledge.
49. Cordesman, A. H., (1999). *Iraq and the War of Sanctions: Conventional Threats and Weapons of Mass Destruction.* Greenwood Publishing Group.
50. Cordesman, A. H., (2018). *Iraq: Sanctions and Beyond*. Routledge.
51. Corrales, J., (2020). Authoritarian survival: Why Maduro hasn't fallen. *Journal of Democracy, 31*(3), 39–53.
52. Cortright, D., Lopez, G. A., Conroy, R. W., Dashti-Gibson, J., Wagler, J., Malone, D. M., & Axworthy, L., (2000). *The Sanctions Decade: Assessing UN Strategies in the 1990s* (Vol. 1). Boulder, CO: Lynne Rienner Publishers.
53. Crabb, J., (2019). OFAC designation of Russian bank a warning to maduro's supporters. *International Financial Law Review*.
54. Cranmer, S. J., Heinrich, T., & Desmarais, B. A., (2014). Reciprocity and the structural determinants of the international sanctions network. *Social Networks, 36*, 5–22.

55. Crawford, N., & Klotz, A., (1999). *How Sanctions Work: Lessons from South Africa*. Springer.

56. Crook, J. R., (2013). Contemporary practice of the United States relating to international law. *American Journal of International Law, 107*(4), 899–951.

57. Curtin, T. R. C., (1969). Total sanctions and economic development in Rhodesia. *Journal of Commonwealth and Comparative Politics, 7*(2), 126–131.

58. Daly, G., (2007). Napoleon and the 'city of smugglers,' 1810–1814. *The Historical Journal, 50*(2), 333–352.

59. David, R., & Holliday, I., (2012). International sanctions or international justice? Shaping political development in Myanmar. *Australian Journal of International Affairs, 66*(2), 121–138.

60. Daviron, B., & Ponte, S., (2007). *The Coffee Paradox: Global Markets, Commodity Trade and the Elusive Promise of Development* (2nd edn.) London: Zed Books.

61. De Visscher, C., (2015). *Theory and Reality in Public International Law*. Princeton: Princeton University Press.

62. De Vos, J., (2010). Christopher Lasch's the culture of narcissism: The failure of a critique of psychological politics. *Theory and Psychology, 20*(4), 528–548.

63. Defourny, J., (2013). Third sector. In: *Handbook on the Economics of Reciprocity and Social Enterprise* (pp. 13–56). London: Edward Elgar Publishing.

64. Delmonte, L. M., (2001). Economic sanctions, Iraq, and US foreign policy. *Transnat'l L. and Contemp. Probs., 11*, 345.

65. Denzin, N., (2008). *Symbolic Interactionism and Cultural Studies: The Politics of Interpretation*. London: John Wiley & Sons.

66. Devarajan, S., & Mottaghi, L., (2015). *Economic Implications of Lifting Sanctions on Iran* (No. 98389, pp. 1–46). The World Bank.

67. Dobler, G., (2008). From scotch whisky Chinese sneakers: International commodity flows and new trade networks in Oshikango, Namibia. *Africa, 78*(3).

68. Dobson, P., (2019). Venezuela: Guaido requests US military cooperation to oust Maduro. *Green Left Weekly*, (1221), 12.

69. Doxey, M. P., (1980). *Economic Sanctions and International Enforcement*. Springer.
70. Doxey, M. P., (1987). *International Sanctions in Contemporary Perspective*. Springer.
71. Doxey, M., (1972). International sanctions: A framework for analysis with special reference to the UN and Southern Africa. *International Organization, 26*(3), 527–550.
72. Doxey, M., (1983). International sanctions in theory and practice. *Case W. Res. J. Int'l. L., 15*, 273.
73. Drain, P. K., & Barry, M., (2010). Fifty years of US embargo: Cuba's health outcomes and lessons. *Science, 328*(5978), 572–573.
74. Drezner, D. W., & Drezner, D. W., (1999). *The Sanctions Paradox: Economic Statecraft and International Relations (No. 65).* Cambridge University Press.
75. Drezner, D. W., (2000). Bargaining, enforcement, and multilateral sanctions: When is cooperation counterproductive? *International Organization*, 73–102.
76. Drezner, D. W., (2011). Sanctions sometimes smart: Targeted sanctions in theory and practice. *International Studies Review, 13*(1), 96–108.
77. Drezner, D. W., (2015). Targeted sanctions in a world of global finance. *International Interactions, 41*(4), 755–764.
78. Drury, A. C., & Peksen, D., (2014). Women and economic statecraft: The negative impact international economic sanctions visit on women. *European Journal of International Relations, 20*(2), 463–490.
79. Dunn, K., & Shaw, T., (2001). *Africa's Challenge to International Relations Theory*. Springer.
80. Dunoff, J. L., Ratner, S. R., & Wippman, D., (2015). *International Law: Norms, Actors, Process*. NY: Wolters Kluwer Law & Business.
81. Dwyer, P. G., & Forrest, A., (2007). *Napoleon and His Empire: Some Issues and Perspectives*. London: Palgrave Macmillan
82. Eliat, Y., & Einav, L., (2004). The determinants of international tourism: A three-dimensional panel data analysis. *Applied Economics, 36*(1), 1315–1328.
83. Ellis, G. J., (1981). *Napoleon's Continental Blockade: The Case of Alsace*. Oxford University Press.

84. Ellner, S., (2015). *After Chavez: The Maduro Government and the 'Economic War in Venezuela*. LAP Exclusives,

85. https://latinamericanperspectives.com/wp-content/uploads/2015/05/01.08.15-After-Chavez-The-Maduro-Government-and-the-Economic-War-in-Venezuela-by-Steve-Ellner1.pdf (accessed on 13 April 2021).

86. Eriksson, M., (2016). *Targeting Peace: Understanding UN and EU Targeted Sanctions.* Routledge.

87. Escribà-Folch, A., & Wright, J., (2010). Dealing with tyranny: International sanctions and the survival of authoritarian rulers. *International Studies Quarterly, 54*(2), 335–359.

88. Escribà-Folch, A., (2010). Economic sanctions and the duration of civil conflicts. *Journal of Peace Research, 47*(2), 129–141.

89. Escribà-Folch, A., (2012). Authoritarian responses to foreign pressure: Spending, repression, and sanctions. *Comparative Political Studies, 45*(6), 683–713.

90. Falk, P. S., (1996). Eyes on Cuba: US business and the embarge. *Foreign Aff., 75*, 14.

91. Falk, R., (2002). Iraq, the United States, and international law: Beyond the sanctions. *The Transnational Foundation for Peace and Future Research, 27*, 2002.

92. Fandl, K. J., (2017). Adios embargo: The case for executive termination of the US Embargo on Cuba. *Am. Bus. LJ., 54*, 293.

93. Farzanegan, M. R., & Hayo, B., (2019). Sanctions and the shadow economy: Empirical evidence from Iranian provinces. *Applied Economics*.

94. Farzanegan, M. R., (2013). Effects of international financial and energy sanctions on Iran's informal economy. *SAIS Review of International Affairs, 33*(1), 13–36.

95. Fenwick, C. G., (1967). When is there a threat to the peace?-Rhodesia. *American Journal of International Law, 61*(3), 753–755.

96. Fisk, D. W., (2000). Economic sanctions: The Cuba embargo revisited. In: *Sanctions as Economic Statecraft* (pp. 65–85). Palgrave Macmillan, London.

97. Franzway, S., & Fonow, M. M., (2011). *Making Feminist Politics: Transnational Alliances Between Women and Labor.* Illinois: University of Illinois Press.

98. Frick, B., & Scheel, F., (2016). Fly like an eagle: Career duration in the FIS ski jumping world cup. *Journal of Sports Economics, 17*(8), 813–831.
99. Fridell, G., (2014). Fairtrade slippages and Vietnam gaps: The ideological fantasies of fair-trade coffee. *Third World Quarterly, 35*(7), 1179–1194.
100. Fu, Q., Chen, Y. E., Jang, C. L., & Chang, C. P., (2020). The impact of international sanctions on environmental performance. *Science of The Total Environment, 745*, 141007.
101. Galbraith, J., (2019). United States recognizes the opposition government in Venezuela and imposes sanctions as tensions escalate. *American Journal of International Law, 113*(3), 601–609.
102. Galtung, J., (1967). On the effects of international economic sanctions: With examples from the case of Rhodesia. *World Politics: A Quarterly Journal of International Relations*, 378–416.
103. Garfield, R., & Santana, S., (1997). The impact of the economic crisis and the US embargo on health in Cuba. *American Journal of Public Health, 87*(1), 15–20.
104. Gause, III. F. G., (1999). Getting it backward on Iraq. *Foreign Affairs, 78*, 54.
105. Genzberger, C. A., et al., (1994). *The Portable Encyclopedia for Doing Business with Japan*. San Rafael (CA): World Trade Press.
106. Gharehgozli, O., (2017). An estimation of the economic cost of recent sanctions on Iran using the synthetic control method. *Economics Letters, 157*, 141–144.
107. Goodhart, M., (2016). *Human Rights: Politics and Practice*. Oxford: Oxford University Press.
108. Gordon, J., (2012). The US embargo against Cuba and the diplomatic challenges to extraterritoriality. *Fletcher F. World Aff., 36*, 63.
109. Grauvogel, J., & Von, S. C., (2014). Claims to legitimacy count: Why sanctions fail to instigate democratization in authoritarian regimes. *European Journal of Political Research, 53*(4), 635–653.
110. Grauvogel, J., Licht, A. A., & Von, S. C., (2017). Sanctions and signals: How international sanction threats trigger domestic protest in targeted regimes. *International Studies Quarterly, 61*(1), 86–97.
111. Gui, B., (1991). The economic rationale for the "third sector". *Annals of Public and Cooperative Economics, 62*(4), 551–572.

112. Guillebaud, C. W., (1940). Hitler's new economic order for Europe. *The Economic Journal*, 449–460.
113. Hafner-Burton, E. M., & Montgomery, A. H., (2008). Power or plenty: How do international trade institutions affect economic sanctions? *Journal of Conflict Resolution, 52*(2), 213–242.
114. Hanushek, E. A., & Woessmann, L., (2010). Education and economic growth. *Economics of Education*, 60–67.
115. Harris, P. B., (1968). Rhodesia: Sanctions, economics and politics. *Rhodesian Journal of Economics, 2*(3), 5–20.
116. Hartley, J., (2003). Russia and napoleon: State, society and the nation. In: *Collaboration and Resistance in Napoleonic Europe* (pp. 186–202). Palgrave Macmillan, London.
117. Haugh, H., & Kitson, M., (2007). The third way and the third sector: New labor's economic policy and the social economy. *Cambridge Journal of Economics, 31*(6), 973–994.
118. Heckscher, E. F., (1922). *The Continental System: An Economic Interpretation* (Vol. 7). Clarendon Press.
119. Hinds, E., (1997). *Private Property: Charles Brockden Brown's Gendered Economics of Virtue*. S.L.: University of Delaware Press.
120. Hintz, S. E., (1972). The political transformation of Rhodesia, 1958–1965. *African Studies Review, 15*(2), 173–183.
121. Hiraide, N., & Chakraborty, K., (2012). Surviving the global recession and the demand for auto industry in the U.S.: A case for ford motor company. *International Journal of Economics and Finance*, *4*(5).
122. Ho-Chuan, H., Yi-Chen, L., & Chih-Chuan, Y., (2012). An appropriate test of the Kuznets hypothesis. *Applied Economics Letters, 19*(1), 47–51.
123. Højen, L., (2015). *US-Venezuela Relations in the 21st Century: Sanctions Against Venezuelan Officials.* Masters Thesis (Aalborg University, Denmark). https://projekter.aau.dk/projekter/files/213145141/Masters_Thesis_LHojen_29.05.2015.pdf (accessed on 13 April 2021).
124. Hovdenak, A., (2009). Hamas in transition: The failure of sanctions. *Democratization, 16*(1), 59–80.
125. Huang, X., Xu, S., & Lu, J., (2011). Trade liberalization and labor income share variation: An interpretation of china's deviation from the Stolper-Samuelson theorem. *The World Economy, 34*(7), 1071–1087.

126. Huebner, A. J., (2009). The conditional optimist: Walt Disney's postwar futurism. *Sixties: A Journal of History, Politics and Culture, 2*(2), 227–244.

127. Hultman, L., & Peksen, D., (2017). Successful or counterproductive coercion? The effect of international sanctions on conflict intensity. *Journal of Conflict Resolution, 61*(6), 1315–1339.

128. Hurd, I., (2017). Targeted killing in international relations theory: Recursive politics of technology, law, and practice. *Contemporary Security Policy, 38*(2), 307–319.

129. Igami, M., (2015). Market power in international commodity trade: The case of coffee. *Journal of Industrial Economics, 63*(2), 225–248.

130. Ismael, T. Y., & Ismael, J. S., (2005). Whither Iraq? beyond Saddam, sanctions and occupation. *Third World Quarterly, 26*(4, 5), 609–629.

131. Ivanov, S., Sypchenko, L., & Webster, C., (2017). International sanctions and Russia's hotel industry: The impact on business and coping mechanisms of hoteliers. *Tourism Planning and Development, 14*(3), 430–441.

132. James, O., (2013). *Office Politics: How to Thrive in a World of Lying, Backstabbing and Dirty Tricks*. London: Vermilion.

133. Jaya, K., (2019). Venezuela's communication dynamics in rejection of humanitarian assistance from the United States of America. *International Journal of Communication and Society*, *1*(1), 26–33.

134. Jiang, L., Chen, Q., & Liu, Y., (2010). FDI and the change of the Chinese culture. *International Journal of Social Economics, 37*(2), 101–118.

135. Jing, C., Kaempfer, W. H., & Lowenberg, A. D., (2003). Instrument choice and the effectiveness of international sanctions: A simultaneous equations approach. *Journal of Peace Research, 40*(5), 519–535.

136. Joyner, C. C., (2003). United Nations sanctions after Iraq: Looking back to see ahead. *Chi. J. Int'l. L., 4*, 329.

137. Kaempfer, W. H., & Lowenberg, A. D., (1999). Unilateral versus multilateral international sanctions: A public choice perspective. *International Studies Quarterly, 43*(1), 37–58.

138. Kaempfer, W. H., & Lowenberg, A. D., (2000). A public choice analysis of the political economy of international sanctions. In: *Sanctions as Economic Statecraft* (pp. 158–186). Palgrave Macmillan, London.

139. Kaempfer, W. H., Lowenberg, A. D., & Mertens, W., (2004). International economic sanctions against a dictator. *Economics and Politics, 16*(1), 29–51.

140. Karsh, E., & Rautsi, I., (1991). Why Saddam Hussein invaded Kuwait. *Survival, 33*(1), 18–30.

141. Kendall, J., (2000). The mainstreaming of the third sector into public policy in England in the late 1990s: Whys and wherefores. *Policy and Politics, 28*(4), 541–562.

142. Kiriya, I., (2017). The impact of international sanctions on Russia's media economy. *Russian Politics, 2*(1), 80–97.

143. Kirkpatrick, A. F., (1996). Role of the USA in shortage of food and medicine in Cuba. *The Lancet, 348*(9040), 1489–1491.

144. Kirshner, J., (1997). The micro-foundations of economic sanctions. *Security Studies, 6*(3), 32–64.

145. Klotz, A., (1995). Norms reconstituting interests: Global racial equality and US sanctions against South Africa. *International Organization, 49*(3), 451–478.

146. Koskenniemi, M., (2014). *Fragmentation of International Law: Difficulties Arising from the Diversification and Expansion of International Law*. NY: Report of the study group of the International Law Commission.

147. Kreczko, A. J., (1980). The unilateral termination of UN sanctions against Southern Rhodesia by the United Kingdom. *Va. J. Int'l. L., 21*, 97.

148. Kuntz, D., & Jackson, C., (1994). The politics of suffering: The impact of the US embargo on the health of the Cuban people: Report of a fact-finding trip to Cuba. *International Journal of Health Services, 24*(1), 161–179.

149. Kunz, J. L., (1960). Sanctions in international law. *The American Journal of International Law, 54*(2), 324–347.

150. Kuyper, P. J., (1975). Sanctions against Rhodesia: The EEC and the implementation of general international legal rules. *Common Market L. Rev., 12*, 231.

151. Laub, Z., (2015). *International Sanctions on Iran*. https://www.cfr.org/backgrounder/international-sanctions-iran (accessed 13 April 2021)

152. Lee, Y. S., (2018). International isolation and regional inequality: Evidence from sanctions on North Korea. *Journal of Urban Economics, 103*, 34–51.

153. Lefebvre, G., & Case, D., (1969). *Napoleon from Tilsit to Waterloo, 1807–1815: Translated from the French by JE Anderson.* Taylor & Francis.

154. LeoGrande, W. M., (1997). Enemies evermore: US policy towards Cuba after helms-burton. *Journal of Latin American Studies, 29*(1), 211–221.

155. Levy, P. I., (1999). Sanctions on South Africa: What did they do? *American Economic Review, 89*(2), 415–420.

156. Leyton-Brown, D., (2017). *The Utility of International Economic Sanctions* (Vol. 32). Routledge.

157. Li, X., & Saghaian, S., (2013). *An Empirical Analysis of Coffee Price Transmission in Vietnam*. Orlando (Florida): South Agricultural Economics Association (SAEA) Annual Meeting.

158. Lopez, G. A., & Cortright, D., (2004). Containing Iraq: Sanctions worked. *Foreign Affairs*, 90–103.

159. Lopez, G. A., (1998). The sanctions dilemma. *Commonweal, 125*(15), 10.

160. Lutz, M., & Lux, K., (1995). Commenting on gendered economics: Mushroom men, straw men, and real persons. *Review of Social Economy, 53*(1), 121–131.

161. Mackey, S., (2003). *The Reckoning: Iraq and the Legacy of Saddam Hussein*. WW Norton & Company.

162. Mahmud, S., (2001). Controlling African states' behavior: International relations theory and international sanctions against Libya and Nigeria. In: *Africa's Challenge to International Relations Theory* (pp. 129–145). Palgrave Macmillan, London.

163. Malhotra, S., (2017). US oil sanctions against Venezuela: Possible effects. *CAPS in Focus, 70*, 17.

164. Markham, J. D., (2003). Napoleon in Russia: Questionable judgement and critical errors. *The RUSI Journal, 148*(6), 62–69.

165. Marquina, C. P., (2018). Venezuela slams new US sanctions. *Green Left Weekly*, (1182), 17.

166. Matsushita, M., Schoenbaum, T. J., Mavroidis, P. C., & Hahn, M., (2015). *The World Trade Organization: Law, Practice, and Policy.* Oxford: Oxford University Press.

167. McCorkell, A., & Gillard, M., (2010). *Sound Familiar? The BAE Scandal, and the Parallels with the Iraq War*. [Online] Available at: http://www.independent.co.uk/news/uk/politics/sound-familiar-the-bae-scandal-and-the-parallels-with-the-iraq-war-1891764.html (accessed on 23 March 2021).

168. McDougal, M. S., & Reisman, W. M., (1968). Rhodesia and the United Nations: The lawfulness of international concern. *Am. J. Int'l. L., 62*, 1.

169. McDowell, D., (2020). Financial sanctions and political risk in the international currency system. *Review of International Political Economy*, 1–27.

170. McKinnell, R. T., (1968). Assessing the economic impact of sanctions against Rhodesia: A note on TRC Curtin's article. *African Affairs, 67*(268), 227–232.

171. Meyer, K. E., & Thein, H. H., (2014). Business under adverse home country institutions: The case of international sanctions against Myanmar. *Journal of World Business, 49*(1), 156–171.

172. Mikhaylova, N. A., Babich, T. V., & Smirnova, O. S., (2017). Improvement of the state support mechanism for regional agro-industrial complex under the conditions of international sanctions and Russia's membership in the WTO. In: *Overcoming Uncertainty of Institutional Environment as a Tool of Global Crisis Management* (pp. 151–157). Springer, Cham.

173. Mills, F., & Højen, L., (2014). *US Sanctions Against Venezuela: A Wrong Turn for Regional Diplomacy*. Council on Hemispheric Affairs.

174. Minter, W., & Schmidt, E., (1988). When sanctions worked: The case of Rhodesia reexamined. *African Affairs, 87*(347), 207–237.

175. Mirzadeh, F., Flowe, Jr. B. H., Ordway, J. A., Fisher-Owens, D., Hoghooghi, B., Bechky, P. S., & Turner, R. M., (2019). Economic sanctions. *IELR*, *35*, 106.

176. Mlambo, A. S., (2005). Prelude to the 1979 Lancaster house constitutional conference on Rhodesia: The role of international economic sanctions reconsidered. *Historia, 50*(1), 147–172.

177. Mobley, R., (2002). The Beira patrol: Britain's broken blockade against Rhodesia. *Naval War College Review, 55*(1), 63–84.

178. Morgan, T. C., & Schwebach, V. L., (1997). Fools suffer gladly: The use of economic sanctions in international crises. *International Studies Quarterly, 41*(1), 27–50.

179. Moya, O. D., (2018). Venezuela elections 2018: Military and institutional backing could keep Maduro in power despite sanctions. *LSE Latin America and Caribbean Blog.*

180. Mueller, J., & Mueller, K., (1999). Sanctions of mass destruction. *Foreign Affairs*, 43–53.

181. Nagy, T., (2001). The secret behind the sanctions. *The Progressive, 65*(9).

182. Nelson, R. M., (2018). *Venezuela's Economic Crisis: Issues for Congress.* Congressional Research Service, the Library of Congress.

183. Nossal, K. R., (1989). International sanctions as international punishment. *International Organization, 43*(2), 301–322.

184. Ogden, C., (2008). Diaspora meets IR's constructivism: An appraisal. *Politics, 28*(1), 1–10.

185. Oner, I., (2020). *Turkey and Venezuela: An Alliance of Convenience.* Woodrow Wilson International Center for Scholars, Latin American program, and the middle east program.

186. Osieja, H., (2006). *Economic Sanctions as an Instrument of US Foreign Policy: The Case of the US Embargo Against Cuba*. Universal-Publishers.

187. Ozawa, T., & Castello, S., (2001). Toward an international business paradigm of endogenous growth: Multinationals and governments as co-endogenisers. *International Journal of the Economics of Business, 8*(2), 211–228.

188. Pape, R. A., (1997). Why economic sanctions do not work. *International Security, 22*(2), 90–136.

189. Pape, R. A., (1998). Why economic sanctions still do not work. *International Security, 23*(1), 66–77.

190. Parry, J. P., (2001). The impact of napoleon III on British politics, 1851–1880. *Transactions of the Royal Historical Society, 11,* 147–175.

191. Pasha, A. K., (2003). *Iraq: Sanctions and Wars*. Sterling Publishers Pvt. Ltd.

192. Ponte, S., (2004). *Standards and Sustainability in the Coffee Sector.* Winnipeg (Manitoba), United Nations Conference on Trade

and Development and the International Institute for Sustainable Development.

193. Porter, R. C., (1978). Economic sanctions: The theory and the evidence from Rhodesia. *Journal of Peace Science, 3*(2), 93–110.

194. Purcell, S. K., & Rothkopf, D. J., (2000). *Cuba: The Contours of Change*. L. Rienner Publishers.

195. Reilly, J., (2012). China's unilateral sanctions. *The Washington Quarterly, 35*(4), 121–133.

196. Reinisch, A., (1996). Widening the US embargo against Cuba extraterritorially: A few public international law comments on the Cuban liberty and democratic solidarity (Libertad) act of 1996. *Eur. J. Int'l. L., 7*, 545.

197. Reisman, W. M., & Stevick, D. L., (1998). The applicability of international law standards to United Nations economic sanctions programs. *European Journal of International Law, 9*(1), 86–141.

198. Richard, N. K., & Raimo, V., (1999). *Liberal-Democratic Regimes, International Sanctions, and Global Governance* (pp. 127–150). Globalization and global governance: Medical Ethics in Conflict with Religious Freedom. London: Rowman & Littlefield.

199. Riley, J. P., (2013). World war-the continental system and the Americas. In: *Napoleon and the World War of 1813* (pp. 45–54). Routledge.

200. Roman, G. C., (1995). *On Politics and Health: An Epidemic of Neurologic Disease in Cuba*. Annals of internal medicine, 122(7), 530-533.

201. Romero, C. A., & Mijares, V. M., (2016). From Chávez to maduro: Continuity and change in Venezuelan foreign policy. *Contexto Internacional, 38*(1), 165–201.

202. Rose, J. H., (1893). Napoleon and English commerce. *The English Historical Review, 8*(32), 704–725.

203. Ross, J. F., (1989). *Neutrality and International Sanctions: Sweden, Switzerland, and Collective Security*. ABC-CLIO.

204. Rothwell, D. R., & Stephens, T., (2016). *The International Law of the Sea*. London: Bloomsbury Publishing.

205. Rowe, D. M., (1999). Economic sanctions do work: Economic statecraft and the oil embargo of Rhodesia. *Security Studies, 9*(1, 2), 254–287.

206. Rowe, D. M., (2001). *Manipulating the Market: Understanding Economic Sanctions, Institutional Change, and the Political Unity of White Rhodesia*. University of Michigan Press.

207. Ruppenthal, R., (1943). Denmark and the continental system. *The Journal of Modern History, 15*(1), 7–23.

208. Ryngaert, C., (2015). *Jurisdiction in International Law*. Oxford: OUP.

209. Saeidnia, S., & Abdollahi, M., (2013). Consequences of international sanctions on Iranian scientists and the basis of science. *Hepatitis Monthly, 13*(9).

210. Sejersen, M., (2020). Winning hearts and minds with economic sanctions? Evidence from a survey experiment in Venezuela. *Foreign Policy Analysis*.

211. Seyfi, S., & Hall, C. M., (2019). International sanctions, tourism destinations and resistive economy. *Journal of Policy Research in Tourism, Leisure and Events, 11*(1), 159–169.

212. Sloane, W. M., (1898a). The continental system of napoleon. *Political Science Quarterly, 13*(2), 213–231.

213. Sloane, W. M., (1898b). The continental system of Napoleon: Part I. *Political Science Quarterly (1886–1905), 13*(2), 0_002.

214. Smugula, J. W., (1995). Redirecting focus: Justifying the US embargo against Cuba and resolving the stalemate. *NCJ Int'l. L. and Com. Reg., 21*, 65.

215. Solingen, E., (2012). *Sanctions, Statecraft, and Nuclear Proliferation*. Cambridge University Press.

216. Spadoni, P., (2010). *Failed Sanctions: Why the US Embargo Against Cuba Could Never Work*. University Press of Florida.

217. Spagat, M., (2010). Truth and death in Iraq under sanctions. *Significance, 7*(3), 116–120.

218. Sponeck, G. H. C., Von, S. H. C., & Amorim, C. N., (2006). *A Different Kind of War: The UN Sanctions Regime in IRAQ*. Berghahn Books.

219. Stephanides, J., Cortright, D., Lopez, G. A., Bondi, L., Biersteker, T. J., Brzoska, M., & Newcomb, R. R., (2002). *Smart Sanctions: Targeting Economic Statecraft*. Rowman & Littlefield.

220. Stephenson, G. V., (1975). The impact of international economic sanctions on the internal viability of Rhodesia. *Geographical Review*, 377–389.

221. Strack, H. R., & Strack, H. R., (1978). *Sanctions: The Case of Rhodesia* (Vol. 15, No. 1–6, p. 126). Choice: Publication of the Association of College and Research Libraries, a Division of the American Library Association.

222. Takian, A., Raoofi, A., & Kazempour-Ardebili, S., (2020). COVID-19 battle during the toughest sanctions against Iran. *Lancet (London, England), 395*(10229), 1035.

223. Taylor, B., (2012). *Sanctions as Grand Strategy*. Routledge.

224. Thaver, R. L., & Ekanayake, E. M., (2010). The impact of apartheid and international sanctions on South Africa's import demand function: An empirical analysis. *The International Journal of Business and Finance Research, 4*(4), 11–22.

225. The French Revolution and Napoleon (1933). *Person, Term, and Thing Definition Place*. Washington (DC): FS Crofts & Company.

226. Tridimas, T., & Guiterrex-Fons, J. A., (2008). EU law, international law, and economic sanctions against terrorism: The judiciary in distress. *Fordham Int'l. LJ., 32*, 660.

227. Von, G. G., & Taulbee, J. L., (2015). *Law Among Nations: An Introduction to Public International Law*. London: Routledge.

228. Wallensteen, P., & Staibano, C., (2005). *International Sanctions: Between Words and Wars in the Global System*. Frank Cass, Routledge.

229. Weisbrot, M., & Sachs, J., (2019). Punishing civilians: US sanctions on Venezuela. *Challenge, 62*(5), 299–321.

230. Ziller, J., (2007). The continental system of administrative legality. *The Handbook of Public Administration* (pp. 167–175). London: Sage Publications Limited.

231. Zimbalist, A., (1993). Dateline Cuba: Hanging on in Havana. *Foreign Policy*, *92*, 151–167.

INDEX